Coaching for Improved Work Performance

Coaching for Improved Work Performance

Revised Edition
Ferdinand F. Fournies

McGraw-Hill
New York   San Francisco   Washington, D.C.   Auckland   Bogotá
Caracas   Lisbon   London   Madrid   Mexico City   Milan
Montreal   New Delhi   San Juan   Singapore
Sydney   Tokyo   Toronto

McGraw-Hill

A Division of The McGraw·Hill Companies

Copyright © 2000 by Ferdinand F. Fournies. All rights reserved. Printed in the United States of America. Except as permitted under the United States Copyright Act of 1976, no part of this publication may be reproduced or distributed in any form or by any means, or stored in a data base or retrieval system, without the prior written permission of the publisher.

34567890 DOC/DOC 09876543210

ISBN 0-07-135293-7

Printed and bound by R. R. Donnelley & Sons Company.

This publication is designed to provide accurate and authoritative information in regard to the subject matter covered. It is sold with the understanding that the publisher is not engaged in rendering legal, accounting, or other professional service. If legal advice or other expert assistance is required, the services of a competent professional person should be sought.

—*From a declaration of principles jointly adopted by a committee of the American Bar Association and a committee of publishers.*

 This book is printed on recycled, acid-free paper containing a minimum of 50% recycled de-inked fiber.

To
BETTY
I couldn't have done it without you.

Contents

Introduction

The first edition of this book was written because of demand by thousands of managers who learned these coaching skills in my seminar, "Coaching for Improved Work Performance." The reason for the overwhelming popularity of this seminar is summed up in one manager's comments, "I have been going to management seminars for years and this is the first time anyone has ever told me how to do specific things to solve my people management problems." In the 20 years since the publication of the first edition, the experience of teaching this coaching process to several hundred thousand supervisors and managers around the world has proven its effectiveness and has provided suggestions for making it even more effective.

The need for managers to be able to coach employees effectively is greater today than ever before. For one thing today's workers approach their jobs with broadened expectations (some unrealistic) of their rights and privileges on the job. Downsizing layoffs and canceled retirement plans have taught employees that the idea of loyalty is a one-way street.

It is probably no news to you that about one-third of job applicants lacks the literacy and/or math skills necessary for the jobs for which they apply. In a recent survey asking small companies to list their biggest problems, "the quality of workers" was listed number one.

Another survey of people in the 18 to 34 age group reported that 79 percent believed there are no absolute standards in ethics. In their view, honesty depends on whether it is convenient. MBA students at one university admitted that they take it for granted that businesses cheat and that they would do it "because everyone does it." What does this do to the idea of a fair day's pay for a fair day's work or taking people at their word? Hackers in some companies are forging and broadcasting embarrassing messages in the boss's name; others are inserting viruses that activate if they are fired. One newspaper requested and then published a popular cartoonist's description of five ways to waste time at the office without getting caught. Employees disgruntled over benefit or policy changes are starting Web-sites to exchange information and plan legal action.

The draconian threat of being sued by an employee for $5 million for a manager's act which would have been considered as merely annoying a few years ago has made a lot of managers fearful of taking any action with problem employees. Although the majority of today's managers recognize that the "shut up and do it" approach does not work, they have stampeded to the opposite ineffective approach of "make them happy." When requesting formal disciplinary action against problem workers, the foremen in one automotive company are told by their bosses, "No you have to learn how to get along better with your employees." So the foremen avoid discipline all together.

Managers are groping for solutions.

The good news is that the worst-performing person you ever intend to fire is probably not more than 20 percent bad; 80 percent of what he or she does is okay. If you fire someone for stealing, it is only about 1 percent of his or her total performance; the rest of performance is 99 percent perfect. Most people who get fired are probably not more than 5 percent bad. Most of what they do is appropriate but the manager can't accept the 5 percent bad and doesn't know how to correct it. But now there is a solution. Experience has proven that the information in this book presents a step-by-step process that guides managers in their daily efforts to manage people's good and bad performance.

It is *not* the objective of this book to help managers make people happier in their work, to make managers more popular, or to raise humanity to some higher level of satisfaction in life, although these things will occur as tangential benefits from the effective use of the coaching process. The coaching process is a management system that helps managers more successfully bring about employee performance achievements that relate directly to the survival of a business. The single purpose of this book is to help managers do better what they get paid to do, to improve their employees' performances, quantitatively and qualitatively, through specific, face-to-face interventions called coaching. If you apply these techniques, you will be able to modify employees' performance as needed.

A few years ago an insurance company executive contacted me. He said, "We have to downsize 10 percent of our employees and I want you to teach my managers the coaching process to be able to terminate the worst employees." I told him that approach would not work because the coaching process helps managers make good workers out of bad workers. If his managers use coaching, the bad workers will improve and the managers would have difficulty deciding who to terminate. His best approach was to do his downsizing then teach his managers coaching to get the best out of the remaining employees.

The book is intended to perform two separate functions. The first deals with certain specific beliefs managers have about their employees, about themselves as bosses or facilitators, and about the seemingly undefinable processes called management and motivation. Some managers fail in their efforts to improve people's performance by not doing the right things and, frequently, by doing the wrong things, because of what they wrongly believe about their employees, themselves, and the work relationship. For example, the president of a food-processing company makes the following statement and practices it, "If I have a manager who is not doing a good job, I give him a big raise. If he doesn't rise to it and get better, I fire him."

Another CEO told me that his method of raising performance was to ask people to do more than they could actually do. He said that although most people failed to achieve their goals they did raise performance levels somewhat. Both of these managers believed that they had discovered a management technique but both were dissatisfied with its effectiveness. One of life's truths is that if you believe the wrong things, you will do wrong things on purpose and, conversely, if you believe the right things, you will do right things on purpose. Therefore, the first function of this book is to change your thinking about certain key beliefs relative to employment, motivation, and management that may be preventing you from being effective.

The second function of this book deals with the techniques you can use as a manager to modify people's performance. Experience shows that even those managers who believe the right things don't know what to do about them. One of the primary reasons for this is that the people-management literature offers abundant theories and philosophies but lacks specific instructions in what to do. As one manager phrased it, "I get the feeling that I am going to be saved but I don't know how that is going to happen or what I should do about it."

After more than 20 years of studying, researching, and teaching people management, it is obvious to me that management is more like bridge building than incantation. People management is a collection of interventions having a cause-effect relationship on employees. Therefore, this book will present specific techniques, to be used when you are faced with specific problems, and will tell you how to use them.

During one in-house coaching seminar at a large pharmaceutical company, the managers asked, "What proof do you have that this stuff really works?" Before I could answer, one manager raised his hand and asked if he could tell a story. He related that when he had been promoted in January of that year as a manager of a 15-person department his boss told him that there was one employee who should be fired right away because he was never anything but trouble. The manager told his boss that he was scheduled to attend a Fournies public Coaching Seminar at the end of January and wanted to put off firing the troublemaker until then. In early February his boss asked when the troublemaker would be fired and the manager told him that he just got back from the coaching seminar and first wanted to try out his newly learned coaching techniques on the problem employee. Around the fifteenth of March the boss again asked the manager when he was going to fire the problem employee and the manager replied, "We don't have to fire him now; he is doing everything he is supposed to do." He then said to the group, "This coaching really works."

It is a natural tendency for most readers, especially experienced managers, to read only those sections of a book that appear exciting from the contents. It may seem logical to go directly to the conclusions without wasting time on the fancy explanations, and it does save time, but frequently it is as unrewarding as hearing only the punch line of a good joke.

I suggest you read the whole book from beginning to end; otherwise it will not perform its function for you. Quite simply, if you do not believe certain things in the beginning of the book, you will not do the things recommended at the end of the book, because they will not make sense to you. Conversely, merely believing the right things is not enough; you must do the right things to be successful.

FERDINAND F. FOURNIES

1

Why Managers Fail as Coaches

In the first national study I conducted to analyze the effectiveness of management-performance-appraisal programs, most companies stated that the most important part of their appraisal program was the appraisal interview—the face-to-face meeting between the manager and the employee. When asked what was the weakest part of their appraisal program, most companies answered, *the face-to-face meeting between the manager and the employee.* Companies frankly admitted that if the appraisal interview was conducted at all it was usually quite ineffective. Individual managers admitted they felt ineffective in handling these face-to-face meetings, especially if the purpose was to solve performance problems. In many instances they admitted that the situation seemed to be worse after the discussion than before it. The strange fact was that most of the companies recognizing managers' failure in the face-to-face coaching process did not provide training in *how to do it.*

It was puzzling that in spite of the abundance of management training programs, the majority of managers were still failing to perform such a vital function of their jobs, the face-to-face coaching process.

After reviewing the kinds of training managers have been exposed to, it became obvious why they were having little more success managing people today than 50 years ago. The reason is that most training requires managers to become psychologists first, before they become successful managers and tells managers *what they should do,* but not *how to do it.*

I had the chance to observe a good illustration of this problem while training one company's sales managers. Prior to the beginning of my seminar, a consulting psychologist, who had been providing salesperson-selection testing for that company for over 20 years, was finishing his presentation. He was recommending how the sales managers could be more successful in their salesperson hiring practices. At the end of his presentation he said, "Ladies and gentlemen, the last and most important advice I want to leave with you is this. Before you hire sales applicants, make sure they are motivated to sell or they will fail. I cannot emphasize this to you too strongly."

Immediately a sales manager in the back of the room raised his hand and asked, "Sir, could you please tell me what questions I should ask to find out whether or not the applicant is motivated to sell?" The speaker's surprising response was, "I can't tell you exactly how to do that." My immediate thought was, "Mr. Consultant, if you can't tell them exactly *how* to do it, why are you telling them they *should* do it?" This problem is common in management training.

From a practical point of view, the real question is this, "If it takes a person seven or eight years of study to get a Ph.D. as a psychologist and another five to ten years of experience to be effective, how is it possible for that person to teach what he or she knows to someone else in two hours, two months, or, for that matter, two years?" The answer is, "It is not possible." What actually happens is that managers attend management training courses and become familiar with the theories psychologists use in their practice. They leave the training course with an even more detailed understanding of how vast their problems are, a more intense sense of urgency regarding their resolutions, and a greater willingness to try to do the right things. But they do not have the specific knowledge of *what to do*.

As a result, managers assume the role of amateur psychologist. Managers can't be blamed for this; the amateur psychological approach feels good and appears to be the only game in town, if you want to give up the Y, S, and T approach (Yelling, Screaming, and Threatening). Besides, if you believe you know your subordinate is schizoid, who is to prove you wrong?

The fact of the matter is that it is unrealistic for a manager to expect to be able to perform as a psychologist without spending time in the study and practice necessary to become one. No matter how current you may be in reading *Psychology Today* or *Reader's Digest* no one is going to send your Ph.D. to you in the mail. If you don't have a couch in your office you don't even have a running start.

I am not blaming managers for their eagerness to play the role of psychologist or their illogical belief that they *are* playing the role successfully. I place the blame squarely on the shoulders of trainers. They are trying to teach in two days what it has taken them years to learn. What they really should be doing is acting as translators. They should be translating theories and technical jargon they have taken years to learn into practical information and techniques a manager needs to know and is able to use successfully. They should be giving you information you can use without going back to college for three years.

My best advice to you is to resist the temptation and the persuasion of pseudotrainers to be an amateur psychologist. There is no such thing. Don't be seduced by the use of words and ideas you really don't know anything about. This is self-destructive behavior. It may seem to you like the only game in town right now, but, when you finish this book, you will know how to use more practical alternatives.

CONFUSION ABOUT WHAT MANAGEMENT IS

In my coaching seminars I start with a simple question, which makes managers shuffle their feet: "What is management?" After some silence the usual responses are

Making a profit
Planning and achieving objectives
Getting results
Getting things done through others

When Lawrence Appley was president of the American Management Association, he made a series of films about management. The first film was directed exclusively to defining management as *getting things done through others*. Mr. Appley said, "When you do things yourself you are a technician, when you get things done through others you are a manager." Most of us in our day-to-day management role frequently change hats. At times we close the door and do things ourselves (technician things); at other times, when we open the door and do management things, we are getting things done through others. Too frequently many of us fail, however, because we spend too much time doing technician things and not enough time getting things done through others. We don't perceive the difference between them. Sometimes this is because we don't know any better. Other times it is because the organization imposes technician tasks on us that prevents us from doing our management tasks.

My first book analyzed the management-performance-appraisal programs in 35 U.S. companies. The smallest employed 100 people, and the largest employed 265,000; all were business organizations managing for profits. One of the objectives in our analysis was to identify all the items that companies measured when assessing management performance and to determine how many of these items were measured in all companies. Before you read further, make your own guess as to how many similar items of performance were measured by the 35 companies.

The answer was none. There was no single item of performance that all companies measured, although they were all appraising management performance. The one item that was measured by most companies was *results* (measured by 78 percent of the companies). The next most frequent item was *leadership* (measured by 69 percent) and *willingness to act* (measured by 65 percent). No doubt you are similarly amazed. Why didn't all companies measure something called *planning* or *delegating,* or *coaching* or *coordinating?* These certainly are elements of performance in all management positions.

I next published a study which analyzed salesperson-performance-appraisal programs in 75 U.S. and Canadian companies. Guess how many similar items of salesperson performance were measured by these companies.

Five items were measured by all companies and three other items were measured by 69 to 100 percent of the companies. Some items, such as *knowledge,* were measured as many as four times by some companies. For example, they measured separately company knowledge, product knowledge, competitive knowledge, and customer knowledge.

One seemingly obvious reason for this big difference is that management is much more dynamic and more difficult to define than selling. Unfortunately, that is not so. There are actually more differences between the different kinds of selling jobs in companies than there are differences between the different management jobs in companies. In other words, there is more similarity in the specific actions managers perform in different companies than similarity in the specific selling activities in different companies. The job of selling varies considerably depending upon the product, the customer group, and the market. There are far fewer variables in the relationship between managers, employees, and the work under the function of management. The obvious conclusion from this survey disparity in what is measured is that *we have applied more effort to defining what selling is than we have in defining what management is.*

If the company experts who design programs to appraise management performance do not know what management is, how can individual managers, who have spent far less time analyzing the process, know any more, or even as much, about it? Ask yourself this question, "If I, as a manager, do not know what I do as a manager, how then can I measure it in others, much less teach them how to do it?" The answer of course is, "You can't."

One of the causes goes back to the way people get to be managers. What happens is that you are called in and asked to kneel down. The big boss touches your shoulder with Excalibur and says the magic words: "I now pronounce you manager; go thither and yon and do it." You jump to your feet and smile happily, saying, "Yes, I will go thither and yon and do it." But let's suppose that instead of knighting you as a manager, the boss says, "I knight you jet pilot; go thither and yon and do it." Will you jump up and say, "Yes, I will"? Or will you respond with, "Are you kidding? I wouldn't know how to start one, much less fly one." The likelihood is that, even if you knew how to start one, you would probably crash if you tried to fly it.

It would be more logical for a person just knighted as a jet pilot to say, "Thank you very much but I don't know how to do it." Flying an airplane is *things you do;* management is *things you do.* Why, in one instance, is a person willing to admit he or she doesn't know how to do the right things, but, in the other instance, assumes he or she knows how to do the right things?

The problem becomes compounded when you realize that the boss who knighted you as a manager now believes you are one. It goes like this: *"You are one because I just made you one; therefore, you must know how to do it."* This assumption sounds just as ridiculous for a manager as it would for a pilot. Unfortunately, we spend a great deal of time in business telling newly appointed managers about the things that should be done, but not the way to do them. Subsequently, when a manager fails, the primary reason for failure is assumed to be an unchangeable, inherent limitation in the individual, rather than an inability to do something because he or she *does not know how to do it.* The first question I ask when someone's failure is pointed out to me is, "Who taught him how to do it?" The usual answer is, "No one."

The emphasis in management training has been primarily theoretical: increasing managers' knowledge, but not teaching them what to do to apply that knowledge. This is evidenced by the difficulties that arise when managers talk about management. It is common for managers not to recognize the difference between management philosophies, practices, strategies, and objectives. Behavior, attitudes and characteristics are viewed as the same thing.

The words managers use when describing other people's performance involves generalizations and undefined metaphors such as the following:

She's sharp.
He's on the ball.
She's dynamic.
He's not in the real world.
She's super.
He needs a push.
She needs to be toned down.
He's flaky.
He needs more polish.

A vice president running a large distribution center told me in confidence that his number two man *was not cutting the mustard*. I asked him what seemed to be the problem and he replied, "The man is not pulling his own weight." When I asked what specifically he was doing wrong, the answer was "He hasn't been on the band wagon since he got the job." The conversation continued like that for another few minutes until I finally told him "I don't know what you are talking about." If that vice president had told one of his peers "My number two man is not cutting the mustard," the likely response would have been, "Do you have a replacement yet?"

In summary, although it seems logical to believe you know how to manage because you are a manager, that kind of thinking is out of touch with reality. If you don't find out what to do, all you have to go on is your good intentions, and good intentions do not justify ineffectual performance. *Management is a system of interventions, things you do* to get things done through others. The things you do might be categorized under the general headings of planning, organizing, directing, coordinating, controlling and coaching, with volumes of specifics under each heading. If you can't describe to somebody else *the things you do* as a manager, then either you don't know what you are doing or what you are doing is magic, and there just isn't any magic in business. If you don't know what you are doing, you can't teach your employees how to do it, much less measure whether or not they are doing it correctly. The only choice left to you is to find out what it is you do, or should do, as a manager. I plan to help you do that.

WHAT DO MANAGERS GET PAID FOR?

Another obstacle to face-to-face management is what managers believe about *what managers get paid for.* When I ask managers what they get paid for, the customary responses are as follows:

For managing

For directing others

For responsibility

For results

I am always surprised at the variety of responses. Many managers say, "The answer depends upon the level of the individual manager in the organization and the type of people he or she is managing." I have had Ph.D. managers and M.D. managers in certain research organizations tell me they thought they were paid *to be there.* One M.D. manager, responsible for the performance of eight subordinates who are also M.D.s, told me that what he did really wasn't management: "It is sort of like a club; we hang around together." You might have assumed that if a person is getting paid for doing something, that person would know what he or she is being paid for.

Picture me at a bowling alley. I'm wearing $100 bowling shoes, $125 bowling slacks, and a $200 bowling shirt, hand-embroidered in Japan. On the back of the shirt is a bowling ball with lightning shooting out of it, pins flying in the air, and, in gold lettering, *Ferd the Champ.* I've got the most expensive bowling ball you can buy, and my bowling bag is made of unborn calfskin. My bowling average is 27. Is it likely, if you know all this, that you will come up to me, pat me on the shoulder, and say, "Ferd, you are a great bowler"? The answer is obviously *no*.

Of course, I protest, and claim that I am being misjudged. I can explain the origins of bowling and how it has changed over time. I can talk fluently about the different styles and nuances of bowling techniques, and I call your attention to the beauty and symmetry of my style, including my body English at the foul line. "I really am a good bowler," I say. But you will probably tell me that although I look good, the final measurement of me as a bowler is my score, how many pins I knock down. It's the results that count.

Now I ask you to picture me as a manager on the job. I wear $800 suits and $100 shirts. I stand tall, and carry myself with a distinguished bearing; I speak well and with authority; I am conversant with all the psychological theories of management and discourse fluently about the nuances of these theories. However, most of my employees are failing in their performance. Is it likely you or anyone else in the organization, knowing all these facts, will pat me on the shoulder and say, "Ferd, you are a great manager"? Once again, the answer is obviously *no*.

You are quite correct, of course, because what you are telling me is that, just as in bowling, managers get paid for results; the achievements or nonachievements of the people they manage. The success or failure of your employees represents your score. What this means to you as a manager is that the rewards and punishments you get as a manager—your raises, promotions, demotions, and nonpromotions—are based on the measurement of your success. These measurements of your success are not the things you do; they are the things your people do, the results. When your people are successful, you will be recognized as a successful manager. When your people are failing, you will be recognized as a nonsuccessful manager no matter what *you* are doing. The *results* of what your people do is your score unless you smell bad at staff meetings.

In other words, if your employees are failing, it would not be appropriate for you to look in the mirror and recognize yourself as an outstanding manager or to commend yourself on the wonderful things you are doing as a manager. A pitfall of not knowing what managers get paid for leads you to believe that it is your prerogative whether you spend your time and effort to help an employee succeed. It is easy to visualize yourself as an important deity who dispenses discipline, favors, and wisdom to those members of the common mass you *wish* to favor. Unfortunately, it is not your choice, it is your job; it is what you get paid to do. It is self-destructive not to help them.

Picture yourself at the bowling alley faced with a split you don't like. You choose not to bowl your next ball; you tell the scorekeeper, "I choose not to try to make that split, just score me down for it." Sounds dumb, doesn't it? Of course it would be dumb if you did that. But I don't believe you would do that, because you know it would hurt your score if you did; you know it would be self-destructive behavior. As a manager, any time you choose not to help your employees succeed you are involved in self-destructive behavior. You are choosing to lower your score.

Your ability as a manager is measured by what your employees do, not by what you do. Therefore, the facts of life dictate that, as a manager, *you don't get paid for what you do, you get paid for what your employees do.*

WHO NEEDS WHOM?

Another reason managers tend to fail in the face-to-face process is because they have disproportionate views of relevant values regarding themselves, their employees, and the company. It causes managers to take the wrong action or no action to solve employees' problems. As a case in point, let's assume you are a manager with 10 people answering directly to you. Let's also assume that today you took the day off for the express purpose of reading this book, but all of the 10 people answering to you went to work. Keeping that in mind, answer this question:

> If the total work activity that is expected to be accomplished by you and your unit on any day represents 100 percent, what percentage would you estimate will be accomplished today with you at home and all of your employees on the job?

When I ask managers this question, their answers range between 70 percent to 110 percent. Now let's suppose that tomorrow you go to work, but all 10 people who answer to you stay home and you don't get replacements. Now answer the question:

> Of the total work activity expected to be accomplished by you and your work unit tomorrow, what percentage will be done tomorrow?

If your answer is above 10 percent, you are kidding yourself. The moral of the story is *you need them more than they need you.* It doesn't mean you are not needed. It doesn't mean you are not important. It just means that you need them more than they need you to get the work done.

You might say this is an unfair example because it is only for one day. So let's do it for a longer period. You stay out for six months and they go to work every day. We will plot daily productivity and average it when the six months are up. Then you go to work and they stay out for six months and you don't get replacements. We also average your productivity for the period. There will still be large differences between the averages no matter how skilled you are or how hard you work.

This is quite contrary to what managers believe when they first become knighted as managers, and many of them never change. What happened when you were knighted? Did you rise from your knee with a smile, nodding agreement? Did you stride back to your area of responsibility with assurance? Perhaps the partitions of your office were extended all the way to the ceiling. You might have received a reserved parking space. Did you look around at the lowly masses with confidence because you knew you were true royalty? After all, you used to be one of them and you were chosen as a manager, not one of them. So why shouldn't you believe you are better than they are?

Almost immediately you realized there were numerous things those employees could not do unless you affixed your signature or otherwise approved. Additionally, you found they frequently came to you and asked for assistance, information, and assurances about the numerous things they had to do. You used to do what they do, and if you were promoted, it must have been because you did it better than they did. Therefore, one of your contributions now is to tell them to stop doing whatever they are doing the way they are doing it and to start doing it your way, because your way is obviously the best way. Slowly you come to the realization that you are the most important person in the group; the others depend on you for your power and the gems of wisdom that drop from your lips. The greater the frequency of their coming to you for information and approval, the more convinced you are that you are the hub of the universe. You truly wonder how they can get along without you. After all if you weren't there to sign and initial all those approvals and give the yeses and noes, and let the gems of wisdom drop from your lips, all those employees of yours would be lost like poor little lambs gone astray. Even on those days when you feel ill you drag yourself to work because you know they can't get along without you.

Another thing that happens to you when they knight you as a manager is that you are corrupted by power. When you are knighted, an invisible sign appears in the center of your forehead and flashes on and off: BOSS . . . BOSS . . . BOSS. You can't see it, but everyone who works for you can. You see lines of people standing around waiting to talk to you. Perhaps the people who talk to you do it with deference. You notice that your employees seem to be concerned about the way they talk to you, but you see no reason why you should be concerned about the way you talk to them. You become aware that when you ask people to do things they do them. After all, they are only there to do your bidding. Quite happily, most of them do so, except the incompetent ones. Because people around you do what you tell them, you become even more impressed with your own importance. But what has happened is that you have become deluded into believing that you are the most important member of that group. Because you believe they need you more than you need them, you treat them accordingly. You get involved in self-destructive behavior. You stop managing; you just keep score.

The sad but true fact is that *you need them more than they need you.* You can't get the job done without them.

2

So What Does
All This Mean?

To be successful as a people manager, you must recognize three very important basic facts about your role as a manager:

Fact No. 1.   Management is the intervention of getting things done through others.

Fact No. 2.   You need your employees more than they need you.

Fact No. 3.   You get paid for what your employees do, not for what you do.

If you accept these three basics, you will come to some very important conclusions about the most appropriate interventions necessary for you to become a successful manager. For example, if management is getting things done through others, and you need them more than they need you, and you get rewarded and punished for what they do, not for what you do, the obvious conclusion is that the only reason for you to be there as a manager is *to do everything in your power to help them be as successful as you need them to be. You succeed only when they succeed.*

If you accept the fact that judgments about your performance are made not on what you do, but on what your people do, a logical conclusion is that the only way for you to get a higher score is to have your people become more successful. This also means that a higher score can be achieved only if you accept full responsibility for the success or failure of your employees. It also means that the more successful you wish to be in the business world, the harder you must work to do everything possible to help your employees achieve, rather than fail.

If you truly believe your primary purpose as a manager is *to do every-*

thing possible to help your employees succeed, you are acknowledging that each time an employee fails, *it is one of your failures.* If you accept full responsibility for the success or failure of your employees, that means the last thing you do before you fire somebody is to look in a mirror and say to yourself, "You failed," and then go out and say to the employee, "You're fired." This is the complete opposite of the common managerial practice which is to look at the employee and say, "You failed; you're fired."

Obviously, there are times when an employee's poor performance is caused by inherent limitations in that individual, and is, therefore, beyond your control. But this rarely occurs as a real cause for failure. This is in contrast to managers' tendency to attribute most instances of nonperformance to inherent and unchangeable inabilities of the employee. When managers do the latter, they are inadvertently catching themselves in cul-de-sacs of nonmanagement. Quite simply, once you believe (or conclude) that an employee's nonperformance is occurring because of unchangeable limitations in him or her, you have closed the door to trying alternative interventions to solving that problem. You have just removed yourself from the management of that employee; now you can just stand around and watch what happens.

One manager told me that after attending my coaching seminar she was trying to coach a problem employee when she concluded that the only solution was to fire the employee. She said she reviewed her seminar notes and thought she had done everything right. As a final step she went into the rest room and was about to say to the mirror, "you failed," but instead said, "I will try one more time." She had another discussion with the problem employee and subsequently his performance improved.

Occasionally managers will respond by saying, "It's not reasonable to expect me to accept responsibility for my employee's success or failure when I take over a department with people I had no hand in hiring." Since the manager did not have a hand in acquiring the resources of that department, it appears appropriate for him or her to point out that the nonperformance was caused by inappropriate resources. It is also assumed that managers have the privilege (or duty) to replace those resources before they can accept responsibility for making it run right. Because of this assumption the first step of many new managers is *to clean out the dead wood.* This *house cleaning* is a common act with lower-level managers and is most common with sales managers.

I ask these same managers what they would do about this right to clean house if someone said to them, "I now pronounce you Vice President and General Manager of our Denver plant." And when they arrived in Denver they found the plant to be 50 years old, the machinery, 25 years old, and all the workers with 20 years' experience. Would they still feel it their right, privilege, and duty to shut down the business, to build a new plant, buy new machinery, and hire new employees? The answer of course is *no.* The fact is that this so-called privilege or duty, exercised by lower-level managers to *clean house,* is logical to them because they don't know what management interventions to use to solve their management problems. Far from being a right or a privilege or a duty, it is *self-destructive behavior.* The purpose of this book is to provide you with more alternatives to solving those problems and help you avoid self-destructive behavior.

DOING WHAT COMES NATURALLY IS SELF-DESTRUCTIVE

Another trap for the new manager is the *I'm only human* approach. Let's pretend the knighting ceremonies have just concluded for you. With the sounds of *go thither and yon and do it* still ringing in your ears, you return to your department to do that thing called management. Since you don't know how to do it, the obvious thing for you to do is *to do what comes naturally.* You are a new manager and you don't yet have all the answers to managing people, so the best way to approach the problem is to be honest and straightforward and sincere in what you do. After all, if you are sincere and try to do the right thing, even though it doesn't come out right, nobody can blame you for that (even those who are hurt by what you do). As a result you blithely go about making honest, straightforward, and heartfelt decisions with the assurance that, even though you may be doing the wrong thing to your employees they will understand because after all, you are only human, *you are sincere and you have emotions just like anyone else.*

For example, picture yourself arriving at work in the morning and saying good morning to each of your 10 employees. You greet each employee, "Good morning, Mr. A. Isn't it a beautiful day? Good morning, Ms. B. Isn't it a beautiful day? Good morning, Mr. C. Isn't it a beautiful day?" By the time you get to employee number ten it is only natural that you begin to feel like a broken record. As a matter of fact, by the time you get to employee number five, the broken-record syndrome may have already set in, so you wave to employees five through ten and take care of the *good morning chore* in one swoop with a "Hi, folks." After all, you are only human, and who wants to feel like a broken record? It feels ridiculous.

As another example, let's assume you hold a brief conversation individually with each of your 10 employees. You say 15 to 20 words to each of them. When you get to employee number ten, I ask you, "What did you say to employee number one?" Your response might be, "What do you think I am, a tape recorder? How do you expect me to remember everything I say?"

It's not fair is it? You are not a computer. You are only human. It is not reasonable to expect you to remember the specifics of 10 conversations. Besides, the repetition in your world bores you. But what you don't realize is that when you hold a conversation with one of your employees, although that employee may be only one out of ten employees to you, you are only *one out of one* to each of your employees. You are the only boss that employee has. If you talk to that employee once today he or she has all day long to think about the things you said in that single conversation. He or she is free to reconstruct the sentences, using synonym and antonym comparisons, and to worry about which words you smiled before or after, and what it all meant. Although you have 10 employees in your work life, each of those 10 employees has only one manager.

Picture yourself at the 87th performance of a famous Broadway show. Before the curtain rises, a member of the cast steps through the curtain and says, "Ladies and gentlemen, we have performed this show 86 times, and we are getting a little bored with the words and music. So today we are going to do something a little different. We are going to do some different dances, tell a few jokes we like, and change the plot around to do something more interesting for us." Or, suppose he says, "Ladies and gentlemen, this will be our third show today. The first show we did this morning was probably the best show we have ever done. The second show was not the best, but it was a good solid show. This one is going to be a bomb because we are pooped. Go talk to the folks who saw the first two shows; they loved it."

It sounds ridiculous, doesn't it? Well, it is just as ridiculous if you believe "just being human" is an excuse to cut short your performance with any of your employees. The day you are knighted as the manager is the day you cease to have the privilege of doing what comes naturally. There is an element of show business in management. You don't have a choice as to whether it is there or not. You can choose only to recognize it or not. You can ignore it, but you can't make it go away. The fact is that when you are in front of your employees, you are on stage.

As an example, let's say there are specific things you should be saying or doing with each of your employees, and it takes 20 minutes to do and say those things. By the time you finish with employee number six you are tired or bored, or feel stale, so you tell employee number seven, "Listen I'm a little bored and tired of talking about this; why don't you go talk to employee number one. I was sharp when I talked to her and she loved it."

That sounds ridiculous, too, doesn't it? Actually you probably wouldn't do that. But you might change what you are doing so it does not bore you or you might take only 10 minutes rather than 20 minutes. Unfortunately, the result is the same; you are rewriting the show for your convenience, and the audience (employee number seven) does not get to see it.

The show-business aspect becomes even more obvious when you realize that whatever you do in the presence of your employees is being interpreted by them individually. They are continuously observing your actions and making their *own* interpretations as to what those actions mean *to them.* If your employees don't know exactly why you are doing what you are doing, they are free and quick to make their own interpretations as to why you are doing it. For example, picture yourself spilling coffee on your clothes at breakfast, getting a ticket on the way to work, and stepping in slush up to your knees in the company parking lot. As a result you are in such a foul mood you don't say your normal *hellos,* but you growl and grump as you walk past your employees. In response, worker number one might think, "Gee, she's still mad at me because of that problem we had yesterday, even though I said I was sorry." Employee number two thinks, "Gee, that was a very small error we made last week, and I cleaned it up before it went too far. I guess she found out about it." Employee number three thinks, "I guess she found out last night that she's not going to get that promotion she was hoping for." Employee number four thinks, "She doesn't have to be mad at me just because I asked for a raise." Onward and onward and onward. As far as you are concerned you arrived at work in a bad mood for logical reasons. But each employee knows only that you their manager didn't give him or her the normal greeting, and each interprets this individually.

Even if you came to work and stood in the middle of the floor with your eyes closed and arms at your sides you would have varied employee interpretations, such as the following:

Employee one.   "He's meditating."
Employee two.   "He's having a heart seizure."
Employee three.   "He's just wet his pants."

Once you become a manager of people you no longer have the luxury of *doing what comes naturally*. In doing what comes naturally you are very likely involved in self-destructive behavior.

Your reactions to this might be: "You mean to say that I have to be false and can't express my normal emotions to my employees?" The answer to that is *no* and *yes*. Falseness is not a part of what we are talking about. We are talking about controlling your self-destructive behavior. I am just asking you to control yourself in the work situation for the same reasons you now control yourself in other social situations, because not to do so is self-destructive behavior.

For example, picture yourself at the bowling alley and it's the last frame of the third game. You bowl a strike and now you have to bowl another ball. Is your reaction to that, "Holy mackerel, I have to bowl again? Gee, I'm tired and I've been bowling all night and now just because I got a strike I have to bowl again." Then you pick up your ball and drag yourself into position and, because you have been bowling all night, you just throw that last ball willy nilly. Do you do that, or do you do what every other bowler does? In spite of how many games bowled that night, you do everything possible to pump yourself up and fight all the tendencies to be tired, because this ball is just as important as all the rest, if not more important. My guess is that you would not do what comes naturally; you would do everything possible to make that last ball count. To not do that would be self-destructive as a bowler. My question is: "If it seems logical to resist tendencies to be just plain human in bowling (and you don't even get paid as a bowler), why don't you resist those tendencies to be just plain human in what you earn your living at, management?"

Can you picture a salesperson making the last call of the day and, because she is tired, she walks up to the customer and says, "Listen, Mr. Customer, I'm a little pooped today and I'm really not going to do a very good job of selling to you. Why don't you call up that customer I visited on my first call this morning? I was really 'up' for him and he bought a lot of products." But salespeople wouldn't do that. What they would do before the last call, as tired as they are, is to check their clothing, use a breath freshener and pump themselves up so their actions on this last call will be as effective as they have to be to make the sale.

I know there are managers who, when aggravated by their employees, slam doors, slam drawers, slam down phones, break pencils, and throw pads on the desk or across the room. These same managers, when aggravated by their managers, do not break pencils or throw pads or slam doors or kick the manager's desk. The reason is they know it would be self-destructive behavior to do that in front of the boss. The reason they continue to do that to their employees is because they don't realize that it is self-destructive behavior to do so. When I ask employees why they don't like their bosses, here are the most frequent answers:

—She criticizes me in front of other people.
—He makes employees look like fools in front of other employees.
—He yells across the room at me.
—He calls employees names; dumb, stupid.
—She insulted me in front of others, yelling, "Why don't you think once in a while?"

You may feel it is quite natural to express your anger and irritation when your employees foul up their performance. It certainly may feel natural, but it has nothing to do with management. It is actually self-destructive. It is just as self-destructive as kicking your bowling ball because you missed a split. People kick a bowling ball only once in a lifetime; they find out it's self-destructive.

Did you ever drive an automobile that burned a lot of oil? If so, did you beat the hood with a tire iron everytime you drove into the gas station to buy more oil? I really believe you didn't even though you may have wanted to. It would have been foolish and self-destructive if you had.

Did you ever have a car cut you off on the road and make you feel like ramming that car to run it off the road? But you didn't. You resisted being just plain normal because you knew it would be self-destructive to do otherwise. To merely yell at another driver these days may cost you your life. I have confidence in you as a human being, that you do not go through the world doing self-destructive things on purpose. That's why I am taking so much time to explain to you that many of the things you do as a manager, which you *believe to be natural and normal,* are really *self-destructive* to you as a manager.

It is not expected that you turn your emotions on and off like a light switch. But it is expected, when you realize that your reactions to your emotions are damaging your effectiveness as a manager, that you will work to improve it. For example, if you get a ticket on the way to work and step in slush up to your knees when you get out of the car, you should take a moment to calm yourself. Say to yourself, "Now look, this has nothing to do with those nice people who work for me, therefore, why should I go in there and emote all over them?" Then enter your office and proceed as you normally do. If you cannot *yet* control yourself to that extent, then, when you enter your office, tell enough people, "I just want to let you know that I'm going to act a little weird today because I am really mad about stepping into slush up to my knees and getting a ticket on the way to work."

Here is how one manager changed his behavior.

I have consciously changed my behavior so as not to show any of my true feelings if I happen to be in a bad mood. In the morning I make a point of saying good morning to everyone on an individual basis, referring to each one by name, rather than a quick, general "good morning." I now also recognize everyone for the job they do by telling them I appreciate their efforts. In the past, I would say nothing if they did their job the way they were supposed to do it. I would only pat them on the back if they did an outstanding job. I am pleased to report that the productivity of these people has increased noticeably which was to me a nice surprise. I did not expect their productivity to go up because I felt that they were producing at their maximum performance level over the long run. I felt that I could not ask them to produce more because I was satisfied with their work and I did not want to alienate them. Without asking them to do anything, just by changing my behavior, the average productivity of the employees has improved. I have noticed also that if a job is running past the 5:30 P.M. quitting time, some of the employees will remain a few extra minutes to complete their assignment. This free overtime never occurred in the past and I can only attribute it to the different way I am doing things.

Let me clarify here that all emotional responses on the job are not self-destructive behavior. If you accidentally smash your hand in a file drawer, I am not recommending that you stuff the bloody stump under your arm and proceed with placid dignity. Screaming, yelling, and some foul language would be quite appropriate. Also, the spontaneous expressions of pleasure over successes (finding solutions to problems, getting the sale, eliminating errors, finishing on time or ahead of schedule, etc.) are not self-destructive to your management.

Not doing what you are supposed to do, however, because you are tired or bored is self-destructive behavior. Giving employees a rear view of your wisdom teeth, or demonstrating how red in the face you can get in fits of rage over their nonperformance is self-destructive. If you must express your rage, do it in a closet; don't louse up your managerial actions by doing it all over your employees. *Doing what comes naturally is self-destructive behavior to a manager.*

SELF-DEVELOPMENT AS A DESTRUCTIVE MANAGEMENT CONCEPT

Another reason managers fail in their face-to-face process with their employees is because they view their employees outside the business parameters within which they embrace all other resources they are paid to manage. When teaching managers about the process of management, I frequently ask them to list the resources they manage. The list usually looks like this:

1. Machines
2. Money
3. Raw materials
4. Facilities (buildings)
5. Finished product
6. People

The reason *people* usually ends up on the bottom of the list is because managers do not generally think of the employees assigned to them as a resource. Managers even ask whether it is dehumanizing to refer to people as a resource. The truth is that many managers are ineffective as people managers because they *do not* recognize the people working for them as a business resource. Therefore, they do not apply the same business rules to managing people as they do to all the other resources they manage.

As an example, let's assume that I am responsible for an office building. Let's also assume there is a raging storm outside and there is a leak in the corner of one room. The water is coming in at the ceiling, dripping down the wall, and wetting the floor. Since I am responsible for the building, you come to me and say, "Ferd, what's going on with that leak in the corner?" My answer to you might be one of the following responses:

"Well, it's an old roof. What can you expect?"

"Well, it's a cheap roof. We didn't pay much money for it. What can you expect?"

"Well, it's a poorly designed roof. Everytime it rains we are going to have that problem."

Those are pretty ridiculous responses, aren't they? If the building were my responsibility, you would expect me to take whatever action necessary to prevent the water from coming in. You would expect me to look for alternatives to solve the problem.

Let's take a look at another situation. Let's make believe I am responsible for a group of production machinery in a certain manufacturing department. You are my manager and you have just come to visit my department to see how things are going. What you hear is a very high-pitched noise similar to that of a bearing in a machine burning out due to lack of lubrication. You say: "Ferd, what's happening with that machine over there?" My possible responses to you might be as follows:

"Well, it's an old machine, you know. You can't expect too much from an old machine."

"Well, it's a cheap machine, you know. We didn't pay too much money for it. What can you expect?"

"Well, that machine has a poorly designed lubricating system. It was that way when we got it, and the bearing is burning out."

I am sure you will again agree with me that those responses would be quite inappropriate. You would expect me to take the necessary action to have the bearing replaced and the proper lubrication provided. As is customary in business, if our company had purchased a machine and it was later discovered that the lubricating system was not the best or didn't suit our needs, we probably would have modified it to make it work. We would seek alternatives to solve the problem.

Let's look at another example. Pretend that I am responsible for the company's cash, and I currently have $26 million in a full-service bank that is giving us 6½ percent return. Today we receive a letter from another bank that is similar in every respect except that it gives 7 percent return. My reaction is as follows:

> "Gee whiz, look at that. We have our money in this bank giving 6½ percent and that bank over there gives 7 percent. Son of a gun. Isn't that a shame?"

Ridiculous again. What most likely would happen is that our $26 million would be moved to the second bank unless there were compelling reasons not to do that.

Now let's pretend I have an employee working for me who is failing, and you, my manager, say to me, "Ferd, what's wrong? Why is that human resource failing?" My possible responses to you are these:

> "Well, it's an old resource, you know. It has been around here for a long time. What can you expect? You can't do anything with it."

> "It's a cheap resource. We don't pay much for it. What else can you expect for the money we pay?"

> "It's poorly designed; it is not qualified and speaks a different language."

How many times have you heard similar reasons given for a worker's non-performance? Isn't it strange that these responses as reasons why the human resource is failing do not sound ridiculous. What we have here is a contradiction in the theoretical approach managers use in managing their nonhuman resources compared to their human resources.

Managers have no difficulty in accepting full responsibility for the success or failure of their nonhuman resources. As a matter of fact managers pride themselves on obtaining performance from their nonhuman resources when others have admitted defeat. In actual practice, managers diligently seek out every possible alternative to solving incidences of nonperformance of nonhuman resources. It is a source of pride to make things work in spite of obstacles. Managers stop seeking alternatives only when it is finally determined that additional efforts to make the resource work are no longer economically feasible. That is, the cost of efforts to make the resource work is greater than the cost of replacing it.

Now, in sharp contrast, when managers are faced with nonperformance of their people, they try only a few alternatives and quickly surrender with, "Oops, it's beyond our control. It's the resource's fault, not ours." The most appropriate solution to correcting nonperformance of a human resource appears to be to replace it. One of the reasons managers do this is because they don't know what other alternatives to try, to make the human resource successful. Another reason is that managers believe in the concept called *self-development,* which in business means the following:

> "We believe that all development is self-development; we, the company, provide the right environment for you, the individual, to develop yourself. We also provide the opportunities, and if you do not take advantage of these opportunities, then it is your decision to fail, not ours."

This belief predisposes managers to place the full responsibility for performance or nonperformance on the shoulders of the *human resource* itself. This is quite contrary to the manager's business approaches with all the other resources. Can you picture yourself, for example, going into your manager's office and stating that a piece of equipment you purchased 12 months ago for $60,000 was not what you really needed; that you had made the wrong purchase? If you are like most managers I know, that would be the last alternative you would select. To admit such a thing would be an embarrassment, a direct reflection on your management ability, and a source of agitation to your manager. It might even damage your career. Instead you would most likely do everything possible to make that piece of equipment work, in spite of the fact that it was a bad purchase. But what happens when you hire a human resource for $60,000 and 12 months later that resource doesn't work out? You walk in and announce to your boss, "I don't think that Charlie is going to work out; I think we made a poor hire." The typical boss's response is, "How long will it take to get his replacement?"

Why is this announcement, which continually echoes through the halls of business, "I think we made a poor hire," made with impunity and without embarrassment? Why aren't managers just as worried about confessing their poor investment in a human resource as they are about a poor investment in a nonhuman resource?

One of the reasons is that companies have not truly calculated the cost of replacing a human resource the way they calculate the cost of replacing their nonhuman resources. When an organization is going to buy a new piece of production equipment they not only calculate the cost of the purchase and delivery of that equipment; they also calculate the cost of everybody's time, including the training time of the operator on the new equipment, until productivity reaches a specified standard. When a company replaces a human resource, however, their calculations include only the hiring fees and relocation costs. They stop calculating cost when the human resource arrives at the front door. They do not calculate the cost of everyone's time invested in that new human resource until he or she achieves performance standard. This can be anywhere from thirty days to six months. They don't even include the cost of everyone's time required in making the hiring decision.

One of the tasks I required of my MBA students at the university is to choose a manager in their organization who has been recently discharged and calculate the true cost of replacing that human resource. Typical of the findings is the case of one student who was surprised to discover that the cost of replacing a $65,000-a-year division controller was over $60,000. When I asked him what his findings meant to him as a manager, he replied "Had I known this beforehand, I would have been willing to invest $10,000 to fix the old one rather than spend $60,000 to get a new one."

One executive, as a result of being exposed to the preceding ideas, calculated the following cost of replacing one of his technical, professional employees.

Estimated Replacement Cost for Technical Professional, Salary $50,000

1. Severance pay @ 1 week/year of service (10 yrs)	$9,615
2. Notice to severed employee, 4 weeks (permitted to job hunt)	3,846
3. Interview expenses, 8 people, $400 ea., avg.	3,200
4. Time spent by interviewers, 12 hrs. @ $45/hr	540
5. Employee orientation (time of all people involved)	1,000
6. Relocation	15,000
7. Agency fee @ 25%	12,500
Subtotal	$45,701
8. Project orientation time (up to 4 months)	11,538
Total	$57,239

As a result of the information he gathered, these were his comments:

> My career has always been in industries where equipment was the tool for production of the product itself. I am, therefore, very familiar with the techniques and decisions relating to the risk/reward probabilities of maintenance and modification versus write-off and replacement. I have seldom considered the human resource in the same way because it seemed too impersonal, inappropriate, or not a useful standard of measurement.
>
> The replacement costs obtained in this project were surprising. Seldom have I viewed my people as an asset that might cost me $40,000 to $50,000 to replace. Never have I considered spending even $15,000 to $20,000 to retrain or modify this asset. It is clearly evident that within the context of total replacement costs, the amount of expense justified for successful rehabilitation can be a high percentage of the annual salary and still be a profitable decision.

Here's how another manager calculated the cost of replacing a word processor who was terminated after 18 months of employment. The costs were as follows:

Severance pay—2 weeks	$910.00
Recruiting advertising	800.00
Supervisor's interviewing time	152.00
Manager's interviewing time (4 hrs)	98.90
Overtime for workload not covered by terminated employee—45 hrs.	585.00
New employee's physical	100.00
Hiring processing costs	225.00
Nonproductive wages (new person)	455.00
Total	$3,325.90

The manager concluded that if the supervisor had spent only half the above cost in trying to correct the previous employee, she could have invested 2–5 weeks of her time (at $673 per week) to fix the problem employee rather than firing her, and it would have been a profitable decision to the company.

Because managers do not realize the cost of replacing a human resource, the logical alternative to solving a people performance problem is to replace the person. Individual managers can't be blamed for this because normal management practice has not required the same specific cost calculation of replacing human resources required for nonhuman replacement. The fact is, in the business world when you fire somebody, you actually suffer more than he or she does. Your troubles begin with the echo of your words, *you are fired.* Consider the losses in your own productive time as a manager because of the time and effort you must devote to covering the empty positions, initiating search, hiring, and training before the new resource becomes as competent as the predecessor. If you calculate all costs, you will discover that in most instances it is more economically profitable for you and your business to improve the performance of the incumbent.

When teaching coaching to sales managers I ask them if they ever devote an entire week or two exclusively to trying to turn around the performance of a failing salesperson. Invariably they laugh and look at me as though I am an idiot and tell me that they might do a day or two but they can't afford to devote that much time to fixing screw ups. I then ask them to calculate how many minutes and hours of their individual time are occupied with a salesperson from the time they say "you are fired" until the time they say "I think the new salesperson is performing up to normal." They include the time spent on paperwork getting rid of the old one, the phone and face-to-face time of the search and hiring process, time handling the situation of the open territory, orientation, and training of the replacement until he or she achieves normal performance. The numbers vary widely depending on the product sold and whether the replacement is experienced in selling that product, but the total time is never less than 30 work days spread over the first year. I then point out to them that if they locked themselves in a room for a week with a problem salesperson determined to fix the problem, they could do a lot of fixing and save themselves a lot of time. Sales managers who have done this, report their surprise in getting performance improvement which previously seemed impossible. When these sales managers fire someone they are saying, "I don't have one or two weeks to help you improve your performance but I have 30 work days to devote to replacing you." When they do that, it leaves only 11 months of their time to manage the rest of their sales force. All things being equal, the manager who has 12 months to manage his or her sales team will sell more than the manager who has only 11 months to do that.

I am not recommending something new to you; I am just telling you to be consistent. You now accept full responsibility for the success or failure of your nonhuman resources, which require you to do everything possible to assist them in being successful. In fact, you demonstrate your outstanding management ability by doing everything to achieve the needed performance in spite of obstacles. The point I am trying to make is that you do not have the prerogative of approaching the management of your human resources outside of these very important business parameters. You do that only because of what you believe about that resource. If you believe the resource must develop itself, you will expect it to improve itself, and this directs you away from managing that resource. This is self-destructive behavior. To be successful as a manager, you must accept full responsibility for the success or failure of *all your resources,* not just your nonhuman ones.

Along about now you are probably saying to yourself, "Wait a minute. My human resource is quite a bit different from my nonhuman resources. After all my machines don't talk back to me. Are you telling me that I should be managing my human resource the same way I manage my machines?"

Of course you are right about your human resources being different from your nonhuman resources. But if you don't stop there, you will also realize that your nonhuman resources are also different from each other. Certainly your financial resources are quite dissimilar from your equipment resources and your equipment resources are quite dissimilar from your raw materials, and so on. But I am not talking about the *way* you manage your resources, I am talking about what you believe about those resources that causes you to mismanage them.

It would be ridiculous to expect you to manage your human resources the same way you manage your nonhuman resources. How can you manage your money the same way you manage your machines or your equipment? You don't put oil on your money or your people, but you certainly need it on your machines. You don't put shingles on your machines, your money, or your people, but you certainly do put them on your facilities. The specific way in which you manage each of your resources is certainly peculiar to that resource. You are right that your people can talk back to you and your other resources cannot, but this ability to talk and to reason is an advantage for you in managing that human resource, not an obstacle. It becomes an obstacle only when you don't know what to do about it, and the purpose of this book is to help you know what to do about it.

The conclusion I want to leave you with is this. The concept of *self-development* may be appropriate for personality development, but it is self-destructive as a management concept. It is in conflict with the business parameters within which you manage all of your other resources. If you believe the resource must develop itself, then you will not exert that influence, which will result in your *self-destructive behavior* as a manager. You, as a manager, must *accept full responsibility for the success or failure of your human resources* the same as you have always accepted full responsibility for your nonhuman resources. You are the greatest influence over the success or failure of your resources.

3
Motivation—The Theories You Can and Can't Use

In an effort to get you and me to the same starting point, I would like to pose the following problem for you. If you had a subordinate manager who came to you today and said, "Please tell me what I can do *tomorrow* to motivate my employees to increase their productivity," what would you say? Use the fly leaf or a piece of scratch paper to write down your answer before you read further.

This is a question I frequently ask managers in my seminars, and it is always surprising how long it takes to get a response. Even more surprising are the responses themselves, which usually are as follows:

"Get to know them better."
"Talk to them."
"Get close to them."
"Let them know you're interested in them."

Occasionally someone will respond with "Enrich their jobs," which has a practical ring to it, but which is quite nonspecific. On rare occasions someone will answer:

"Set goals for them."
"Recognize their achievement."

The scarcity and impracticality of the responses are even more surprising when you realize that managers asked this question are not neophytes. They are company presidents, vice presidents, directors, and experienced managers at all levels in all kinds of organizations, who have been exposed to the prevalent management training literature. It is also quite common for these same managers to state the reason for employee poor performance as *lack of motivation,* which leads us to the next logical question, *What is motivation?*

Quite often a group of 25 managers will spend 15 minutes trying to define *motivation,* a word they use so freely. Invariably they settle on two definitions as follows:

1. Motivation is a thing you do to get others to do something.
2. Motivation is something that happens inside people that gets them to do something.

It is a wonder there is not more unanimity in defining a concept that is so heavily threaded through management training and which appears to be vitally related to success in people management. Why is it that despite all of the management training to which managers are exposed, they are able to talk about motivational theories and reasons for nonperformance, but are unable to specify practical things in their control to influence motivation? A review of some of the theories may give us a clue.

HIERARCHY OF NEEDS

One theory of motivation is that humans do the things they do because of their needs; that is, humans direct their own actions to satisfy their own needs. Therefore, humans' needs are considered the source of all of their actions; that is, they prompt their actions. And because humans have many needs at any one time, the strongest need is the need that determines the human's actions at that time.

According to one behavioral scientist,* these needs motivate humans' actions only as long as they are not satisfied; once a need is satisfied it no longer motivates. According to Maslow, these needs, to which human actions are directed, can be categorized and compared in their relative importance as they influence human actions. He arranges these needs in the following hierarchy. When a need at any one level is satisfied, the next level need becomes predominant.

---

*Abraham H. Maslow, *Motivation and Personality,* Harper & Row, New York, 1954.

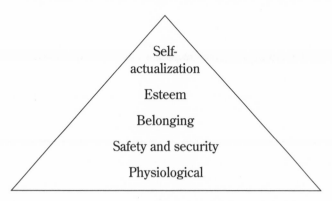

As indicated in the hierarchy, the first-level need is the basic human need related to the sustenance of life itself, such as food, clothing, and shelter. Once these physiological needs become satisfied, the next-level need, *safety and security,* becomes predominant as a motivator. This would be equivalent to the need for self-preservation. It is not only the need to be free from physical endangerments, but also the perception that this is so.

Once these needs, which are primarily physiological, are satisfied the next-level need, *affiliation or belonging,* emerges as the dominant need. This, considered as the first sociological need, is the need to share a physical propinquity with others, but also to perceive that acceptance by the group. Once this need is satisfied, it is theorized that *esteem* becomes dominant. This is the need for the individual to be recognized by the group as being outstanding for some reason, as well as the need for self-esteem, which is based on the recognition of others.

Once esteem needs have been satisfied, the need for self-actualization becomes more dominant as the motivator. Maslow says this is difficult to describe. Described in different ways by different individuals, it has to do with the individual's concepts of life and humanity and those things that each individual feels are needed to maximize one's potential whatever it may be. You know you have it when you feel you are doing or accomplishing in life those things you feel you should be doing.

Although it is accepted that each individual varies widely as to where he or she will be in the hierarchy, and that people will move to different levels of needs even though a previous level has not been fully satisfied, the assumption of this theory is that people will act in specific ways because of the dominant need that influences their behavior. For example, the need for esteem is considered to be related to prestige, power, self-confidence, and control.

When this theory is presented to managers in training seminars, the participants usually leave the seminar with the assumption that they know or will be able to know what level need is predominant with a particular individual they manage. They then assume they will be able to identify elements in the work environment that will satisfy that dominant need. Therefore, managers faced with a problem employee will attempt to translate the hierarchy theory of needs into specific actions, by having long conversations *to get to know the employee better.* These interesting conversations cover broad areas about the employee's past and present life in and out of business, and past disappointments, achievements, and aspirations. Through these conversations the manager tries to identify the needs that occur between the employee's ears. The assumption is that if the boss talks to the employee long enough, the boss will know what is going on inside the employee's head.

There are two problems with this approach for managers, however. In the first place, to know what is going on between someone's ears just by talking to him is not an easy process even for a psychologist, and it is very difficult, if not impossible, for a nonpsychologist. In the second place, if you did know what was going on between someone's ears today, you would not know forever. If you wanted to know next month you would have to play amateur psychologist again. I am not questioning whether Maslow's theory is valid or whether it can be used by a psychologist. What I am questioning is whether you, as a manager, can use it. As a teacher, I am faced with the problem of not only telling managers what they should do but also telling them *how to do it.* And I can't tell managers how to put that theory to work tomorrow with any certainty of gauging success. Therefore, it is not appropriate for me as a basis for teaching you a face-to-face technique for managing employees' performance. Not being able to tell you *how to do it* prohibits me from telling you that *you should do it.*

THEORY X VERSUS *THEORY Y*

Perhaps you are familiar with the work of another noted behavioral scientist, Douglas McGregor, who is famous for his classification of management approaches as *Theory X versus Theory Y.** According to McGregor,

---

*Douglas McGregor, *The Human Side of Enterprise,* McGraw-Hill, New York, 1960.

the structure of organizations is based on certain assumptions about human nature and human motivations. *Theory X* assumes that most people find work inherently distasteful, lack ambition, have little desire for responsibility, and prefer to be directed; they are not creative in solving organizational problems, and they want safety above all. Managers who accept *Theory X* believe that people are motivated by money, fringe benefits, and threats of punishments. *Theory X* managers believe that people work only as long as they are watched; therefore, the best management approach is to design exactly what it is that these people must do, tell them specifically what they must do, and closely control them or coerce them to make sure they do it. Managers in companies that accept *Theory X* build a top-heavy organization with many levels of managers who are planning, deciding, and policing what everyone is doing.

McGregor presented an alternate theory, *Theory Y,* which assumes that people are not naturally lazy or unreliable, and that a properly motivated worker is capable of directing his or her own efforts to accomplish organized goals. According to *Theory Y,* work is considered as natural as play if the conditions are favorable; people do have the capacity and creativity for solving organizational problems; they can be self-directed and creative at work if properly motivated and they do want to do a good job when they are working. Managers in organizations that accept *Theory Y* push information and responsibility downward, explaining to workers the reasons why things should be done, assuming they have an interest in doing them and a willingness to do them. Managers also spend time with workers discussing problems and asking for their ideas and suggestions as to how the job can be done better.

Unfortunately, managers who thought they were following *Theory Y* assumptions got themselves involved in something called *democratic management.* They met with their workers and not only explained what had to be done, but took votes on what things would be done and when. In McGregor's view, this was a misdirection and misinterpretation of his theory. Business is one of the most undemocratic organizations in our democracy. Employees do not vote on who is going to be the company president, much less who is going to be their manager. Because of the information available to any manager concerning the unit's relevancy to the entire organization, as well as that manager's upward and lateral interface relationships in the organization, there are certain decisions that can be made only by the manager. It is one thing to collect ideas and suggestions from employees on how a job might be done better, but it is another thing to make the decision whether to change the job. McGregor stressed that a manager must manage; managers must make those decisions that only the manager is able to make.

The most important conclusion that can be drawn from McGregor's *Theory X* versus *Theory Y* concept is not about workers, but about managers: *managers do what they do for or to workers because of what they believe about workers.* As mentioned earlier, managers are not as successful as they should be in the face-to-face process primarily because of their unfounded and erroneous (and self-destructive) beliefs about workers. Ask yourself if you would act differently as a manager if you *really believed* all your workers wanted to and were capable of being successful.

SATISFACTION AND DISSATISFACTION

Another noted behavioral scientist, Frederick Herzberg, initiated some revealing studies of motivational influences on the nonblue-collar worker.* One of the most interesting realizations that comes from Herzberg's research is that the things that *dissatisfy* workers are not just the opposites of the things that *satisfy* workers. According to Herzberg's findings, things that dissatisfy workers are entirely different from those that satisfy them. The factors or relationships of the job that lead to each are distinctly different. A few of the dissatisfiers and satisfiers Herzberg found in his initial research are listed here:

Dissatisfiers	*Satisfiers*
Company policy administration	Achievement
Supervision	Recognition
Work conditions	Work itself
Salary	Responsibility

The important implication of this is the realization that elimination of a dissatisfaction does not automatically provide a satisfaction. If you, as a

---

*Frederick Herzberg et al. *The Motivation to Work,* Wiley & Sons, New York, 1959.

manager, eliminate a dissatisfaction for your workers, you should not assume that you have created a *satisfaction*. You have only eliminated a dissatisfaction.

For example, Herzberg listed compensation inequities as a common source of dissatisfaction. A compensation inequity occurs when you pay two workers doing a highly similar job, highly dissimilar compensations, or when you pay two workers doing highly dissimilar jobs, highly similar compensations. What you have is unfairness, an inequity, a dissatisfaction. This kind of dissatisfaction is a common one and has nothing to do with whether your company is the highest-paying or lowest-paying company in town. If you do the proper thing and eliminate this inequity, using sound wage and salary administration, you will only have eliminated a dissatisfaction.

Another source of dissatisfaction in many organizations relates to the supervisory relationship caused by managers using the Y, S, and T approach (yelling, screaming, and threatening). If this is a source of dissatisfaction to workers you can take steps to eliminate it by teaching the managers to smile a lot, be friendly, and not to scream so much. If you succeed, you will merely eliminate a dissatisfaction.

The same thing relates to working conditions. You may have complaints that the work area is hot in summer and cold in winter, that the old paint is grimy, and that the seats are hard and worn. If you take steps to improve these conditions by making it warm in the winter and cool in the summer, painting the walls, and replacing the seats with softer ones, and even providing music, you certainly have taken steps to eliminate dissatisfactions. But according to Herzberg's theory, you have not created a satisfaction or motivator. When you eliminate these dissatisfiers you are merely cleaning up the environment. Herzberg refers to these activities as improving the hygiene factors. For example, picture yourself with a cavity in one of your teeth. If you take the positive action of brushing your teeth three times a day you may be successful in preventing the cavity from getting any worse, and your breath may smell nicer, but your efforts did not fill the cavity or make it go away.

Herzberg labeled the satisfiers as motivators because they had the positive effect of increasing the individual's output. Of these satisfiers he found *achievement* to be the single strongest motivator. Herzberg said that people are not motivated by failure; they are motivated by achievement. Small achievements act as motivators for someone to go on to try to achieve a *little bit more*. This *achievement* is the perception that occurs in a person's mind that he or she has done something for the first time or has done it better than he or she ever did it before. For example, picture someone who usually falls down six times every time he tries to stand up. If once he falls down only five times, he could perceive that as an achievement. That achievement then influences that person to try to stand more frequently and perhaps to try to walk. Further achievement (falling down less) acts to influence him to attempt more achievements. Failing by less influences people to improve performance.

The second strongest motivator, as indicated by Herzberg, is *recognition*. This occurs when someone achieves something and someone else recognizes that accomplishment in some way. For example, suppose an individual has only fallen down five times instead of six and you run over to her and say, "Hey, you are improving your ability to stand up; you fell down less than you normally do." Your words of praise for that achievement are *recognition*.

Herzberg tells us that the dissatisfiers on a job have no influence as motivators for high-level performance. The satisfiers are considered as actual influences to motivate people to higher levels of productivity. If achievement and recognition are the strongest motivational influences in the work environment, one effective way to increase productivity would be to provide more opportunities in each job for achievement to occur, which would give you, the manager, more opportunities to apply recognition. Makes sense doesn't it?

Herzberg conducted his research and published his findings over 30 years ago. A logical question would be "What do managers do today in business because of these important findings?" For example, if achievement and recognition are the strongest motivators and lead to increased productivity, what do we managers do as a general practice to take advantage of that? The answer is *little* or *nothing*. In fact we behave contrary to his findings; we spend a lot of time convincing people that the good work they produce is normal—that what they *achieve* is what was expected anyhow, and that's what they get paid for. How often have you heard managers make statements similar to these:

> "I wish (so and so) would grow up; every time he solves a problem he runs in here to tell me about it."

"Some people around here think they should get a medal when they do something right; I wish they would get the message that doing things right is what they get paid for."

"(So and so) would be great if she would just stop looking for a pat on the head when she does something right."

In spite of the fact that Herzberg's first work on the subject was published in 1959, it appears that managers continue to ignore the motivational influences of *achievement* and *recognition*.

A game I play with managers in my seminars is to ask them to think of the possible number of achievements that might have been accomplished by their employees during the last 90 days. I ask them also to include achievements that might have occurred three months ago that they just recently found out about.

Once they have written down that number I then ask them to think of a second number, the number of times they did something that might have been considered as recognition of that achievement. Then I ask them to compare their two numbers. No one has ever had two equal numbers. Rarely is anyone's first number less than four times larger than the second number. This means that for every four achievements occurring in the work place the manager is only recognizing one of them. Managers get embarrassed by this and quickly defend themselves by stating they never pass up the opportunity to recognize somebody's achievement as long as they are aware of it. They also complain they have very busy schedules and don't really have time to stroll around to find out what their subordinates are doing. They say "The theory is fine, but in the real world we have to address ourselves to the bottom line." These managers are saying they don't have time to seek out the achievements of their workers so they can recognize those achievements and thereby motivate their workers to improve, because they, the managers, are spending all their time trying to increase productivity. Sounds foolish, doesn't it?

I know an experienced manager who has had serious discussions about an employee's level of maturity because the employee persisted in waving his achievements in front of the boss. The conversation went something like this.

You have been on the job 18 months now and you are doing a fine job. You certainly have the kind of creativity, experience, and insight that we expected you to have when we hired you. I certainly have no complaints about the problems you have helped us to solve and the systems you have helped design. However, I am seriously concerned about your maturity and self-confidence. You appear to have a great need for me to pat you on the head each time you come up with a new idea, a solution to our problems, or an innovative system change. I think it is important for you to realize that the nature of your job is to be creative, to seek out solutions, and to be innovative in implementing them. We know you are very creative and have a lot of good ideas. That's why we hired you and that's why we pay you so well. You should learn to have a little more confidence in yourself and realize that for someone as gifted as you the innovative and creative processes are what you should expect as normal for yourself. We certainly expect it as normal for you. We like you and we think we have made the right choice in putting you on that job. Therefore, you should have no reasons for feeling insecure in that job. If you continue to produce as you are now producing, there certainly will be no doubts about your long-range future in this organization. I will certainly take care of you at raise time. But you should stop wasting your time and my time by expecting me to pat you on the head like a little boy each time you come up with a solution. Neither one of us has time for that. There is no need for you to worry whether we are aware of your accomplishments. Although it may not appear so at times, we are aware of what is going on and will quickly let you know if things are not as they should be.

The real message is, "Why don't you go back to your office, chain yourself to your desk, and keep pumping out those good ideas and solutions. Remember that those good ideas are really just normal productivity for you; that's exactly what is expected."

I have been with managers when they have tried to avoid recognizing achievement saying, "Uh oh, let's take a walk. Here comes so and so who wants to tell me what a wonderful job she did today." These managers think they are responding normally to an aggravation in their otherwise busy work schedules. What is actually happening, however, is that the worker is trying to communicate to the manager, "Look boss, I'm motivated because I think I just achieved something. Why don't you recognize my achievement, which will motivate me to go out and achieve more things?" The managers are responding with, "Get out of here, kid, you bother me. I don't have time to waste; I'm too busy trying to increase productivity."

One manager told me "since we are all high achievers in our organization we rarely compliment anyone for a job well done because we all know that there are still many problems to be solved and the job is never done."

Metaphorically speaking, what we have is a situation where someone (Herzberg) has told us that if you tickle people under their right earlobe they will jump over all the tall buildings in town, but managers are running around scratching everybody's left kneecap. If managers are interested in increasing productivity, and they are aware of Herzberg's findings that recognition is the second strongest influence to improve productivity, why aren't they spending more time seeking out achievements, which would present them with an opportunity to apply recognition. For example, why shouldn't the second number *recognizing achievements,* be 80 to 90 percent of the achievements occurring?

One of the reasons given is *not enough time.* Managers claim they don't have enough time to manage. For the last 10 years I have been asking managers during seminars if they hand paychecks personally to their employees. Half or fewer do this. Checks are usually distributed by the manager's secretary, the payroll department, or, at worst, through the mails. Some companies have direct deposits to the worker's bank. Of those managers who do personally hand out paychecks I ask, "How many of you say 'thank you' to your employees when you give them their checks?" Only one out of a thousand managers do that. The rest, like one bank vice president, think I am crazy. He said, "Why should I thank them? I am giving them their paychecks, they should thank me." The assumption is that the manager is presenting a gift to the employees; therefore, the employee should express the proper gratitude. The fact of the matter is that a paycheck must be given for past work done; the law requires you to do it. If you decided not to do it, there would be legal recourse to make you do it. You are not giving them a gift; you are only giving them the compensation they have earned for the work performed. And if you have not taken specific action to thank an employee for something (or talked to him or her) during the past work period, paycheck time gives you the opportunity to express your thanks for merely coming to work every day during the period.

Another reason managers don't recognize achievement is because they are not aware of the numerous forms of recognition at their disposal. Most managers believe the only forms of recognition that have any impact on the employee are raises, bonuses, or promotions. Managers do not realize that one of the major sources of recognition is the sounds that come out of their mouth directed to their employees, such as the following:

"Thank you."

"It looks like a very good job."

"I appreciate all your effort on that."

"Thank you for working so hard to get this to me in the short time available."

"You certainly seem to be making a lot fewer errors than you used to."

"I could never do it that well."

The third and most important reason managers do not score higher recognizing employee achievement is because managers have a warped sense of what an achievement is. Most managers, when they become aware of an outstanding achievement by an employee, will quickly recognize it. Managers are ready and willing to recognize those who win races or scale the highest mountains; achievements that are clearly evident. But what about the numerous people in the organization who are failing by lesser amounts today than yesterday? For example, when someone who was always a day late in delivering something now delivers it only half a day late, she is achieving by improving her performance. Achievement occurs when someone who always wastes a dollar on something now wastes only 75 cents, or when someone who makes everybody mad at her, now only makes half that many mad at her.

Managers confess to me they have difficulty perceiving *failing by less* as an achievement. Some even confess they find it difficult to thank someone for a lesser degree of failure if that individual is still failing. They believe that recognizing improvements in failing is really condoning failing (a little amateur psychology gets in the way here). There are really two difficulties. The first difficulty is the managers' inability to view *degrees of less failure* as *achievement.* It is easy to see the winners. Secondly, when managers try to compliment degrees of less failure they don't know what to say without being sarcastic, misunderstood, or embarrassed. They also wonder what the good worker will think when the failing worker is seemingly thanked for failure. The solution is: *Don't thank people for failing; thank them for achieving more* (more about this later).

The following guidelines will help you make your recognition comments most effective:

1. Your comment should be positive; talk about success rates not failure rates.
2. It should describe behavior.
3. It should occur soon after the achievement.
4. It should include a business benefit of the achievement if possible.

Following are some examples of achievement situations and possible recognition statements.

Situation 1. After checking Tom's attendance records for the past two months you find that he is 15 to 20 minutes late to work every Monday. You speak to him about it on Friday and ask him to come to work on time. The next Monday morning you are at his desk as he arrives 2 minutes late.

Recognition. "Hi, Tom. I see you made an effort to fix the lateness problem. Today is about a 90 percent improvement. Keep that up and you will help us meet our company standard of one late day per month."

Situation 2. Four times during the past five days when you passed Sally's work station after lunch break had ended you noticed that she was not there. You speak to her about it and find that these absences are not work related and you ask her to return to her workstation as soon as a lunch break has ended. The next day you check her workstation right after the lunch break and she is there working.

Recognition. "Sally, thank you for coming back to work right after lunch. It will help eliminate complaints about unanswered phones."

Situation 3. Twice during the past week you have observed Fred deviating from the prescribed procedure he normally follows on a specific task. You remind him that the prescribed procedure must be followed. The next time you observe him he is following procedure.

Recognition. "Hi, Fred. I see you are following procedure as we discussed. Thanks! It helps increase our acceptable work score."

Situation 4. On occasion you assign a special problem to Kathy, the supervisor under you. You always tell her to keep you advised of her progress. You realize that she usually solves the problem but does not report back to you with her progress. Two hours after bringing this to her attention, she contacts you to report progress on problems she is working on.

Recognition. "Kathy, thanks for keeping me informed on your progress. It prevents me from looking like an idiot when my boss asks me what is going on."

Situation 4. During your staff meetings Howard usually presents information and material which is unrelated to the agenda of the meeting. You make a general statement to the group asking them to keep discussion to areas of the meeting agenda. During the remainder of the meeting Howard only talks about pertinent information.

Recognition. After the meeting in private you say, "Howard, thanks for helping to keep the meeting on track by limiting your comments to the agenda. It helps us finish sooner."

Most managers view *recognition of achievement* as hanging medals on those individuals who win the races. It is easy enough to hang medals on winners. In fact there are winners in the business world who will win in spite of your helpful efforts (the high achievers). But management is not a function of playing head scorekeeper, where all you have to do is hang medals on the winners. Management is doing something during the race to influence the outcome of the race.

Management is recognizing those runners *during the race* who have never won, but have run the first hundred yards faster than they ever did before. That recognition will influence how they run the second hundred yards, and, eventually, will influence their position at the finish. Management is doing everything possible during the race so all your employees will tie for first place. If, as Herzberg says, people are influenced by little bits of achievements to try other little bits of achievement, managers should be recognizing degrees of less failure in their employees and thereby influencing them to increase their efforts to fail by less.

When managers try using recognition of achievement, they are surprised at the quick response. Here are some of their stories.

Case 1. The biggest changes occurred with one particular employee I had previously judged as uncooperative and antagonistic. Anytime he was given an assignment he would always botch it up in some way. Of course, he would also receive the wrath he deserved. His position in the company is such that I felt it would be worth the effort to try to make him more productive rather than terminating him and having to start from scratch with a new employee.

My behavior changed in that I started to praise him for the right things he did after each assignment, making sure that I did so to a greater degree than when we discussed negative comments on things he did wrong. I also singled him out in front of others to praise him so that the rest of the staff would be aware that he was not a total loser. In some instances I would pair him with a coworker doing the identical job so that he would get immediate feedback as to how he was performing that particular job. In the past I would always wait until he had finished his assignment before going over it with him.

Now I have taken time to walk over to his desk while he is in the midst of his work [during the race] to see how he was doing and to compliment him if his work is correct.

I find now by my showing more interest in his work and by the combination of praise and lack of negative comments, his productivity has risen drastically. The amount of errors has diminished and he is actually asking about new assignments. There is still a lot of room for this individual's improvement but I now have him heading in the right direction.

Case 2. My secretary produces a rather complicated monthly report. For years, I have considered this report a part of her normal work and usually did nothing more than quickly glance at it and say, "Okay, send it out." This time I read it rather carefully in her presence and complimented her on the fine job in putting it together. I thanked her for the neatness of the report and the content, which required no changes. I was surprised at her reaction, when she said, "Thank you, this is a nice compliment." I noticed also as the day wore on that my coffee cup was always refilled when I was in need of a cup of coffee and she seemed more friendly. I made it a point over the next several days (and I will continue) to thank her for a job well done and not just recognize things that are done above and beyond.

Case 3.   We were having trouble getting some work done by our landlord through our maintenance department and over the past several weeks, I had become rather impatient. Last week, my maintenance supervisor presented me with a copy of a certified letter which he had prepared and sent to our landlord suggesting we spend our money to get the work done and deduct the expense from our monthly rent. I thanked the supervisor for putting the letter together and said that I felt with this approach we would certainly get the work finished. In retrospect, my normal approach to his letter would have been, "It's about time we started getting after the landlord." The supervisor's reaction was one of thanks and since then he has approached me on three different occasions to keep me informed. His latest visit was to proudly announce that the job has been completed. Again, I thanked him for a job well done.

Case 4.   We have a statistician who has been on board approximately six weeks. On Mondays she prepares the weekly sales figures from sources around the country which entails about five hours' work and complete accuracy. During the first several weeks she made a great many errors making people doubt the credibility of the actual sales and production figures. Each week I spoke to her and showed her the errors and told her the importance of her job and the fact that I could not put up with errors. On the fifth week I found only one insignificant error in her report. Having just completed your lecture on achievement and recognition, I was quick to go to her and thank her for the fine job. I rather causally mentioned that the only error made was on this one figure and I could understand what she did incorrectly. I took a minute to show her how to correct it and when I left she thanked me and was beaming with smiles. This past Monday she made no errors and again I was quick to recognize that she now has the job completely under control and I told her I was delighted.

Case 5.   We are in the supermarket business and each month my two operations managers have individual meetings with their store managers. When these meetings are held, I usually like to talk to the store managers for approximately 30 minutes, to let them know what is going on and what we expect from them. This year has been a poor year in the supermarket business and to date, our results have not been encouraging. Last week we received the profit and loss results for the latest period and although not spectacular, they showed considerable improvement. My usual approach is one of doom and gloom, spelling out the fact that none of us will survive unless the results improve. This time I started the meeting by congratulating the 10 store managers on the improvement shown in the latest period. I pointed out several areas regarding gross profit and also the control of expenses that they as a group had improved. The expressions on their faces were enough to tell me that I was using the correct approach and before long one of the store managers raised her hand and indicated that she had just begun. This prompted a flurry of comments by the other managers about things that were being done in each of their stores to make the next period even more profitable. In the past, this type of participation did not take place after spelling out bad news. In the past everyone became quiet and I had a tendency to do all the talking. I found with the approach of using recognition, I did not even have to ask questions. They were there to volunteer the solutions toward becoming more profitable. I learned an important lesson: everybody likes their achievements recognized, no matter how small they are.

Case 6.   Shortly after I started thanking people for things they did which I normally considered part of their normal job and took for granted there was an increased tendency for people to openly discuss things with me. In fact, two managers who previously came into my office only when I summoned them began to approach me quite regularly to discuss problems within their sphere of influence. They were asking advice that in the past they may not have felt comfortable asking. I am convinced that a dedication toward changing one's behavior can go a long way toward increasing my employee productivity. The experiment that started two weeks ago, will now become part of my everyday activity.

If achievement and recognition are the single strongest motivators, the things you should do as a manager to increase productivity are as follows:

1. Get out from behind your desk so you can discover more incidents of achievement.
2. Be sure to recognize achievement as soon as you become aware of it; one-liner e-mails are fine.
3. Interpret incidents of *lesser degrees of failure* as achievements; recognize them.
4. Make up a list of how many hundred ways you can show appreciation.
5. Be conscious of the percentage of words you use when talking to employees about bad things they do as compared to the percentage you use talking about good things and increase the good-things percentage.
6. Write the initials of each person answering to you on your calendar each day. Then each day before you go home, put an *x* beside each one who achieved something and circle each *x* if you have recognized that achievement. Then do more of steps 1, 2, and 3 to increase the number of *x*s and circles.

PEOPLE ARE DIFFERENT—BUT DOES IT MATTER IN BUSINESS?

One theoretical obstacle to managers carrying out the face-to-face process is the invariable admonition they get from books and seminars that they recognize each of their employees as being different and that they treat them as individuals according to their differences. This is usually supported with detailed explanations of the personality anomalies throughout the population. It is assumed that knowledge of these anomalies will equip managers to identify individual personality differences and, therefore, to adapt their management efforts accordingly. This seems logical in view of all the literature describing the psychological complexities of humans, but it leaves me with the important question, "Do managers have to understand as much about people as psychologists do, to successfully manage them in business?" This seems like an important question to me because if the answer is *yes* the next question is even tougher to answer: "How the heck do they do that without getting their Ph.D. in psychology?"

Let's explore this question to determine whether managers are really faced with the same problems psychologists are faced with. For example, visualize a large office building with 2000 people in it. Let's make believe you and I could somehow get those 2000 people to exit the building, one at a time, through the same door, at sunset when it is getting a little difficult to see. Meanwhile you and I will hide behind a bush or a parked car very close to the exit they will be using. As each person comes out the door one at a time, you and I jump out from our hiding place with guns and yell, "Stick 'em up!"

Now if we did that to each of the 2000 people, do you think we would get 2000 *different* alternative reactions? The answer, of course, is no. Some individuals will faint, some will pull out their own guns, some will hand over their cash, some will cry, some will run away, some will fight, and some will wet their pants. Of course, there would be some combinations of reactions such as handing over the cash and wetting the pants, or throwing a punch and wetting the pants, and so on. There might be 25 or 30 different alternative reactions, but there would not be 2000. Why not? If everyone is different why aren't there 2000 different alternative reactions?

You probably have guessed the answer already: *there are not 2000 possible alternative reactions.* Because you and I restricted the parameters of the situation, we restricted the number of possible alternative actions. If we had held up the same 2000 people (one at a time) in a phone booth, there would have been even fewer alternative actions available to them.

Let's go one step further; we will take these same 2000 people, select a dozen at a time and place them in a lifeboat somewhere in the Caribbean. We make believe their cruise ship has just sunk. Some of them have to row, someone has to steer, someone has to fish, someone has to catch rainwater, and someone has to hit sea gulls on the head for lunch. After you get everything settled down, someone jumps up, says, "I want to dance," and proceeds to do so.

Now what are you going to do? Are you going to sit this person down and try to get to know him better by talking about his previous life and work experience? Are you going to discuss family background, whether he loved mom or dad the best, what his brothers and sisters were like, whether he had a lot of toys to play with? Are you going to try to learn what his disappointments were in life, his achievements, and life's aspirations? Or will you most likely point out that he can row, steer, fish, hit sea gulls on the head, or catch rainwater, but dancing is not an alternative?

Let's assume you do either, but the individual responds by saying, "I just want to dance," and continues to do so. Will you talk more about the individual's life and ambitions or will you say, "You can do any of the things I mentioned previously, but dancing is not an alternative because you are rocking the boat. If you don't stop dancing we are either going to throw you overboard or tie you up and put you in the bottom of the boat."

In a lifeboat situation the participants have limited alternatives of appropriate behavior available to them. If one persists in inappropriate behavior, it is most likely destructive to themselves and the group. The captain or leader is left with few alternatives.

This example is used because there is considerable similarity between *business* and a *lifeboat*. There is no business that has its name written in the sky by the hand of any god that says, "This business will be here forever, no matter what it does." The opposite is true, "A business will be there only as long as it continues to do those things necessary for survival." Every year companies that someone assumed *would be here forever* fail and go out of business.

The reason is that these companies ceased to do those things necessary for survival; they ceased to be profitable; they ceased to survive. Your company is a lifeboat; if everyone does not do the right things, it will not survive. The division, department, or unit you manage is a lifeboat. If you and your employees don't do the right things, you and they will not survive.

When psychologists think about humans, they consider what they are in the womb; they view humans relative to their total environment, including parents, mate, and children; what they do when asleep and when awake; their lives, loves, work, joys, and sorrows. The task of understanding the individual complexities of people is never ending for psychologists. Fortunately, managers are not faced with solving the same problems as the psychologists; that is trying to understand humans as they relate to their total environment. Managers are faced only with the problem of managing *human behavior* in the restricted environment of the work situation, their lifeboat.

When a person seeking employment comes to your company and says, "I would like to come into your company," she is really saying, "I would like to come into your lifeboat." The implied agreement (written or not) goes something like this:

She: I will do what you tell me to do as long as you pay me with a check that doesn't bounce.

You: I will tell you what to do, give you some tools to do it with, and try not to dismember you in the process.

When you hire people as employees you do not buy people, or their bodies, or their brains, or their values. You merely rent their behavior. This might be broom-pushing behavior, word-processing behavior, code-writing behavior, selling behavior, problem analysis behavior, idea-giving behavior, and so on. Each job that must be done in your company is a collection of specific behaviors that, when done by the worker correctly, constitute that specific job. The opposite is also true. If a worker does not behave in a certain way, which constitutes a specific job, the worker is, in fact, not doing that job.

In business the appropriate behavior of any job is quite specific and limited. That is, if a worker behaves in certain ways, that behavior is appropriate, and if the worker behaves in certain other ways, that behavior is not appropriate. And because most jobs in any organization are interrelated, any one job not performed correctly affects other job performances causing delays, failures, and poor customer service. There is a major contrast between appropriate behavior in business jobs and appropriate behavior in other activities of life. There is a myriad of behaviors available to people throughout life that neither has constructive or destructive influences over their existence. In other words, there are a lot of weird things people can do outside of work that may get some puzzling looks but will not land them in jail. In business, however, in any specific job, the alternatives for appropriate behavior for that job are limited. There is not a wide choice of behavioral alternatives available to the worker if the job is to be done the correct way to achieve the needed business result.

When individuals come to work for your company, they are, in fact, offering to restrict their selection of alternative behaviors to those that you are willing to pay for. When one of your employees says, "I will not sweep the floor, I will not operate the computer console, I will not come to work on time, I will not complete my reports on time, I will not call on new customers," he is saying, to you "I *want to dance; I refuse to give you the behavior I previously offered to rent to you.*"

When managers ask me what to say to an employee who, when faced with limited choices in how to do the job, claim a democratic right, I tell them the conversation should go like this:

Employee: But what about my democratic right?

You: The country may be democratic but the company is not. Congress didn't pass laws requiring employees to vote on how we do our job. And employees don't vote on who the managers will be. Besides when you asked to be hired I don't recall you saying you would do the job only if you could do it your way.

A lot of employees think they should have a lot of latitude in choosing how they do their jobs but their choices are usually in conflict with what needs to be done in the *job*. You must help the employee understand the rules of the game.

Employee: How do you want me to do this?

You: You can do it either of these two ways.

Employee: Which way is best?

You: We can't tell the difference, they are both pretty good.

Employee: You mean you don't care how I do it?

You: As long as you do it one of these two ways, we don't care how you do it.

Employee: Well, how do you want me to do the other thing?

You: We have four alternative ways for you to do that.

Employee: I prefer this fifth way.

You: All of us would prefer the fifth way but we don't use the fifth way here.

Employee: But I think the fifth way is easier.

You: It may be easier but it does not deliver the results we need so we don't do the fifth way here, we only have four ways.

Employee: But supposing I have a fifth way which is better than your four, don't you want new ideas?

You: We love new ideas. We will take a look at your fifth way and test it. If it works, we will have five ways, but in the meantime, we will have four ways and a test.

Employee: You mean I don't have a choice?

You: Sure you do, you have four alternatives to choose from.

Employee: But I feel restricted.

You: That is a reasonable feeling.

Employee: I don't like doing it your way.

You: That's okay.

Employee: You mean I don't have to do it?

You: No. I mean it's okay not to like it. It's not okay to fail to do it. As long as I've been here, I haven't known anybody who liked that job but they all did it well.

When employees refuse to behave in those specific ways required of that specific job, they are involved in *self-destructive behavior.* If the success of your unit depends on their behavior to survive, their inappropriate behavior is destructive to your unit. If you can't get them to stop their self-destructive behavior, you are involved in *self-destructive behavior.* The survival of your lifeboat (your unit) is at stake, and you, as the captain, are in equal danger of survival.

One management fallacy is the belief that managers have a complete freedom of action. Not only is each management job composed of specific appropriate behaviors, just like any other job, but the higher the level the job is, the less freedom of action there is. Even more important, the behavior of employees has a direct influence over the alternative behaviors of the manager. When employees do what they are supposed to do, the manager has available a normal spectrum of alternative behavior. When an employee says, "I'm not going to do it," the manager's alternatives become limited by the employee's behavior; the manager's behavior must be directed to dealing with that nonperformance.

It is okay to explain to employees, "Look, when you do what you are supposed to do, I have a lot of alternatives available to me which are good for you. I can give you choices of work assignments, good appraisals, raises, time off, extra training, transfers if you desire, recommendations for promotion, and stock options. But when you don't do what you are supposed to do, you have me backed into a corner; my alternatives are limited. I have to give you reprimands, bad appraisals, demotion, time off without pay, and termination. I work here like you do. I have to take action to correct the problem or I will be in trouble."

In conclusion, although people are different, managers need not deal with that fact in the same way psychologists do. The manager's job is not managing people, but managing people's behavior within the restricted parameters of the business environment, which is significantly more restrictive than a person's total aspect of life. When people accept employment in your company, they choose to give up the privilege of behaving as differently as they would like to do because they want the money you will pay for the specific behavior you want. The behaviors that are appropriate in any job are quite specific. The survival of employees (in that job), your unit, you, and your company depends upon employees doing those specific things necessary for survival. *When employees do not do what they are supposed to do, they are involved in self-destructive behavior.*

This recognition of employment as a behavior rental agreement is not another exciting bit of management buzz wordism; it just happens to be the plain facts about a simple relationship we have made complicated beyond recognition and control. You might say, "That sounds like a practical understanding of the relationship, but most employees don't see it that way."

Of course you are right; most employees don't see it that way because you haven't made the effort to explain the facts of business life to them. People are hired in business to do jobs only because we don't have a machine that can do those jobs. You might say that people are doing jobs machines should be doing, but the machine has not yet arrived. In business a machine performs a profitable function when the results of what the machine does exceeds the cost of maintaining and operating that machine. The same relationship holds true of a worker. Any business resource must make a contribution to the business greater than the cost of maintaining that resource. The point at which a worker is paid exactly what he is worth is the point when that worker is no longer making a profitable contribution to that business. When the costs of maintaining a worker equal the value of the contribution the worker makes to the business, that relationship becomes a charitable relationship.

If you want the majority of employees in your business to understand the profit and loss aspects of business survival and the practical relationship of workers to work, teach them about profit and loss. Why should the words *profit* and *loss* be heard only in the executive wing or the accounting department? Tell people when you hire them that you are only renting their behavior, not purchasing their bodies and souls; then concentrate on managing people's behavior, not managing people.

Of course, recognizing employment as a behavior rental agreement eliminates some major aggravation managers get from people complaining that they don't like the work they are doing. It is easy to explain that not liking the work is okay but not doing the work is not okay. You can explain that the nature of most work is that it is repetitive so if you take a job doing something you like to do, you will have to do it so much that eventually you will not like it anymore. But that is okay as long as you do it right. Some of the most interesting work can eventually become boring, tedious, and tiresome, that is why we have to pay you for it. If people really enjoyed all the work in your company, you could call it an amusement park and charge people to come in. But because most people would rather be doing something else than working, you have to pay for it. It is reasonable to expect people to do what you pay them to do even though they don't enjoy or even like it, the same way they do all those other things in life they don't enjoy and don't get paid to do, like changing diapers, exercising, and being nice to people they don't like.

But it is important to give people a list of the behaviors which constitute the job before you hire them. One woman who was hired as a mail clerk in one company's mailroom was told in her second week that it was her turn to sweep the floor. She refused saying she was hired as a mail clerk not a janitor. It didn't matter when her supervisor explained that the sweeping job was rotated through all the mail clerks; no one had told her that when she was hired. She didn't have a complete list of the behaviors for which she was receiving the rent money. This is a common problem in business which surfaces when people say "that's not my job," or "you're asking me to do more than I am supposed to do," or "you don't pay me enough to do that."

You can correct this problem with your current employees by asking them to write down what they think they are supposed to *do* and you write down what you think they are supposed to *do*. Working with both lists, compose the behavioral rental list for each job. But the key word is *do*. Responsibilities are not actions; write down what people must *do* to meet a responsibility. Also don't include goals or objectives because they are not a part of the behavior rental list. They describe results you expect to achieve over a specified period of time if the employee executes the standard job behaviors. For example think of "piloting an airplane" as the job and your destination and time of arrival as the goal or objective. Once you have completed the behavioral list you will not have to do it again unless the job changes. Once you list the behaviors, you have described perfect job performance; doing the behaviors is acceptable performance, not doing the behaviors is unacceptable.

4

An Alternative to Psychotherapy

The vast majority of the theoretical people management techniques taught to managers are based on the psychodynamic approach. This approach assumes that humans are inert organisms and move only when pushed or pulled by needs or drives.

Managers are taught that if you want to understand why people do things, you must first understand their *motives*. And further, if you want people to behave differently, you must first change their motives; the assumed result will be a change in their behavior. As previously mentioned, this places managers in the position of playing *amateur psychologist*. Happily for all you managers out there, there is another alternative. Part of this alternative comes from George A. Kelly, Ph.D., who was a professor and director of clinical psychology at the Ohio State University for 20 years.

According to Kelly, we need a theory about motives to explain why people move only if we believe that they are inert. If we believe that people are *active* by the very nature of the fact that they are alive, we do not need a theory to explain why people move because they are active and moving all the time. In his paper, "Man's Construction of His Alternatives,"* Kelly described some of his experiences as part of a traveling psychological clinic servicing schools in Kansas. He related how when a teacher complained that a pupil was lazy, he would proceed to diagnose

---

*Brendan Maher, *Clinical Psychology and Personality: The Selected Papers of George Kelly,* John Wiley & Sons, New York, 1969.

whether the child was lazy or was not lazy. If they worked at it long enough, they could usually find *some grounds* to justify any teacher's complaint. But eventually Kelly discovered something he called *the law of the excluded middle*. This law implies that once you give a name to something, the only two alternatives available are *it is or it isn't* what you have named it. When a teacher called a pupil *lazy,* the only alternatives to the diagnostician was to find whether the child was *lazy* or *not lazy.* Kelly said, "When the teacher called a pupil lazy, we looked at the pupil as if it was so. But it was the teacher who called the pupil lazy, not the pupil."

To paraphrase one of his examples, let's suppose you and I were in a room full of people and I pointed to your left shoe and said *it is an introvert.* Because I have called the shoe an introvert the assumption is that somehow the shoe is responsible for it. We may even try to look closer to be sure whether it is or is not an introvert, when, in actual fact, introversion may not be an appropriate description for describing what your left shoe is. Since I called your shoe an introvert why do we look at the shoe rather than at me? It is I who placed the label of introversion on the shoe; why do we assume that because I say it *that makes it so?*

The importance of this concept to managers is the realization that labeling people because of what they do does not necessarily make them what we call them. Even more important to managers is the realization that *labeling* leads away from problem solutions rather than to them. For example, managers observe employee problem behavior and label the worker (lazy is a good example). What happens in the real world is that we observe people who are not doing what we think they should be doing and, because it is clear to us that the worker knows there is something he or she should be doing, the obvious reason for the *not doing* is he or she is *lazy.* We construe laziness as a kind of malady that certain people suffer from either because they were born that way or because of a certain sociological influence. Because we managers have labeled the worker, that label becomes the accepted cause of the problem behavior. Now that the employee has been labeled *lazy,* we can understand laziness as the reason for the *nonperformance.*

PEOPLE DON'T DO DUMB THINGS ON PURPOSE

Kelly's next important observations came when he talked to pupils identified by their teacher as *uncooperative.* He frequently found the pupils had no idea they were being *uncooperative*. In fact, he found they were doing what they thought was perfectly logical to them at that time.

Kelly observed that humans are active organisms, always in motion, always taking action. Because humans are active organisms they are always faced with choosing alternative actions from those alternatives they see available to them. Kelly describes how people view the world through their personal construct systems. Each person views the world, the good, the bad, the happy, the unhappy on an individual basis. The assumption is that people will select what they believe to be the best alternative for them, from those alternatives they see available at that time.

The implication from the preceding is that people do not go through the world doing *illogical things* on purpose. They do what they believe to be the right thing at that moment in time. They have selected (they believe) the best alternatives for them, from those alternatives they see available to them. What they do appears illogical to them only when they find out it didn't work. It appears illogical to someone else who is watching because that someone else sees more alternatives, or knows the one selected will not work.

Did you know that every year between 60 and 70 percent of the murders in this country do not occur in bank holdups, hijackings, and street corner muggings? They are not committed by criminals. They occur between best friends, relatives, loved ones, and next-door neighbors. When you ask Charlie why he stuck that butcher knife in his brother-in-law's throat, he says, "I had to shut him up and it seemed like a good idea at the time." To those of us not involved, that seems horrific and illogical. Perhaps if we talk to Charlie sitting in his cell waiting for sentencing, he also may agree that it was illogical (in retrospect). Perhaps if you or I were there when Charlie picked up the knife, we could have grabbed his wrist and said, "Do you realize you might get life for this or not get out of prison until you are 67; is there anything else you could do to shut him up?" Charlie then might have dropped the knife and walked away.

If we believe humans are active organisms, and we view their actions as a continuous process of *selection of alternatives,* we quickly realize that *experience is merely adding to the number of alternatives an individual has to select from, when faced with a requirement to take action (alternative selection), and hanging around long enough to see if the results of any action turns out as expected.*

For example, when you were seven years old and faced with a situation requiring a decision or action, you might have had only two alternatives to select from. They both may have been bad alternatives. If you were later faced with the same problem at age twelve, you might have had seventeen alternatives to select from. Your experience increased the number of alternatives to select from to solve the problem and you discovered over time which ones worked. It is likely that some of those seventeen alternatives were better than the two you had when you were seven.

Let's relate this to your work experience. Was there ever a time when you were stumped with a technical problem, couldn't land a sale, or couldn't handle a people management problem, and you went to your boss and said, "I tried A, B, and C but I just don't know how to solve this problem."? Your boss responded with, "Why don't you try E?" and gave you a workable solution. Your response might be, "Why didn't I think of that?" No matter how many alternative solutions you had, your boss needed only *one more* to help you solve your problem. He or she might have had 35 more alternatives to choose from.

There is no mystery or magic in experience. The function of experience is merely the act of adding to the number of alternatives you have to select from, when you are required to act. This means that when you point to someone and say, "She does not have enough experience to do that," you are really saying, "That person does not have enough alternatives to choose from when required to act in that situation." In business the problem "needs more experience" is too frequently solved through the equivalent of making someone do something for *more years,* when the actual learning (acquiring additional alternatives) could have been accomplished in two weeks.

Training adds to the number of *effective* alternatives an individual sees available when faced with a specific requirement to take action. Learning by experience wastes a lot of time and leads to bumps and bruises while discovering that alternatives which were thought to be good, were not so good. Training compresses time making people smarter without getting older and avoids the unnecessary bumps and bruises. Therefore, the solution to the *not enough experience* problem is not to require the individual to live more days, weeks, or years in that work situation, but to help them acquire those additional alternatives that are needed. If you know what those alternatives are, you can solve the problem by giving them to the worker. It's called training.

What this means to you as a manager is that there is an alternative to the requirement that you become a psychologist before you become a successful manager. That alternative is to forget about people's motives; you don't know for sure what they are anyhow. If you want to know why people do things, try to understand the practical alternatives they were confronted with, and ask them why they selected the alternatives they did. Recognize that people's behavior takes place within the dimensions of their own personal construct systems, their own views of the good, the bad, the hurt, and the happiness in the world. Stop interpreting the actions of your workers in view of the alternatives *you see* available to them. Interpret what they do in view of the alternatives *they see* available to them. *They do not see the alternatives that you see available.*

If you want them to select better alternatives, give them more alternatives to select from, or let them know now the future consequence of the alternatives they are selecting.

ATTITUDE—A BARRIER TO EFFECTIVE MANAGEMENT

How many times have you felt you knew what people's attitudes were? How many times have you interpreted a worker's good or poor performance as related to his or her attitudes? Do you assume that people do good work because of good (or positive) attitudes and poor work because of poor (or negative) attitudes? Therefore, do you believe that when you change their attitudes they will do better work? Have you ever criticized an employee's unsatisfactory work performance, stating the reason for the poor performance as his or her poor or negative attitude, and pointed out that the solution to solving the performance problem was for the individual to change his or her attitude?

If you are similar to 90 percent of the managers out there in the world, you will admit to all or part of the preceding. Most managers I have taught or worked with in the last 25 years have readily admitted to the same. Once managers tell me they know their employees' attitudes (even sometimes) I ask them how they know. The answers are always the same:

1. I see what they do (their actions, nonactions, reactions, achievements).
2. They tell me.
3. Self yardstick (I did that and I know what my attitude was, so they must feel the same way).

Some managers say they know what people's attitudes are because *other people* tell them, but the only method the *other people* actually have is one of the three preceding.

Next, I ask them: "What is attitude?" The answer to this usually requires a lengthy discussion because most people have difficulty defining *attitude,* although they freely talk about it. Finally, we end up with something like this:

> "Attitude is how people feel about themselves and the world around them and can include quite specific feelings or values, such as likes and dislikes."

After we have defined attitude, I ask: "Where does attitude occur?" The unanimous answer is "in the person's head" or "between the ears." Then I ask them to explain to me how they actually use the three sources of information previously given to determine what people's attitudes are.

For example, "If attitude occurs between people's ears, tell me how your observations of the things they do (their actions) lets you know what is occurring between their ears?" This usually leads to a long discussion of people's stereotyped behavior and the supposition that certain attitudes are unalterably linked to certain behavior, that is, "People do best what they like and do poorly what they don't like." But then it takes little effort to get managers to admit that they do things everyday they don't like to do or don't want to do but they do them anyhow and do them well. Therefore, if you and I saw them doing those things we might assume they loved doing those things.

As the discussion progresses, managers admit there are some things in life they used to like to do and did well, but they have done it so frequently they no longer like to do it; but they have to do it well so they do. They also admit there are some things in life they didn't like to do but had to do, and now, because they have done it so much, they have begun to like it. The realization slowly becomes accepted that there is no permanent link between any specific attitude and any specific action. It is quite possible for people to do something five times in a row but have five changes in attitudes in relation to that thing.

Eventually managers admit they do not know what a person's attitude is by observing behavior. Of course they are right. What they were really doing was observing someone's behavior and guessing about the attitude between that person's ears as related to the behavior. Still, they hasten to add that their guesses get better the longer they do it. "It is difficult," they say, "to know if any specific guess is right or wrong, but over a period of time your guesses will improve." This is ridiculous. If you observe an employee's behavior and make guesses about the attitude connected with that behavior over a five-year period, some of your guesses will be right and some of your guesses will be wrong. The real problem is: *how will you know which of your guesses were right and which of your guesses were wrong?*

For example, let's suppose you and I are face to face, and I ask you to guess how much change I have in my pocket. I will shake my pocket to let you hear what it sounds like. After you guess I say, "Well, isn't that interesting," and walk away, depriving you of knowing how much change there really is in my pocket. How would you know whether your guess was right or wrong? Your single guess has not been verified. It may have been correct, but without verification you would not know whether it was.

You may complain that this example is unrealistic because the guesses you make about your employees' attitudes are more numerous and occur over a longer period of time. You believe that your guesses will improve over time. You think it will be more reasonable for you to make 2000 guesses as to how much change is in my pocket. I will shake my pocket each time to give you some behavior to observe. Because you are clever, you will also record my reactions each time you make a guess (did I smile, or frown, or shift from one foot to the other, or slump my shoulders, etc.). At the end of your 2000 guesses you will analyze your data and relate my smiles, frowns, and body posture to the amounts you guessed. Clever as you are, you will surmise that certain of my reactions were related to a correct guess. For example, it may appear obvious to you that I smiled when you were incorrect and frowned when you were correct. You will probably isolate those guesses that appear to correspond with those reactions. But, after you have analyzed all the information you have collected and make your final best guess, I say, "Well, isn't that interesting," and walk away without telling you the true amount of the change in my pocket. Again you are without verification whether your guess was correct or even close. There is no question that many of your 2000 guesses would be correct. Many of them would also be wrong. The critical question again is: "How will you know which of your guesses is right and which is wrong, if your guesses are never verified?"

When managers realize that number one in the preceding list, as a method for knowing what people's attitudes are, is really *guessing,* they agree that guessing is not an effective or businesslike basis for identifying people's attitudes. But they quickly go on to number 2, *I know what their attitudes are because they tell me.* This sounds like pretty firm ground, but it presents two problems. The first problem is related to the fact that *we do not always know what our attitudes are, even though we say we do.* Research has demonstrated that people frequently do things that are in contrast with what they state to be their attitudes. When this contradiction is shown to them they often restate their attitudes. We are not our own psychotherapists. What we talk about as being important to us frequently is not what is really important to us. I, for example, drive an economy car for the obvious reason that it is economical to operate. It is a Mercedes diesel. Diesel fuel costs about 5 cents less than gasoline. If you talk to the dealer who sold me my car, and tell him what I believe about my economy car, he will probably laugh and suggest that I would have to drive a lot of miles to make up in fuel savings the added cost of a $50,000 car. But I believe I know why I drive it regardless of what he says. The fact is that people do not always know what their attitudes are even though they say they do. Therefore, when someone tells you what his or her attitude is, how do you know he or she knows what it is?

The second problem we face is that even if individuals knew what their attitudes were, how do we know they are telling the truth? Strange as it may seem, patients lie even to their own psychotherapist, or tell them *what they think they want to hear,* even though the patient went there for healing purposes. So why in the world would you expect anyone to be totally truthful to you, the boss, who wields power over employees' destiny?

How many times have you heard managers say, "I think my employees only tell me what they think I want to hear"? There is a lot of truth in that statement. Sometimes managers respond by stating they believe their people are honest with them. Usually I ask them if they are honest in their dealings with the people they work with and the answer is *yes.* Then I ask them if they ever have to deal with someone they dislike, and would it be self-destructive if that person discovered the manager disliked that person. The answer is usually *yes.* Then I ask them what they would do if that person asked them, "Do you dislike me?" The answer invariably is: "I would say no."

In the real world, people must sustain numerous relationships with other people. In the interest of preserving those relationships, people tend to say what they believe to be appropriate, rather than what they actually think. These decisions to say one thing rather than another during the numerous interactions are considered a social grace rather than lying. In a boss-employee relationship, it might be considered self-preservation. It is usually easy to get managers to recognize that number two from the preceding list is not a practical or businesslike basis for knowing people's attitudes.

This leaves the third basis for knowing what people's attitudes are: *I used to do that and I know how I felt about it, so they must feel the same way.* Some managers are quick to recognize: *if I just learned that I don't always know what my attitudes are, then I can't very well do this.* Of course they are right, but even if you were certain of your own attitudes, I would have to ask you, "Who registered you in Washington with the National Bureau of Standards as having the 'normal' attitudes for humanity or for anyone?" As a matter of fact, if you are a successful manager you probably do not have normal attitudes. To be a successful manager (at least in this country) you have to be a high achiever. The higher you go up the management ladder, the greater is the requirement you be a high achiever to get there.

Let's look at the difference between high achievers and normal people. The normal people come to work on time and leave work on time; sometimes they arrive early and sometimes they work late. They hurry home to spend time with their families, Little League sports, civic activities, hobbies, and so on. The high achievers come to work early most of the time and stay late most of the time. They work until 6, 7, 8, 9, and 10 o'clock at night, six or seven days a week. The average work week of a high-level executive varies from 60 to 90 hours. Their luncheon and dinner engagements are with businesspeople for business reasons. Their golf, tennis, or handball games are with businesspeople for business reasons. Even vacations are scheduled at times and places where business can be combined with pleasure. For example, a two-week vacation with the family is spent in Thailand because the company's plant there can be visited at the same time. If a high achiever were going to visit a hospitalized spouse or friend but received a call about a business problem that just came up in Chicago, the high achiever would most likely send flowers to the hospital and catch a plane to Chicago.

We high achievers are not normal; we are a little neurotic like olympic athletes. Olympic athletes give up doing a lot of things normal people do so they can spend inordinate amounts of time perfecting an athletic skill. But because it is for the Olympics, we don't think of them as weird. But we do not want to be changed. The life of a high achiever can be very satisfying. We try a lot of things and we accomplish a lot of things. We work hard at what we do, and we win a lot. When we win a lot in the business world, it usually means we make a lot of money that can buy a lot of tangible benefits. Most of us high achievers got where we are with little help from others. Frequently we achieved despite the helpful efforts from others, including our bosses.

The first mistake we high achievers make after we get knighted as managers is in how we classify the people who work for us. If we are lucky enough to hire a high achiever, our first reaction is to say to ourselves, "Wow, I finally acquired a normal person; someone who believes in the protestant ethic; someone who understands the agony of defeat and the ecstasy of success." We may even go home at night and pray to our favorite deity, "Thank you, God, for sending me a normal person like me. If you get a chance will you send me a couple more normal people, and help me get rid of those subnormal goofoffs who can't accomplish anything without looking over their shoulders all the time." It seems logical that we should compare the people who work for us to what we think we know best—ourselves. Unfortunately, we assume we are normal. We should really be praying like this: "Dear God, thank you for sending me a high achiever. If you get a chance, could you please send me a few more neurotics like me? But please give me the knowledge, understanding, and strength to do what they pay me to do, which is to manage those normal people to help them be as successful as we need them to be." Because we high achievers were successful without assistance, or in spite of it, we assume that is the only way it should be, and we perceive our management job as *pointing high achievers in the right direction and whispering in their ears, "Go get 'em!"*

In two studies I made of performance-appraisal programs in U.S. and Canadian companies I frequently found statements like these on their appraisal forms:

"Does the individual do that little bit more, or only what's expected?"

"Is this person able to work effectively with minimum supervision?"

The first statement, which was used to identify a normal performer, assumes that if the individual is a normal performer (a high achiever like us), he or she will always do more than what is expected. Have you ever heard a manager say, "If I have to tell them what to do, they are wrong for the job"? This also means, "Those who do only what is expected are below-normal performers."

The second statement was also used to identify *good* or *normal* performance. What is most interesting is there was no corresponding statement, such as "Is this person able to work effectively with normal supervision?" The underlying assumption is that the normal manager-subordinate relationship is one of only minimum supervision. This means that any amount of supervision more than minimum (whatever that is) is indicative of poor worker performance. But in the real world managers don't get paid for *minimum supervision;* they get paid for *maximum supervision,* whatever is necessary to achieve results. Managers must construe supervision as those things a manager does to guide, help, and support the success of their employees, and they must recognize that managers don't get paid for minimum effort, but for maximum effort to achieve results. The only reason you are there as a manager is to do everything possible to help your employees to be as successful as you need them to be.

Not only is point number three, *self-yardstick,* just as fallacious as the other two as a basis for knowing people's attitudes, but if you use it, you will expect your employees to perform just like you, with minimum assistance. Therefore, they will be deprived of the help they need to be successful, and you will be involved in self-destructive behavior.

So, the only conclusion left is *we really don't know what people's attitudes are.* We only guess at what they are and then become trapped into believing our guesses are correct. The insidious part of this self-delusion is that once you believe you know what an employee's attitude is, you then believe you can blame that bad or negative attitude for causing poor performance. Since it is the worker's attitude that is wrong, it is the worker who must change it. Your only alternative is to tell them they must change it, and step back to keep score whether they do it. Since it is obviously the worker's fault and the worker must correct it, you just put yourself out of the management of that human resource.

There is another trap for you when you believe you know what people's attitudes are. If you really believe you are able to know what people's attitudes are, then you are in the *mind-reading business.* If you believe you are able to read minds when talking to other people you are really talking to yourself. What you do is project your thoughts into somebody else's head and then direct your conversation to those thoughts you obviously know are there; you are talking to yourself. A sure sign that you are doing this is when the person you are talking to is acting in ways that are not related to what you are talking about. The problem is that you are not responding to that person's communication signals; you are holding both sides of the conversation in your own head.

If you finally recognize that you can't read minds, you will find yourself somewhat alone in the world because everybody else believes they are able to do it. For example, an article written by an associate professor of psychology recently appeared in the journal of a guidance counselors' professional organization. It started like this:

> All counselors use extrasensory perception (ESP) and experience residing beyond the ordinary senses without even realizing it.

> How many times have counselors looked at their clients and immediately had distinct feelings about them? These feelings can be a form of ESP.

Of course there have been numerous times when we all have looked at other people and immediately had distinct feelings about them. But our feelings tell us what is going on inside our head, not what is going on inside their heads. If you believe you know what is going on inside somebody else's head, you know you are right, *because you know you are right;* no one can prove you are wrong. Even if the other person claims what you believe about him or her is incorrect, you still know you are right; that person simply will not admit it.

It is unfortunate for both the manager and the employee if the manager believes he or she has some undefined powers to assist in the management process. But for professionals, schooled in the people-helping professions, to believe they have undefined powers to assist them is not only ludicrous, it is tragic.

I have been in the people management business for 30 years, and I discovered 29½ years ago that I couldn't read minds. My best advice to you as a manager is to get out of the mind-reading business. The necessity for you to be a successful people manager is too important to you to base it on mysticism.

I realize it is not easy for you to give up something that is such a familiar part of our way of life; everybody talks about everybody else's attitude. When a waitress places a plate noisily on your table in a restaurant, the natural response is to comment about her poor attitude. You do not know whether the plate was greasy, her arthritis was acting up, or her doctor called to tell her the rabbit test was positive. In this casual situation there is no harmful consequence to you in playing the attitude game. Your choice will be to leave a smaller tip, which leaves more money in your pocket. It doesn't make any difference to you what the real reason was for the sloppy service. To play the *Attitude-Guessing Game* as a manager, however, is *self-destructive behavior.*

5

A Theory You Can Put to Practical Use

As mentioned earlier, the predominant management training in the people management process uses the internalized theories as a basis to describe why people do things, that is, people do things because of their inner drives, motives, and attitudes. Happily, there is another alternative, the scientific perspective of human behavior called *behaviorism*. This scientifically derived body of knowledge is based on the premise that *all behavior is a function of its consequences.* Specifically translated, it means that people do the things they do because of the results or consequences to them for those actions. This scientific approach to people management, sometimes called *behavior modification,* has demonstrated that not only can people's behavior be changed regardless of what their attitudes might be, but, once the behavior has been changed, the attitude usually follows.

Behavioral science as a conceptual approach to understanding why people do things is perhaps ninety years old. Behavior modification, as a scientific practice of changing or directing the behavior of people as therapy, training, or management practice, has made quantum jumps in acceptance in the last thirty years. If you feel the word *scientific* is heavily used here, you are right. Behavior modification deals only with measurable behavior, in contrast to the theoretical, internalized activities of people's minds, which are not measurable.

WHY PEOPLE DO WHAT THEY DO

The behaviorists tell us that for every human action there are two possible categories of consequences to the individual: there could be a positive consequence and there could be a negative consequence. One primary rule of the behavior modification concept, which is most meaningful to you, is as follows:

> *Behavior that is followed by a positive consequence (to the individual behaving) will tend to repeat itself.*

As an example let's take a look at how the action of mowing the lawn might look in this concept.

MOWING THE LAWN TODAY

Positive Consequences	*Negative Consequences*
1. Lawn looks nice	1. Don't play golf today
2. Easier to do because grass is not too long	2. Perspire in hot sun
3. Neighbors tell you how nice it looks	3. Physical effort

NOT MOWING THE LAWN TODAY

Positive Consequences	*Negative Consequences*
1. Play golf	1. Lawn looks terrible
2. No perspiration	2. Grass too long next weekend— hard to cut
3. No physical effort	3. Neighbors make snide remarks about lawn

Although this is a very simple analysis of some of the possible alternative consequences to doing or not doing something called *mowing the lawn,* it can be easily seen how the positive consequence for not mowing the lawn might result in some very long grass.

If you accept the fact that people do the things they do because of the consequences to them for what they do, it is easy to understand why people will increase the frequency of doing something if each time they do it, a positive consequence usually results. Quite frankly, if you do something and the result is a pleasant experience to you, isn't it likely you are going to do that something again? The idea is simple enough to grasp, but there are some nuances that must be explained. For example, when a person does something there can be many consequences: short-range consequences, long-range consequences, consequences to them, consequences to people around them, and also negative consequences or painful events. The preceding principle works if

1. The consequence is to the individual.
2. The consequence is positive.
3. The consequence occurs soon after the action.

The second rule, which is important for you to understand, is as follows:

Any consequence that occurs after an action and increases the frequency of that action is called a positive reinforcer.

For example, if you give jelly beans, hugs and kisses, or gold stars to people after they do a certain thing, and the frequency of that thing increases, the jelly beans, hugs and kisses, and gold stars are *positive reinforcers.* More specifically, we could make some pretty good guesses that under certain conditions jelly beans, hugs and kisses, and gold stars are considered positive consequences by the individuals acting. We can know for sure whether these are positive reinforcers only if the frequency of behavior we are reinforcing increases.

If we look back at what Herzberg told us about achievement and recognition we realize that he is talking about consequences of performance. He called these motivators but we now know they function as reinforcers with verbal or written recognition as one kind of reinforcer.

Let's look at the possible ways positive consequences of an action may influence that action. For example, let's say I have a four-year-old daughter who I am encouraging to practice the social amenities. Let's assume I am now standing in a room full of guests and I say to my daughter, "Tondalayo, be a good little girl and say hello to everybody." I accompany this with a gentle shove from behind to initiate Tondalayo's movement into the room. Tondalayo takes the necessary steps to maintain her balance, looks around the room, begins to cry, and rushes to me, burying her head on my knee. My reaction is to bend down and stroke Tondalayo's head, hug and kiss her, and, perhaps, give her candy or ice cream.

Let me ask you: "Did Tondalayo do what I wanted her to do?" The answer is obviously *no*. What consequence followed that *not doing?* Was it a positive consequence or a negative consequence to Tondalayo? We probably would be safe in assuming that the hugging and kissing and candy or ice cream were positive consequences to her.

I am concerned about my daughter learning the social amenities. If I use my typical amateur psychological approach, I might try to converse with her asking why didn't she socialize, what is she afraid of, and I might explain the importance of her socializing and how she must grow up to be a socially oriented person. But I know in advance that my chances of holding such a discussion will not be successful with my four-year-old daughter, so I turn to the behaviorist and ask: "What can I do to get my daughter to do more social things?" The behaviorist's first response is likely to be: "Stop rewarding her for not doing what you want her to do." And the conversation might go something like this.

Me: But after all she was crying.

Behaviorist: Does she cry a lot?

Me: Yes.

Behaviorist: Do you hug and kiss her everytime she cries?

Me: Yes.

Behaviorist: Looks like Tondalayo is controlling your behavior. It appears that Tondalayo has learned that good things can be made to happen by crying. If you want to decrease her frequency of crying, one way is to stop rewarding it.

Me: You mean when I ask her to say hello to friends and she cries and hugs my leg, I should remove the positive consequences of kissing and hugging?

Behaviorist: Right. Do not reward her for nonperformance.

Me: When do I kiss and hug her?

Behaviorist: When her behavior approximates what you want. For example, if she goes a longer period without crying, or takes a step closer to your friends, or she smiles, or talks, or touches them, then run up to her and hug and kiss her.

The important point here for you to perceive is that although we both thought I was being nice to my daughter in displaying parental love and affection in her moment of frustration, what I was actually doing was rewarding her for not performing. Now if I, in fact, did ignore Tondalayo's nonperforming behavior (crying and not being social), and I hugged and kissed her when I saw the behavior I did want (longer periods without crying, talking, etc.), we would expect to see an increase in the desired behavior. The periods of not crying would get longer and the incidents of talking would increase.

If you take a minute to think about it I am sure you could name many situations in life where positive consequences are reinforcing people's actions. For example, in our modern society, at least here in the United States, half of the population successfully manages the behavior of the other half. As an example let me ask you this question: "When a man is pressuring a woman what does the man do when the woman cries?" You are right. He usually stops pressuring the woman. The consequence to the woman who is crying is that pressure goes away because of crying behavior. To the man who is pressuring the woman the positive consequence of removing the pressure is that the crying behavior stops. This crying behavior, which is predominant in females, is a learned response rather than inborn. At very early ages both male and female children are quite successful in using crying behavior to bring about positive consequences. When boys and girls reach a certain age, however, the boy is usually punished for crying behavior, but the girl isn't. As further growth continues there are social influences that decrease crying in boys and permit it to increase in girls. For example, one of the positive consequences of a boy not crying in situations where he formerly did is to be recognized as a *brave little man.* The female's behavior continues to be reinforced; that is, her crying behavior brings positive consequences to her.

THE DOWNSIDE OF USING PUNISHMENT

Another aspect of behavior modification deals with the negative consequences, or painful events, that occur following an action. One important principle that relates to negative consequence is as follows:

Behavior that is followed by a negative consequence or a painful event will decrease in frequency.

In fact, the most effective method of decreasing the frequency of behavior is to administer punishment or painful events to the person behaving. But before you say, "Aha, I always knew that," let me tell you something else. There are several aspects of the administering of painful events to decrease a behavior frequency that create more problems than benefits.

One of the first problems in the administration of negative consequences or painful events is that the person handing out these consequences often misinterprets what is, and what is not a negative consequence. For example, have you ever witnessed a situation where a child was misbehaving on purpose, with the result that the child received some kind of physical punishment or chastisement? Afterward you or the other adults involved might have wondered why a child would appear to want to be punished. In the meantime the child may have walked away rubbing the spanked area, but thinking: "They still love me." As with positive consequences, a consequence is positive or negative only as interpreted by the receiver of that consequence. If love and attention are a positive consequence to a child and there isn't much of that happening, then any attention, even chastisement, may be a positive consequence to that child. Attention is a powerful reinforcer even if it is chastisement. So the first problem in using negative consequences or painful events to decrease the frequency of a behavior is that the negative consequence you are passing out may in fact be a positive consequence, and, therefore, will increase the frequency of the behavior you don't want.

The second aspect of using negative consequences is that it creates unwanted side effects. In situations where people receive negative consequences or painful events, they become apprehensive. Therefore, if your management style is typical of most managers, and you use negative consequences to change people's behavior, you will be dealing with very apprehensive people.

Another serious side effect to negative consequences is aggression. When people are subjected to punishment or painful events, they may decrease the frequency of the behavior that is causing the painful consequence, but they may also react aggressively by holding work back, causing disruptive actions, sabotaging work performance, or even shooting the boss. When I ask managers, "Why don't employees do what they are supposed to do?" one answer that comes up fairly often is *because they don't like the boss.* When I get them to explain what they mean by that, they usually tell me that because the employees don't like the boss, they will foul up performance to injure the boss or the boss's reputation. That, clearly, is an act of aggression by that employee. In other words, the positive consequences of not doing work as a worker is to get the boss in hot water. It is difficult enough for managers to manage the productivity of employees who are neutral at best. It becomes almost impossible if the employees are aggressively trying to achieve the downfall of the manager.

So, the most important observation we can make from these comments about the side effects of negative consequences and painful events is to avoid them whenever possible. Instead of directing your attention to decreasing the employees' behavior *you don't want,* direct your attention to increasing the employees' behavior *you do want.*

Much of the work in behavior modification has been applied in educational situations. For example, one study found that one of the reasons students didn't do their homework was because of social rejection. Those who did their homework were labeled as eggheads. The long-range positive consequence to those children who did their homework was that they would get higher grades and do better at higher levels of education and, eventually, get into the college of their choice. Unfortunately, those long-range consequences are extremely difficult to perceive as a value to children in grade school. There was no immediate positive consequence to outweigh the immediate negative consequence of being labeled an egghead by peers. The action taken by the teacher was to advise the students that for every completed homework assignment, they were permitted to write their name on a sheet of paper and place it in a jar at the back of the room. At the end of each week one name would be drawn out of the jar and the student whose name was drawn would receive a prize (the value of the prize was under $2.00). By this action the teacher provided an immediate positive consequence for doing homework, which was more important than the negative consequence of peer pressure. As a result of this change, the number of children completing their homework assignments rose from less than a quarter of the class to almost two-thirds of the class in a 60-day period. Please note that this is not an isolated circumstance that has occurred once in the last 50 years. This is an example of a common practice of providing an immediate positive consequence where none existed before, to increase the frequency of desired behavior.

APPLYING BEHAVIOR MANAGEMENT IN BUSINESS

Let's consider how consequences affect behavior in business. Every business has certain jobs that people don't do too well. These jobs may be considered tedious or very difficult or annoying to do. Think of one of these jobs in your own organization, and ask yourself what happens when a person does not do it well. If your organization is like most, the answer is, *you never ask them to do it again.* In other words the positive consequence for a worker who does a certain job poorly is that he or she is not asked to do that job again. When someone comes along who does that tedious or difficult or annoying job well, the manager's immediate response is to schedule all of the crummy work for that individual. In other words, the consequence for doing an undesirable job well is, *you get to do that unpleasant work all the time.*

Let me ask you another question: When you have a critical task that must be done in a hurry, or without errors, to whom do you give it? Do you give it to your employees who always do the best work, or to those who screw up occasionally? Most managers would consider that an easy choice. "I always give that priority work to my best workers." Sounds logical, doesn't it? But what you don't realize is that you are changing the behavior of the other workers, the *screwups.* They are learning, *the less I do around here, the less they ask me to do.* It is unlikely they will ever verbalize it, but that is what they are learning. Isn't that a nice positive consequence for nonperformance?

If you consistently load up the same people with the hot projects, three possible things generally occur: they get promoted; their level of performance begins to drop off; or they resign. If they do resign, you naturally ask why they are leaving, and the answer is always *for more money.* This is why managers complain about not being able to pay their high performers enough to keep them. Unfortunately, managers are deluded because they don't ask the right questions. The fact is that almost everyone leaving your company for another job will be paid more in their new job. The same thing is true of the people your company hires; they will be paid more money working for you than on their last job. The new employer probably asked the right question, which is, "Why do you want to leave your job?" The most likely answer is, "The more you do over there, the more they ask you to do; there are people over there doing half as much work as I do and the managers don't ask them to do any more. I would like to work where the work is distributed fairly." This is not a fairy tale; this is what is happening out there when the consequences of doing an unpleasant job well is to get to do all the unpleasant work!

Now picture a manager who has an employee with an absentee problem. This manager has been exposed to the standard management training programs that lead her to believe she is capable of functioning as an amateur psychologist. Her first step to solve the absentee problem is to get to know the employee better. She calls the employee in, perhaps offers him a cup of coffee, and talks about the employee's background, the satisfactions and dissatisfactions in his life, and his future hopes and aspirations. They might discuss things the manager could do to make the company a better place to work, and she might even ask what job he would really like to have. The manager hopes that, as a result of this discussion, the employee will recognize the manager's interest and concern and will, therefore, be absent less. What is actually happening is that one of the consequences of absenteeism behavior is to get free coffee and to spend a lot of time sitting in the boss's office talking about yourself. What do you suppose the same manager does to all of those employees who come to work every day? Nothing. According to the manager's logic, nothing is required; they come to work every day.

If you have spent a considerable amount of time interviewing people for hire, you undoubtedly asked them how they were treated where they previously worked. If your experience is typical, one of the most common responses you would have gotten is, *The only time the boss talks to you over there is when you foul up something.* What this means from a behavioral point of view is that the consequence (a negative one) for doing everything you are supposed to do correctly is to be ignored by the boss.

Of course many managers tell me they don't buy coffee for their problem employees. They call them in and really make it hot for them, although the absentee problem doesn't get any better. It is inconceivable to them that their yelling, screaming, and threatening could be anything but a negative consequence to the employee. In school situations it frequently occurs that children who are yelled at by the teacher for pulling hair and throwing spitballs increase their frequency of hair pulling and spitball throwing. This is mystifying to the teacher until she is helped to realize that her attention is a positive consequence to the child, and, because the misbehavior is increasing in frequency, her attention must be reinforcing it. The situation is usually corrected when the teacher ignores the behavior she does not want but gives her *attention* to the child following behavior she does want. The result is a decrease in inattentive behavior and an increase in attentive behavior. It is important for managers to realize that whether they think a consequence is positive or negative is irrelevant; only the view of the individual receiving the consequence is relevant.

Not too long ago, a manager in one of my MBA classes told me it appeared he had people working for him who seemed to do things wrong on purpose so they could confess it to him. He said, "It seemed they really wanted me to yell at them." The puzzle disappeared when he described his relationship with his employees in more detail. His employees were highly educated, technically oriented individuals who worked independently at a professional level. Because their responsibilities were clearly identified, everyone was expected to work relatively unsupervised. He went on to explain that because everybody was experienced and knew what they were supposed to do, his contacts with them were quite infrequent. Except for the planning meetings at the beginning of the year, subsequent meetings occurred only when performance problems came up. These meetings were usually initiated by the employees. Although the meetings were initiated to discuss problems, he described the meetings as very low key. It was usually a pleasant discussion with mutual agreement on solutions and both parties pleased at the outcome. I asked him: "Because your discussions throughout the year with your employees are infrequent, and you describe these problem-solving meetings as very pleasant discussions, is it possible your employees view these problem-solving discussions as a positive consequence?" His response was, "My God, am I one of those bosses who only talks to their employees when they screw up?" He was right.

Another illustration of the relationship between an individual's behavior and the consequences is apparent in the case of a sixteen-year-old girl who was a *thumb sucker.* If you were to use the internalized approach in an effort to determine the causes and possible solutions for a sixteen-year-old girl sucking her thumb, you might conjure up visions of childhood privation. Analysis of this *thumb sucking* in a behavior/consequence framework, however, determined that the only time this girl sucked her thumb was when her parents yelled at her. The mystery became even less mysterious when it was further learned that when she sucked her thumb, *her parents stopped yelling at her. Thumb sucking* appeared to be a purely logical behavior on the part of this sixteen-year-old girl. If you want your parents to stop yelling at you, you stick your thumb in your mouth. What can be more practical than that? If the parents wanted the child to stop sucking her thumb, all they had to do was *stop yelling at her.*

A corollary to this in business might be the manager who is surprised and insulted when employees storm out of her office. She might not be so surprised if she were to learn that the only time her employees storm out of the office is when she yells at them. If she wants them to stop storming out of the office, the correct solution may be for her to change her behavior and talk to them rather than yell at them. Remember what we learned from the ideas of George Kelly? *People do not do illogical things on purpose. What they do appears perfectly logical to them at the time they are doing it.*

THE THREE SOURCES OF REWARD AND PUNISHMENT ON THE JOB

Rewards and punishment to workers come from only three sources.

Source 1. *The work.* This includes positive consequences from the worker's point of view (achievement) such as "getting them all correct," "finishing on time," "making no errors," "playing games on the computer for two hours without getting caught," or a customer saying, "Thanks! You helped solve my problem."

Negative consequences may be customers yelling every time he or she answers the phone in customer service, paper cuts, splinters and bruises, boring repetition, sore feet, back pain, and headaches.

Source 2. *Fellow workers.* Positive comments from fellow employees (very rare); "that was a good presentation. I wish I could do it like you"; "Boy, you have guts. I would be afraid to play games on my computer for two hours"; get well cards when they are ill.

Negative consequences such as: "Hey slow down, are you trying to make us look bad?", sarcasm following employee's suggestion, social ostracism, and possible flat tires for high producers.

Source 3. *The manager.* Rewards from the employee's point of view would be positive comments from the manager (verbal, e-mail) reinforcing performance throughout the day following appropriate performance, "I see you are right on schedule—nice work," "I just read your report and found it quite interesting," "Finishing your part on time is going to help us meet the schedule—thank you for your effort."

Negative consequences may be "You did that (unpleasant) project so well, you will get all the rest of those (unpleasant) projects," "Since you finished early I have more work for you," "I'm glad you called, I want to tell you how bad your last report was," "Why are you asking me for help, can't you think for yourself?"

Some jobs have a lot of beginnings and endings during the day with the opportunity for employees to win or lose (positive or negative consequences). But unfortunately the prevailing situation is that most jobs are just doing this hour what you did the last hour without any immediate consequence for performance. And few workers are running around complimenting other workers for the good work they are doing. That leaves the managers as the only source of positive consequences (positive reinforcers) to employees for performing well any day.

The process of behavior modification is much more scientific in practice and involves more variables and techniques than presented here. It would be ridiculous of me, however, to convince you to stop being one type of amateur psychologist only to become another type of amateur psychologist. I don't plan to do that. The purpose of this book is to help you improve your face-to-face techniques to improve the productivity of your employees. The only way for you to be successful at that is to get out of the business of being any kind of amateur psychologist and manage the variables over which you have control.

Therefore, from a practical management view point, the only alternative to the psychodynamic approach is the management of behavior. Behavior is the only thing you can deal with. You can see it when it is bad, you can measure it, and you can talk about it unemotionally. You can see it when it changes, and you can measure it after it changes. If you separate yourself from the internalized reasons for behavior, and start dealing with that behavior itself, you will be able to separate people from their behavior. You will learn how appropriate it is to be able to say, "I like you very much, but I dislike your behavior. If you would change your behavior I would like it as much as I like you." And if you start trying to change behavior rather than trying to change people, you will no longer be faced with the resistance people naturally present, because *they don't want to be changed.*

Here is how one student manager described his experience using positive reinforcement.

My job function is to manage 15 people whose jobs range from truck driver to clerk to office manager. Most of the time I do not get involved with the lower echelon, unless the office manager has a problem he can't solve. It so happened that he came to me about a particular problem he was having with a truck driver who was fast at his work, but who ignored the details. The manager explained that on numerous occasions he had instructed the driver to make sure he filled out his pickup tags completely, but the driver was not responding to his request. Rather than try to explain to my manager what to do and how to do it, I decided to make the driver part of my class project.

I instructed my manager not to say anything further to the driver about the pickup tags until I had a chance to talk to him. The next day as soon as the driver returned to the office from his morning rounds I immediately approached him and proceeded to compliment him on how well and how fast he was making his pickups and deliveries. Ordinarily, the only time I would talk to the driver was to register some complaints, so it was easily understandable why he had a puzzled look on his face. After I complimented him, I suggested that he might try to fill out his pickup tags completely, as this would facilitate the handling of the equipment and eliminate errors. The driver said he would fill out the tags completely. The next day I checked to see if he had performed his job correctly and he had. At this point I congratulated him for his improvement, and I followed up again in a few days. I found at this point that he was still doing his job correctly, whereupon I expressed my satisfaction and thanked him again for the fine job he was doing. My manager has not had any further problem with him along these lines. Badgering and threatening about the unsatisfactory performance did no good, whereas praise and recognition (positive reinforcement) for desired performance were the answer.

The moral of this story is that it's okay to talk about bad performance and ask people to improve but the most important step managers rarely use is to reinforce performance improvement.

As a manager, you will probably never become an expert on people, although it is highly likely that you are already an expert on behavior. You probably are thoroughly familiar with the behaviors that are appropriate for your employees in their specific jobs. *Start managing those behaviors.*

BELIEVING THE RIGHT THINGS FOR SUCCESS

I assume that one of the reasons you are reading this book is to learn how to be more successful as a people manager, or, more specifically, how to be more successful in carrying out the face-to-face process with your employees. As mentioned earlier, it is quite evident to me that one of the major reasons managers are not as successful as they could be in this process is because of what they believe about their employees and the people management process. Erroneous beliefs lead managers into the self-destructive behavior of disrupting relationships, rather than helping to improve them. Stated another way, *if you believe the wrong things about your employees those beliefs will be the basis for you to do the wrong things to solve problems with them.*

To put the information already covered into the proper perspective I would like to summarize for you as follows.

Point Number 1

Accept the idea that *the management function is getting things done through others.* Accept the idea that *you need them more than they need you.* Recognize that *the rewards and punishments you get as a manager are not based on what you do, but on what your employees do; your employees are your score card. No matter what your style or skills or knowledge might be, their success or failure reflects upon you.*

If all of the preceding are true, then you will recognize that the only reason for being there as a manager is for you to *do everything possible to help your employees be as successful as you need them to be.* The last thing you should do before firing someone is to look at yourself in the mirror and say "You have failed"; then tell your employee, "You're fired."

Point Number 2

Recognize that management is a series of interventions, *things you do,* the way you behave. Your behavior as interventions are the greatest influence over your employees in the work environment. If you don't *do* the right things you will not be successful as a manager. There is an element of *show biz* in management. You can't influence whether it is there or not, you can choose only whether to recognize it or not. All of your behavior on the job is interpreted by your employees as either for them or against them. It is not enough to do what feels right, or to do what comes naturally, or to have good intentions. If you don't do the right things, you cannot expect the appropriate results. The wrong things you do are self-destructive behavior. If you don't know what to do, find out before you act. If what you are doing doesn't work, stop doing it.

Point Number 3

There is no such thing as an *amateur psychologist,* so stop trying to be one. Besides, there is no need for you to be a psychologist to be a successful manager. If you want to be a psychologist, get your Ph.D.; otherwise forget it.

Point Number 4

When you employ someone, you are not buying people, or their minds, or their values; you are only renting their behavior. As a manager, your job is not to change people, but to manage and change their behavior in your restricted environment—your lifeboat. A good first step would be to rewrite your job descriptions to list the behaviors you are renting.

Point Number 5

If you want to know why people do things, forget about their motives and attitudes; you can only guess about those and you never know which of your guesses are right. Realize that people do not go through the world behaving illogically. Behavior appears illogical to them later when they discover it didn't work, or to an observer who knows a better alternative. Don't interpret the things people do in view of the alternatives you see available to them; interpret what they do in terms of the alternatives they see available to them. They don't see your alternatives, only their own. Find out what alternatives they saw, and ask why they selected the alternative they did.

If you want people to select better alternatives, let them understand the consequences of the alternative they are selecting and give them more alternatives to select from. Experience gives people more alternatives good and bad. Training gives people more *effective* alternatives without requiring them to grow older.

Point Number 6

The scientific management of people called *behavior modification* is more appropriate for you as a basis for people management, because behavior is something you are eminently qualified to deal with. You can see it when it is wrong; you can measure it; you can talk about it unemotionally; and you can see it when it changes.

6

Avoiding the Communication Problem

It has become quite common in recent years to blame performance problems and organizational conflicts on *poor communication.*

The face-to-face medium is the predominant medium of communication between manager and employee; therefore, it is of critical importance. Managers harm more than help themselves in their efforts to deal with employees because of poor communication.

I remember a story in the *New York Times,* following a baseball game between the Boston Red Sox and the Yankees in Yankee Stadium. The story explained that when the score was Boston 5, Yankees 3 in the ninth inning, and the Yankees were at bat with two out and two men on base, a new relief pitcher was sent in. The coach instructed him to *pitch tough.* The first pitch resulted in a home run. Afterward the coach was quoted by the *New York Times:* "If that's pitching tough, I don't know what pitching soft would be like." Obviously there was a communication problem.

When training managers I usually ask: "What kind of problems, obstacles, or frustrations arise when you are trying to get employees to do something they should be doing or to stop doing something they shouldn't be doing?" Their frequent response is "they don't listen, they don't respond, they don't understand." Managers blame their employees for failure of the communication process. A more accurate observation would be that the manager is failing, not the employee. One of the major reasons managers are not as effective as they could be (for the purpose of influencing others) is because they are operating with the wrong definition of communication.

For example, when I ask groups of managers: "What is communication?" the usual first response is "the transmission of information." After some discussion the definition is amended to "the transmission of information between two or more parties so that it is understood." Unfortunately, this, too, is incorrect, and precisely why managers fail in their efforts.

I first learned about communication in the third grade. The teacher first described the elements of communication as similar to electrical communication. She said there must be a sender, a receiver, and a transmission. For example, in telegraphic communication between two cities, if you transmit "dot dot dash dot" from San Francisco, New York City will receive "dot dot dash dot," unless someone chops down the poles. If New York sends a signal back to San Francisco, for example, "dot dash," San Francisco will know that New York has received the message.

The teacher described how this was similar to what happens when people talk to each other. One person (the sender), through vibrations of the vocal cords, makes vibrations in the air (the transmission), and these vibrations travel through the air to the other person's ear (receiver). These vibrations activate the mechanism in the inner ear that transmits impulses through nerve synapses to the brain. Because we have learned to interpret the meaning of these impulses, we are able to understand words and, therefore, to communicate. The teacher then gave a rule as a basic guide to communication, which you are probably familiar with: "Say what you mean and mean what you say."

As a result I went through the world communicating like the wife of a once-famous television personality. On one of his television programs he explained how his wife communicated in a foreign country when she could not speak their language and they could not speak English. He said she believed that if she spoke to the natives clearly, slowly, and loud enough in English, they would understand what she was talking about, even though they did not speak English. This is not as strange as it seems; this is how many of us communicate with others, even those who speak English. Did you ever tell someone to do something and that person did not do it? Wasn't your reaction to repeat it louder? You might even have said, "Did you hear what I said?" You assumed the communication failed because your dot dot dash dot was not loud enough.

UNDERSTANDING THOUGHT TRANSMISSION

The problem is not a hearing problem. The problem is that there is no similarity between electrical or electronic communication and the communication between people. In the first place, the mind thinks at least six times faster than we can speak, and because the mind thinks so much faster, its primary function is a *reactive function*. Of course, the mind receives the information transmitted, but the information is received so fast that the mind reacts even before the message is completed. You can demonstrate this reactive principle yourself by saying to a number of people, "Say what comes to mind when I say something to you." Then say a single word to each of them, such as black, up, or hard. The responses you will most likely get will be white, down, and soft, but no one will respond with the word you said. As a matter of fact, you can say any word you choose and they will never repeat what you said. If you said to them dot dot dash dot their response might be "you are crazy."

If communication really was information transmission, and you said white they would say white; if you said black they would say black. Because the mind is primarily a reactive instrument it does not think of what you said, it thinks of something else *because of what you said.* The things you say act as triggers to create other thoughts as a reaction.

This means that if you have an idea in your head that you want to communicate to someone else, the worst thing you can do is to put that idea into the most precise and correct words you can think of and speak them. Because as soon as you say these words, the listener will hear them, *but think something else.* Because the mind is primarily a reactive instrument, successful communication is a function of *thought transmission,* rather than information transmission. Therefore, if you have an idea you wish to transmit to someone else, you must say or do something that will cause that idea to appear in the other's head as a reaction to what you said or did.

For example, let's assume you and I are face to face, and my aim is to impress you with my honesty. I might begin to talk about my early childhood, my religious upbringing, and all the times I performed in an honest and trustworthy manner. As I continued relating my resistance to temptation and unrewarded honest dealings with others you might begin to wonder, "What is this guy trying to get out of me?" Voila! Thought transmission (unintended).

Let's take another example. Let's say I wanted you to be frightened, and I said to you, "Be frightened! Be frightened! Be frightened!" Obviously you will not be frightened, so I will improve my diction and say the same words even louder. Is it likely that you are going to be frightened? More likely you will be wondering what kind of a nut I am, and why I am carrying on this way. If I recognize that communication is thought transmission, however, and I want to transmit the thought *fright* to your mind, I might wait until you are relaxed, sneak up behind you, and yell as loud as I can "Boo!"; or I may approach you with a glass of water and stumble theatrically in front of you to make believe I am going to spill water all over you. In both instances you would probably jump out of your chair.

In neither instance did I say the word *fright,* but I successfully communicated the thought of *fright* to you. I did something in front of the thought called *fright* so it appeared in your head. I used thought transmission. By the same token, if I wanted the thought of my honesty to appear in your head I would be more successful if I did something in front of you that you could perceive as honest. For example, I could plant money in your path and before you get there I could come along and pick it up and ask you if it was yours. If you said *no,* I might suggest you turn it in to lost and found, or ask you to take care of it because someone may show up having lost it. You may think I'm soft in the head, but you will also think I am honest.

COMMUNICATING WITHOUT FAILURE

If you recognize that communication is thought transmission and not information transmission, you will realize that your communication efforts must be directed to doing something in front of the thoughts you want to appear in someone's head.

I know that communication as *thought transmission* is really not a new concept to you. For example, have you ever sent a gift to someone as an expression of your feelings? Did that person respond by saying, "Ah, he loves me," or "I wonder what he's up to now" (or both)? Have you ever winked at someone, or shaken your fist, or held up the middle finger, or nodded your head, or shrugged your shoulder? If you did you were using thought transmission; you acted in a way to transmit a thought; your action caused a thought to occur.

In recent years several books have appeared on the subject of something called *body language*. The writers explain in detail the message communicated by the various positions of your body. Actually, body language is an ideal example of the process of thought transmission, intended or not. What actually happens is that someone observes the position of someone else's body and because of that observation a thought appears in the head of the observer. The writings on body language are merely telling us that, regardless of your intentions, the things you do with your body are transmitting thoughts to others. Those thoughts may not be what you intended to communicate but it is occurring.

In fact, many times our facial expressions or body movements accurately transmit the thoughts we are trying to conceal with our words. For example, what thoughts are transmitted to your employee's head when she is talking and in the middle of her presentation you begin to read something on your desk? Intentionally or not, you have communicated, "I am bored with what's going on," or "What is on my desk is more important than what you are talking about," or "I don't really care about what you are talking about."

Information transmission as a concept interferes with managers because they waste time controlling the transmission of information and losing control over the transmission of thoughts. Managers make speeches to employees. They tend to do all the talking, whether it be praising, giving help, reprimanding, or trying to eliminate problems. What happens is that the manager calls in the employee and starts talking. While the manager is talking, she has no idea what thoughts are going through the employee's mind. The manager assumes the employee is thinking about what she is talking about, but the employee may be wondering how many martinis the boss had for lunch, whether she is in a good mood or a bad mood, or whether she found out about the problem they had but cleaned up and hoped she wouldn't discover. The simple fact of communication is that when you are talking to others, the only things you can be sure are *working* on the subject you are talking about are your brain, your mouth, and maybe their ears. If you want to know what a person's brain is working on, *you have to make sounds come out of that person's mouth.*

One manager who used thought transmission for the first time sent me this note:

> This week I tried to use thought transmission as a major communication tool when working with my employees. Although I need a good

deal more practice, and I must learn to take my time, I am thoroughly convinced of the value of this method. This is the first time I have experienced anything in management that resembles the feelings I experienced in my technical work when I solved a difficult problem or mastered a demanding procedure (the great "aha" feeling).

Instead of concentrating on different ways to say things so there will be no doubt of what is intended, I have only to think of a way to make the other person say it. The qualitative evidence of the success of this technique is overwhelming.

When I ask managers what they really want from their employees, they invariably answer *involvement*. When I ask them what they mean by involvement, they describe something that occurs in the employees' heads. What they really mean is they want the employees' heads involved in (thinking about) the subject the manager is thinking about, when the manager wants them to think about it.

The way to get this involvement and the only way to know whether you have it, is to *make sounds come out of their mouths*. The sounds that come out of their mouths had to be in their heads. This is the most fundamental way of knowing whether you are successfully transmitting thoughts, and it completely changes the emphasis of your communication techniques with employees. Rather than making the sounds come out of your mouth (telling people all the things you want them to know), you must do something to make the sounds come out of their mouths. That something is *ask questions the answer to which, is what you want to tell them.*

For example, in my coaching seminars for experienced managers, my desire is to transmit the thought to the heads of the participants that (1) what they are doing is not working all the time; (2) in some instances they are doing some things that are no longer appropriate; and (3) although what they are doing may be working there may be better ways of doing it to achieve better results. The worst way for me to approach this would be for me to make a statement to them about their obvious failures. If I did do that, my guess would be that some of the thoughts appearing in their heads might be:

"This guy never saw me before today. How the hell does he know what kind of a manager I am?"

"You mean I'm going to have to sit here and listen to this abuse all day?"

"He doesn't know what I am doing, so how can he tell me that what I am doing is failing."

"Look at the funny shoes he is wearing."

"I wouldn't be seen dead in a tie like that."

"I wonder if we will get out of here in time to beat the traffic."

To circumvent that reaction, I use thought transmission. That is, I do something in front of those thoughts I wish to appear in their heads, and that something I do is to ask them a question, like this:

"It appears obvious to me, looking around the room, that the majority of you managers have been managers for quite a long time; therefore, I assume you have been doing that thing called coaching or counseling or appraising for a long time. The question that occurs to me is this: 'Realizing how important time is to you managers, I wonder why you would want to take a day of your time and spend it on a subject that you obviously have been doing for many years.' " (And I shut up.)

They then tell me all the reasons why they should spend a day of time on this subject, and these answers are exactly what I would have told them, had I done it the other way. The major difference is that the sounds came out of their mouths rather than mine. And because the sounds came out of their mouths I know those thoughts were in their heads. Voila! I have been successful at transferring those thoughts from my head to their heads.

I actually did two things in this example. The first was to ask them a question and the second was to shut up. One of the reasons managers have difficulty communicating with employees is because employees use silence to intimidate them. Why is it that managers get so nervous when they ask a question and it is followed by silence? Because that silence seems so intolerable, managers answer their own questions. *Stop doing that.* When you answer your own questions you are reinforcing employees *not answering.*

If you ask somebody a question and you really believe he or she is going to answer it, *don't answer it yourself.* Frequently in seminars when I ask management groups a question, as previously mentioned, it is followed by long periods of silence. If the participants do not respond to that question right away, I will use body language to transmit the additional thought to their heads that I do not intend to answer the question I just asked. For example, I will put down the chalk or magic marker I am holding and sit in a chair very comfortably as though I am prepared to sit there for the rest of the day. I will also *shut up.* I will wait perhaps five minutes and if I speak again it will only be to say, "Does anybody want me to repeat the question?" I will never answer the question myself.

The fact is that silence is intimidating, but I am not going to be intimidated by silence; I am going to use silence to intimidate the people I expect to talk to me, so they will talk to me.

Another problem with communication occurs when managers accept noncommunication. For example, how many times have you explained something to an employee and, after you finished, you wanted to know whether he understood it or not so you asked "Do you understand this?" The employee answered "Yes." The only sound you had coming out of his mouth was "yes." You do not know, in fact, whether the thing you just explained actually arrived between his ears. If you want to know whether he knows what you just explained, the only appropriate kind of question is: "Would you now explain to me what we just talked about?" or "Would you describe now how you are going to do that job based on what we just discussed?" *If you make the sounds come out of their mouths then you know the thought had to be in their heads.* If the only thing you get is a "yes," then that's all you know for sure was between their ears.

In conclusion, for you to communicate effectively for the purpose of influencing others, you must recognize that communication between people is not information transmission, but is *thought transmission.* It is the process of getting a thought from your head to their heads.

Because the mind is primarily a reactive instrument, the most *ineffective* way of getting a thought from your head to their heads is to put the thought in your head in the most specific and precise words you can think of. When you do that, their minds will react to the information they have heard and, therefore, think something else.

Thought transmission is the process of saying or doing something in front of the thought you wish to appear in their heads. The only way for

you to verify whether thought transmission has occurred is to make the
sounds come out of their mouths, make the thoughts come out of the end
of their pencils, or make them behave in a way that will occur only as a
result of the thought you have transmitted (such as jumping out of a chair
in response to your transmitting the thought of *fright*). This is the
dilemma you are faced with:

Problem: I know I said what I want you to hear, but I'm not sure you
are thinking what you heard me say.

Solution: Thought transmission. Ask a question the answer to which
is what you want to tell them.

7

A Practical Approach to Managing People in Business

The concept that *authoritarian management* and *participative management* are at opposite ends of a single line of alternative choices has established a narrow playing field which limits managers' full understanding of why employees do what they do.

By accepting the idea of authoritarian management as one thing and participative management as its opposite thing, we are duped into limiting our understanding and choices between them. With this approach as the only game in town, managers see themselves stuck with the choice of workers either being browbeaten, punished, and unmotivated on the one hand or loved, recognized, and motivated on the other hand. All of our people performance problems are viewed as being hinged to unhappy unmotivated workers with solutions being hinged to happy motivated workers without consideration of all the other influences on people's performance.

In analyzing managers' failures in correcting employees' performance problems, the most frequent cause is misdirection of their corrective efforts, that is, they concentrate on the symptoms rather than the causes of the problem. It is interesting that this phenomenon occurs only when managers are dealing with their people resources. Rarely do managers make this mistake when dealing with nonpeople resources. Wouldn't you consider it preposterous if you observed a manager who discovered an inadequacy in the lubricating system of a piece of production equipment and responded by having the equipment painted? Well, it appears just as preposterous to me when a manager discovers an employee's nonperformance and reacts by modifying the compensation plan to create incentives for the employee to improve performance, when the reason for nonperformance was that the employee *didn't know how to do it.*

Virgil Rowland described how he gained insight into one aspect of management's problems. For several years he collected responses from 8000 managers in answer to a single question: "What areas of knowledge do you feel that you yourself need to know more about to do your own management job better, to do your direction-of-people job better?" He collected answers from first line managers, vice presidents, and the various jobs in between, including department heads and plant managers from all kinds of companies, governmental agencies, and other organizations. After considerable analysis, he determined that all the answers fell into four categories as follows:

1. We need to know what we are supposed to do.
2. We need to know how far we are expected to go in discharging our responsibilities and authorities.
3. We need to know how well we are expected to do our jobs.
4. We need to know how well we are doing our management jobs.

The answers are disappointing, aren't they? You would think 8000 managers of various levels would be able to describe much more sophisticated or exciting needs. Nevertheless, they are real needs.

What is even more disappointing is that these responses from managers over 30 years ago are the same responses employees at all levels give me today when discussing barriers to their effectiveness. This is especially true in high-tech companies growing 50 to 80 percent annually where technicians may be promoted three times in a year.

The real revelation here is that something as simple as the lack of direction and feedback could be an endemic obstacle to peoples' performance in business.

WHY EMPLOYEES DON'T DO WHAT THEY ARE SUPPOSED TO DO

An even bigger revelation comes out of my own research looking for practical explanations for employee good and bad performance. Prior to writing the first edition of this book I had collected responses from 4000 managers answering the question, "Why don't employees do what they are supposed to do?" These managers varied in education from high school graduates to MDs; they were from banking, manufacturing, retailing, utilities, and governmental organizations, and they represented every level from first-line manager to president, and included every function such as research, manufacturing, marketing, sales, and administration.

The initial surprising observation was that managers after being forced to be specific gave very specific and practical answers not requiring a psychologist to interpret. The second surprising observation was that these managers with their varied backgrounds gave highly similar answers. This was so intriguing I continued the project and eventually collected and analyzed responses from 25,000 supervisors and managers around the world. The additional data expanded the original list of why employees don't do what they are supposed to do from 13 to 16 as follows.

1. They don't know what they are supposed to do.
2. They don't know how to do it.
3. They don't know why they should do it.
4. They think they are doing it (lack of feedback).
5. There are obstacles beyond their control.
6. They think it will not work.
7. They think their way is better.
8. They think something is more important (priorities).
9. There is no positive consequence to them for doing it.
10. There is a negative consequence to them for doing it.
11. There is a positive consequence to them for not doing it.
12. There is no negative consequence to them for not doing it.
13. Personal limits (incapacity).
14. Personal problems.
15. Fear (they anticipate future negative consequences).
16. No one could do it.

These are listed in the order they are usually given by managers. The first item on the list is given as an answer, first or second 99 percent of the time. What is surprising about this is that when managers try to solve individual nonperformance problems they *rarely* select this first answer as the place to start solving the problem. Another interesting aspect of the list is that only two items point to something inherently wrong with the worker, such as personal limits (incapacity), or personal problems.

The majority of the reasons for nonperformance are obviously there because management didn't do something right or did something wrong.

Most of the reasons appear to be the result of a communication problem—*lack of direction and lack of feedback.*

The big revelation to me and my associates was that there are only 16 reasons why employees at any level, by any title don't do what they are supposed to do. We looked hard for other reasons and found different wording but they always fit under one of the above 16 reasons. We also found that the concept of "motivation" no longer had relevance since many of the 16 reasons more specifically explained why people did what they did without invoking the idea of motivation. It seemed ridiculous to say, "If you tell people why they should do something they will be motivated" when in fact all you are doing is eliminating the problem, "they don't know why they should do it."

We found that the concept of *choice* had more relevance than the idea of motivation. Asking why they are *choosing* not to do it got more specific solutions than why aren't they motivated. Looking at the 16 reasons, you can see that reasons 1, 2, 4, 5, 13, and 16 have nothing to do with the employee choosing not to do it. Reasons 3, 6, 7, 8, 9, 10, 11, 12, 14, and 15 are logical reasons why they would choose not to do it. To put it mildly, I was blown away with these findings which changed my entire understanding of the people management process, and I wrote a book, *Why Employees Don't Do What They Are Supposed to Do and What to Do About It.*

It has always appeared to me a strange contradiction that in a seminar environment, managers respond to the question, "Why don't employees do what they are supposed to do?" by telling me such things as "they don't know what they are supposed to do, they don't know why they should, and they don't know how to." Yet, when I discuss specific employee failures with individual managers they invariably state the reasons as personal, inherent, and unchangeable things in that employee that are beyond the control of the manager. If it appears to you that I am accusing managers of doing illogical things when dealing with individual employee problems, you are right. One of the major reasons managers fail to improve employees' performance problems is that their solutions are not related to the problems.

When managers tell me they want to improve performance they are really talking about improving results; they want the outcome of performance to be better. But you cannot manage a result. If it didn't happen yet it is an expectation, goal, or objective. Once it happens it is history. You can only manage the things people do; their behavior which causes results.

If you think of a result as the end of a foot race, you can see that managing what people do during the race is what influences the outcome of the race. This is true of results in business for a day, a month, a quarter, or two years. Management intervention during a day will influence that day's output. Management intervention at the end of the day has no influence over that day's output, the race is over. Setting a goal and expecting specific results is a good thing to do but managing what people do during that period is the only way to guarantee a result. The earliest point in the work relationship when management decisions influence the results is when the employee is hired. If you hire a 4'8" person to do a 6'3" job, there is no ladder available, you can't lower the job, and the person can't jump that high, your results will suffer. Your selection of a worker based on your evaluation of his or her abilities, learned and innate, will result in how closely you match the individual to the job requirements. If your selection is wrong, your future results begin to be influenced at this point.

Performance is the *things the employee is paid to do* such as punching keys, pushing and pulling levers, walking, talking, sitting, standing, analyzing and solving problems, writing lines of code, pushing brooms, or flying airplanes. The employee's performance is the behavior you rent that is expected to produce desired results. Rarely do workers (at any level) perform the way we want them to perform as they walk in off the street. It is necessary to change and guide the quality, quantity, and appropriateness of their actions, or even just to tell them where the tools are (brooms, airplanes). This *telling* is the next most common influence we apply in business with the hopes of improving the performance. It is usually called training, and at times is called orientation. Sometimes it isn't called any thing because it is *rapping over cups of coffee,* and because it isn't called anything it is usually ineffective. One aspect of this training influence is that you could conceivably hire someone who has the capacity necessary to do the things you want them to do, but they do not have the ability; they don't *know how* to do them. If you don't train them, your future result will suffer.

BEYOND MOTIVATION

When I ask managers, "Why don't employees do what they are supposed to do?" one frequent answer is, "They don't want to do it." When I ask them, "Why don't employees want to do it?" their response is, "They are not motivated." Oddly enough if the first answer is, "They are not motivated," the second response usually is, "They don't want to." This occurs because the majority of managers today are dealing with the internalized concepts of motivation, and blame nonperformance of employees who are obviously capable of performing, on self-motivation deficiencies. When I ask them, "Why aren't your employees motivated?" or "Why don't they want to do what they are supposed to do?" they give practical answers such as:

"It's boring." (no consequence)

"They think it's beneath them." (negative consequence)

"They would rather do something else."

"Peer pressure." (negative consequence)

"They don't think they are being paid enough." (no positive consequence)

"They want to hurt the boss." (positive consequence for not doing it)

"They are not recognized for what they do." (no positive consequence)

"Fear." (they anticipate future negative consequence)

These reasons for the lack of motivation do not seem so mysterious when we compare them with what we know about behavior management: *people do what they do because of the consequences to them for what they do.* For example, it is easy to understand why people would not do certain things if the negative consequences to them are: it is boring; they believe they would look foolish doing it; or there would be social rejection (peer pressure) if they did it. Conversely, why would people do something if they enjoyed positive consequences for not doing it? For example, by not doing what they were supposed to do, they could do something else they would rather do, or if they don't do it someone else will do it, or they will receive attention for not performing.

If your employees have the ability to do something and have been trained how to do it, but the consequences are not reinforcing for doing it, you can reasonably expect performance not to occur. Therefore, your future results will suffer. Delivering consequences to performers for doing or not doing what you want done must become part of your management interventions.

Another category of major influence over performance, one that is usually overlooked by managers trying to improve performance, is the external influences; the obstacles to performance. These are the things needed to support performance that fail to occur, or things that occur that should not occur and that interrupt performance. These are conditions beyond the performers' control, such as heavy snow, power failure, hurricane, fire, or theft. They can be failures of other sources to provide the required ingredients, information, or tools needed by the performer. Persons could fail to do what they were supposed to do because no one provided security clearance to permit entrance to the building or area where the work must be done; or they didn't get the correct password to access a databank; or one person showed up to do it, but the coworker did not.

I know of one company that is being strangled by its data processing system. The manager responsible for selecting the hardware knew it was not capable of handling the company's needs when he ordered it, but his boss had led him to believe the executive committee would not approve a bigger expenditure. So the employee *did not ask for more money;* he recommended the less-expensive hardware that was inappropriate. Guess who bit the dust? It was not the manager. Another category of obstacles, rarely recognized is conflicting instructions from two or more managers.

As you read this, you may wonder why it is necessary to describe what must seem perfectly logical to every manager. "Why," you might wonder, "wouldn't every manager understand these influences, and, although having never written them down, follow this analysis when trying to solve performance problems?" I wonder the same thing. But I can tell you with confidence that the majority of managers in American business do not analyze their people performance problems this way. They treat a training problem with motivational efforts or an obstacle problem with training efforts.

My favorite example of this occurred in a large distribution center of a retail organization that daily loaded and shipped 15 to 20 trucks of merchandise to their 600 stores. It seemed the trucks were arriving at the stores with heavy cases of hardware loaded on top of cartons of lamp shades, which were crushed and destroyed in the process. Cases of paint were loaded upside down and paint from the cans, which usually opened during the trip, dripped onto other merchandise, destroying it. The operations manager felt the only solution was a training program to teach the truck loaders how to load heavy items on the bottom and place cartons so the arrows on them were pointing upward. He told me that although he made speeches to the truck loaders about the cost of damage and the importance of their doing the job right, the situation was getting worse rather than better.

Before I agreed to design the training program, I told him it was necessary to observe the actual work environment. This is what I found. Each truck was 40 feet long and fully enclosed. A conveyor belt extended from the warehouse past the loading dock, and into each truck. The conveyor was retracted in stages as the truck was loaded. The merchandise to be loaded on the truck was prestacked in the warehouse area approximately 100 feet from the truck itself. When a truck was ready to be loaded, the merchandise in the warehouse was placed on the conveyor, which moved at a constant rate carrying the merchandise into the truck. Inside the truck were two truck loaders who removed the merchandise from the conveyor belt and stacked it in the truck from floor to ceiling. The conveyor ran continuously whether it carried merchandise or not. As a matter of fact one of the rules on the loading dock was: "No one turns off the conveyor except the shipping foreman."

When loading was ready to begin, the foreman made sure the truck loaders were in position inside the truck. He then signaled the people in the warehouse to load the merchandise on the conveyor. The foreman then left to inspect other trucks being loaded simultaneously. Once the merchandise began to be loaded on the conveyor in the warehouse it flowed almost continuously into the truck.

What was happening inside the truck was similar to an old "Candid Camera" episode, where a man was placed in a room with a conveyor belt coming out of a wall. He was told that pies would come out on the conveyor belt and his job was to place the pies in individual boxes. Everything went fine for a few minutes, but the speed of the conveyor was slowly increased. The man also speeded up his efforts but he couldn't keep up. It was hilarious, he was slamming pies into boxes, while other pies fell to the floor.

The situation was similar inside the truck. When a truck loader lifted a heavy case off the conveyor and was faced with placing it on top of a carton of lamp shades, the logical alternative would have been to put down the heavy carton, move the lamp shades out of the way, put the heavy case in its place and put the lamp shades on top of it. Unfortunately, if one of the truck loaders stopped to scratch his nose, a box would fall off the end of the conveyor on to the floor and sometimes his foot. In fact the loaders were not lifting boxes off the conveyor, they were catching them as they came off the end of the conveyor. If he stopped to move the box of lamp shades on the floor, he would have been buried under boxes falling off the conveyor. He could not turn off the conveyor, and there was no signal he could make to the dock foreman or the people in the warehouse loading the conveyor belt. As a result, he kept stacking boxes; hardware on top of lamp shades, arrows pointing downward or sideways; whichever way the boxes came off the conveyor, is the way he stacked them. There wasn't time for anything else.

The solution to the problem was not a training program. A shutoff switch was placed on the end of the conveyor *in the truck,* and the truck loaders were given authority to shut off the conveyor anytime it was necessary to shift cartons. After switches were installed the merchandise damaged by poor loading decreased.

The reason for poor performance seemed fairly obvious; it was the external influences beyond the control of the loaders. The manager of the operation did not correctly analyze the reason for nonperformance. If I had designed and conducted a training program the problem would not have been solved.

Each of the preceding 16 reasons influence performance, hence results. All of them don't have to be bad at the same time to hurt performance. You could have an employee who has the ability to do a job, knows how to do it and wants to do it, but can't do it because of obstacles beyond his or her control. You could have an employee who does not have the ability to do what you want done, or does not know how to do it, but who wants to do it, and the unfortunate result will be the same: nonperformance and nonachievement of the end result.

It is clearly evident that an incorrect conclusion about the cause of unsatisfactory performance could lead you to apply the wrong solution. You can accurately analyze the cause of nonperformance problems by following the step-by-step process of the coaching analysis described in Chapter 9. It will lead you through a systematic, functional analysis of worker performance to pinpoint the reason why performance is not what the job requires.

8

The Magic of Feedback

In the study of human behavior psychologists have discovered a long time ago that feedback is one of the most critical requirements for sustained high-level performance of any human act. Without frequent and specific feedback, performance varies and often fails.

Picture yourself in a bowling alley all by yourself ready to begin a bowling game. Everything seems fine except, when you release the ball for the first time, the lights go out over the pins. You hear the pins falling but you can't see how many you knocked down. Looking around you, you see no one, so you yell out, "Hey, the lights are out over the pins and I can't see what I knocked down." A voice replies from somewhere in the area of the pins, "There are two standing." You shout, "Which two?" The voice replies, "Don't bother me. Just bowl again." Apparently there is no other alternative, so you bowl again toward the pins you cannot see. You don't hear any pins fall. After a moment the lights go on and you see the pins are set up again. So you say to yourself, "Ah, that's better," and you get ready for your second frame. As you release the ball, the lights over the pins go out again. You yell, "Hey, how about putting the lights on or tell me what is going on?" You hear the voice again say, "Please stop bothering me. I have enough to do back here. Keep bowling. I'll be back in two hours to tell you how you did."

Let's pretend you continue to bowl under those conditions. At the end of two hours the voice says, "I'm back." You say, "How did I do?" The voice replies, "Not too good." You say, "What's my score?" The voice says, "I don't know but it's terrible." Even if you were a good bowler, that would be no surprise. The reason is that you were deprived of feedback.

You were not permitted to see the results of each of your actions and, therefore, you could not make effective corrections in your performance.

One of the major reasons for unsatisfactory performance by workers at all levels is the lack of feedback to them about the work they are doing. It has been estimated that approximately 50 percent of the nonperformance problems in business occur because of the lack of feedback. Workers don't know how well or badly they are doing what they are doing. If workers think they are doing okay, they have no reason to change what they are doing.

The most widely publicized application of feedback to improve performance in business was in the Emery Air Freight Corporation. One of the processes of this freight-forwarding company was to consolidate smaller shipments from several customers into a single large container, which was then shipped as a single item by air. It was the intent of the company that 95 percent of all those items that could be so containerized would be containerized. Although there was no measurement of the actual percentage that was containerized, it was generally assumed in the organization that the 95 percent goal was being met. The managers at various levels, as well as the dock workers who actually did the work, believed they were containerizing 95 percent of those items that should be containerized. Eventually an audit of the process revealed that consolidation was occurring at the 45 percent level. This news was a big surprise to everyone.

The problem was corrected by providing feedback to each individual dock worker about that worker's actual level of performance. This was accomplished with a form that required the dock worker to write the name of the shipper for each item, to note whether each package being processed met the requirements to be containerized, and to indicate whether it actually was containerized. At the end of the shift, the dock worker calculated the actual percentage of those containerized against those that should have been containerized, and turned the form over to his or her supervisor. When this form was introduced nationwide, the overnight result was an increase in containerization from a national average of 45 percent to 95 percent. Yes, you read it right; overnight.

Before you relegate this to the realm of magic, consider these aspects of the problem.

1. The worker knew how to do that thing called containerization.
2. The worker knew that he or she was supposed to do that thing called containerization.
3. All of the tools and supplies for containerization were available.
4. The worker *thought it was being done.*

This was clearly a feedback problem. The company was not demanding 100 percent performance; it wanted only 95 percent. The dock workers *thought they were doing it* at the 95 percent level, so why should they do anything different. Everytime they passed up a box, they perceived it as being part of the 5 percent. Because there were no counts available to the workers, they had no way of knowing whether they were passing up 5 percent, 10 percent, or 55 percent. It was a feedback problem that was fixed by providing feedback to the workers. About 50 percent of what appear to be motivational problems in business are actually feedback problems.

THE THREE TYPES OF FEEDBACK

If workers at any level believe they are doing what they are supposed to be doing, why should it occur to them to do anything different? Because lack of specific and frequent feedback is one of the most common causes of inappropriate performance, giving specific feedback is the quickest, cheapest, and most effective intervention for improving performance. Effective face-to-face feedback does not have to be more complicated than the following statements:

"Do you know that you are the only one whose weekly reports are more than a day late?"

"Do you know that you frequently interrupt people when you speak at staff meetings?"

"Do you know that your employees are complaining that you don't permit them to express themselves?"

"Do you know that your typing produces two typing errors per page?"

"Are you aware that you are embarrassing employees by criticizing them in public?"

"Do you know that you begin to mumble after you present your first product in your sales presentation?"

When you ask questions this way you are actually giving what is called neutral feedback. *Neutral, positive,* or *negative* refers to the manner in which the feedback is delivered. Negative feedback would be as follows:

What is wrong with you? Can't you concentrate long enough to get your report in on time? (late reports)

You better get rid of your obnoxious attitude and stop treating people like idiots. (interrupting people)

You don't have the professionalism to become successful in sales. (mumbling)

Notice how these feedback comments are put-downs rather than useful exchanges of information. Also notice that they are not specific enough to be useful. When someone is standing on your foot and you say, "Do you know you are standing on my foot?" you will get immediate appropriate action. But if instead you say, "Pardon me but when a person is in crowded social settings it is their social responsibility to be aware and considerate of the space occupied by those around them so as to avoid unwelcome and accidental physical contacts," you will get some weird looks. Of course, you could say, "Get off my foot, you jerk," and perhaps lose some teeth.

Positive feedback would be, "Hey, I see you got all of your reports in on time. Keep up the good work."

You will discover that workers frequently do not know how many errors they are making or how many days they actually come to work late. At times a worker will know how many errors he or she is making, but will assume everyone else is making the same number of errors. In other words, workers know their own levels of performance, but think everyone else's performance is just as bad.

Sometimes workers know they are doing things they should not be doing, *but they don't know it is a problem.* The feedback you give them is to let them know that what they are doing is not satisfactory. The first step to solve a tardiness problem is to tell the worker how many times he or she has been tardy, that you don't accept it, and ask that employee to correct it, as follows:

You: Charlie, I notice that for the last week you have been late
       for work three out of the five days. This is not acceptable
       performance; would you please come to work on time?
Charlie: Okay, I sure will try.
You: Thank you.

That is called a *feedback discussion*. Notice that your statement also referred to expected performance: "Would you please come to work on time?" The usual response to a feedback discussion is improved performance.

You will eliminate a lot of performance problems by giving feedback to the worker on a one-time basis. If you have identified a problem behavior, such as *excessive time away from the workstation*, the first conversation with your employee should be a feedback statement such as, "Tondalayo, I notice you have been away from your workstation more than six times each day this week. Would you please restrict your absence to the scheduled rest periods?"

If workers' productivity is unsatisfactory because they don't know how they are doing, they may need feedback on an hour-to-hour basis. You can, in fact, increase productivity in certain jobs by providing feedback about individual productivity by the minute or the hour. I am not recommending that you spend all your time telling people how they are doing each hour. This requires the creation of a feedback system that operates between the worker and the work so the feedback does not pass through you to get to the worker. This can be simple actions of checking or counting or comparing by the worker at established intervals of the work process, according to time or phase completion. If bowlers keep their own bowling scores, they are operating their own feedback systems.

One interesting aspect of feedback occurred with the vice president of a division of a large corporation. He told me about one of his employees who was responsible for preparing some comprehensive marketing reports involving market analysis of specific projects. The vice president complained that these reports, when submitted, were usually incomplete, because they didn't answer all the questions the vice president thought should be answered. At my suggestion that the employee might not know what finished was supposed to look like, the vice president and the employees together worked up a list of key questions that should be answered in all reports.

The vice president contacted me shortly afterward to tell me he did that but that the next report also had been incomplete. I asked the vice president whether the employee was checking that list of questions against the completed report before the report was forwarded to the vice president. The vice president said he didn't know but would find out. He got back to me shortly afterward, and told me that, amazingly enough, although the employee had the list of questions, he was not checking the list against the completed report before submitting it to the boss. The vice president instructed the employee to check all future reports against the list before submitting the report. Subsequently all reports submitted were satisfactory.

In this instance the first thing the vice president did to correct the problem was to establish a *basis* for feedback for the employee (what *finished* was supposed to look like). This provided an ideal basis for the employee to give feedback to himself after completing the report, to determine whether the report was finished.

In summary, performance problems caused by lack of feedback can only be solved by providing feedback to the worker. It seems logical and easier to do that with routine or highly repetitive jobs, but it is also critically important in the so-called creative or unmeasurable jobs. If you don't know how to measure the performance of a certain job, it doesn't mean the job performance can't be measured; it just means you don't know how to measure it yet.

9

Coaching Analysis

Now we will get down to the nitty gritty of what you can do when people are not doing what they are supposed to be doing, or are doing something they shouldn't be doing. The process you can use is called coaching. It is a four-step process which will guide you in using the simplest to the most sophisticated interventions as needed to correct performance problems:

Step 1. Neutral feedback. Tell employee about bad performance and ask employee to correct it. Follow up to check for improvement; reinforce any improvement.

Step 2. Neutral feedback. If performance has not improved, tell employee about bad performance; ask why performance is bad; ask for specific behavior change; give assistance if needed. Follow up to check for improvement; reinforce any improvement.

Step 3. Coaching analysis. If performance does not improve, use coaching analysis to understand why performance is unsatisfactory and take action to eliminate what, if anything, is influencing the poor performance.

Step 4. Coaching discussion. If poor performance is by employee choice, use the coaching discussion to get employee to change his or her choices.

The first step in coaching analysis is critically important to your success as a coach. The purpose of the analysis is to help you answer the question "What is influencing performance?" This is not a rhetorical question, but one in search of facts, in contrast to the more common responses from managers after they observe a performance discrepancy, such as the following:

"I know what's wrong, he just needs a kick in the . . ."

"What's wrong is that we don't pay enough for the job; what else can you expect?"

"You know these young kids nowadays. You can't expect much more."

"You just can't get any more out of these old timers."

"We just have to get some people in here with the right kind of attitudes."

"Well, I guess it's time for another pep talk."

"She must be having personal problems at home."

Once stated, these reasons become accepted as the real reason for unsatisfactory performance, and the *stater* acts accordingly without further analysis.

A common occupational hazard of managers is to be afflicted with the *all-seeing, all-knowing* disease. In most instances the affliction takes hold slowly and the victims don't know they have it; they just have it. Characteristic of the affliction, although it is never visible to the afflicted, is the ability to close the eyes or stare into space and know what is happening beyond the limits of one's senses. With confidence, the afflicted state they know what is going on and why things are happening, without being encumbered with mere facts. Managers ailing from this occupational disease would never ask the question, "What is influencing poor performance?" They would immediately announce that they *know* the reasons why performance is unsatisfactory and exactly what to do about it.

Needless to say, this syndrome leads managers to the self-destructive behavior of aggressively applying solutions to correct nonexistent reasons for poor performance. The moral of the story is if your first response to the question "What is influencing poor performance?" is "I know what it is," *start to worry.*

To help you avoid this problem, the Coaching Analysis (Fig. 9.1) will lead you through a step-by-step analysis to help you identify specifically

Figure 9.1 Coaching analysis: what is influencing unsatisfactory performance?

the problem it causes and appropriate corrective action. The coaching analysis looks long and complicated but after you read the explanation of each step you will realize that it will take you only a few minutes to complete it. The coaching analysis is generally done by you the manager alone, if you have sufficient information to do it. If you lack sufficient information to answer all the questions in the analysis, it is necessary to collect that information either by talking to someone else who is familiar with the situation or by talking to the employee. If you talk to the employee to collect information to complete the coaching analysis, the purpose is not to discipline the employee or to bite him or her on the ankle. In other words after you observe a performance discrepancy, your first discussion with the employee may be to collect information about what has happened. This is separate and distinct from any discussion you might have after you have completed your analysis and identified the reason for nonperformance.

IDENTIFY THE UNSATISFACTORY PERFORMANCE

The first step in coaching analysis is to *identify the unsatisfactory performance.* This may seem like a pointless step to talk about because unsatisfactory performance has a way of jumping up and biting you. But more precisely, what really jumps up and bites you is the *result* of the unsatisfactory performance.

For example, it is easy to observe from available reports that someone's sales have decreased, or someone's scrap rate has increased, or someone's error rate has increased. These observations are only results or consequences of the worker's performance. You still don't know what is causing these results. It is necessary to know what specific things a person is doing wrong, or failing to do right, to cause sales to go down, scrap rate to go up, or error rate to increase. Workers' performance is the workers' behavior, the things they do called *work.* As a manager, you must know what the inappropriate behavior is before you can select a correct solution to change it.

It seems that it would be a lot easier just to call the employee in and tell him or her to get the sales up or the scrap rate down. But have you ever done that? If you have, what was the result? Most managers tell me it works sometimes but not often enough. The reason it doesn't work is because the employee too frequently doesn't know *what to do differently so the result will change.*

Think of the last time you did that, and let's pretend the employee's response to you was, "I would be glad to, boss. Please tell me what I should do differently so the result will change." Could you have told the employee, specifically? If you couldn't, how do you expect the worker to know what to do? Don't feel bad; lots of managers are saved that embarrassment because workers generally don't ask that question.

One of the most common reasons why managers do not get promoted or get demoted is something called "inability to get along with others" or ineffective people-to-people relationships. This is a common problem because the way it is described excludes practical corrective efforts.

For example, I know one manager who was told "you are abrasive," "you are rubbing people the wrong way," and "you are ruffling people's feathers." He was advised to correct that problem, otherwise, his future with the organization was limited. The obvious actions he could take to correct the problem were wear softer suits to be less abrasive, leave more space between himself and other people and keep his hands in his pockets so he doesn't rub anybody anyway, and when he is next to someone with feathers, don't blow on them.

Now you might respond by saying, "That's ridiculous, I know what they mean." But you are guessing about what is specifically being done wrong. You know there is a problem, but you don't know actually *what* the employee is doing wrong. But suppose the employee was actually doing this:

1. When he gives work to peers he doesn't ask for their help, he demands it.
2. When employees give finished work to him he never says thank you.
3. If the work is 99 percent perfect when they give it to him, he never talks about how good it is, he always emphasizes the 1 percent error.

If you describe that to the individual, he can write down specific things he can do to correct the problem such as, "say please," "ask for help when requesting work," "express thanks both verbally and in writing when something is completed," and "talk proportionately about how perfect something is as well as how bad it may be."

These specific corrective actions will solve the problem but we wouldn't get there from a generalized description of the problem. To help you get better at analyzing human behavior take a look at the following statements, some of which describe measurable behavior and some do not.

- "My accounting supervisor is afraid to make decisions."   (Fear is inside a person's head; you can't measure that or even know it is there. If your accounting supervisor told you he or she was afraid to make decisions the "telling" would be measurable. "Not making decisions" is measurable.)
- "My secretary's mind is not on the work." (Minds are inside people's heads and are not measurable. If you say the secretary is wasting time on personal phone calls, reading non-business-related magazines, socializing, or just sitting staring into space, that would be measurable.)
- "My secretary gives me too much personal advice." (This is measurable. Advice is someone telling you what you should or should not do and you can put advice in lots of categories such as personal, financial, child rearing, car buying, business, or politics. *Too much* can be measured against what you consider to be enough. You could say, "It is OK to tell me when my clothing is messy, but don't tell me how to talk to my boss."
- "My chief engineer thinks she (or he) has all the answers." (You don't know what people think. If they tell you what they think, the telling is measurable. What prompted this comment is the measurable behavior in the next statement.)
- "My chief engineer interrupts me when I am speaking." (You can measure when and how often it happens.)
- "My credit manager ruffles people's feathers." (People don't have feathers. You have to get the facts. What does the employee do that leads you to say he or she ruffles people's feathers?)
- "I have one employee who forgets who the boss is." (Forgetting is in a person's head—you can't measure it. If the employee is walking around saying, "Who is the boss? Can someone tell me who is the boss?" you would have measurable behavior. Some managers conclude employees forget who the boss is when they act like intelligent people and ask questions or disagree with the manager or yell back when the manager is yelling.)

- "My head programmer has lost enthusiasm for giving me work." (Enthusiasm is a quality you assign to people who behave in certain ways such as moving fast, showing high interest, or smiling while they work. You can't measure enthusiasm but you could measure the behavior you think denotes enthusiasm.)
- "The line supervisor delegates but doesn't follow up to find out if they are doing it." (The act and frequency of following up is measurable.)
- "The receptionist just doesn't want to follow the rules." (*Want* is a thought inside a person's head; not measurable. But you can measure which rules and how many times an employee does not follow them. Most people don't want to follow a lot of rules but we follow them because of the consequences.)

You need to know what the employee is doing wrong, or failing to do right, which is giving you an unsatisfactory result. For example, are reports late because the employee doesn't start on time, wastes time on less-important work, or is absent too often from the workplace? Each of these is a separate worker behavior you can observe and discuss and manage. Therefore, when identifying unsatisfactory performance, keep asking yourself *why* until you come up with a specific behavior causing the discrepancy. Avoid the useless generalizations such as the following:

He is a negative thinker.

Her head is in outer space.

He is not tough enough.

She is lazy.

He needs a push.

He doesn't use his head.

She needs to be toned down.

He's flaky.

She needs more polish.

In one seminar a manager described a performance discrepancy as, "My secretary wants to mother me." He was not describing behavior, he was describing what he assumed to be an intent or a desire between his secretary's ears. When I asked him, "What does your secretary *do* because she wants to mother you," he replied with an identifiable performance discrepancy, "She gives me too much advice about my personal life." If the purpose of the coaching process is to get somebody to stop doing what he or she shouldn't be doing or to start doing what he or she should be doing, you have to identify the *behavior that is the problem.*

One sales manager told me he had a long meeting with a salesman whose sales were down but, after the discussion, the sales did not go up. He asked, "What should I do now?" When I asked why the sales were down his response was, "Because he is not selling." I then asked, "What is the salesman doing wrong or failing to do right that results in what you call 'not selling'?" His answer was, "I don't know." The only logical alternative was to tell the manager to go out in the field with the salesman to observe what the salesman was doing wrong or not doing right to cause lower sales.

One of the difficulties of identifying performance discrepancies is that most managers think they do it, even though they don't. For example, if a manager is trying to correct the tardiness problem, she will talk to the employee about *being late too much.* Rarely will the manager have an accurate list of the frequency of latenesses related to scheduled starting times and the specific extent of the lateness. If time cards are available, some managers might go to the trouble of extracting that information. But if time cards are not available, rarely does the manager trouble herself to keep a record. Even more important, the manager rarely knows what normal tardiness is for all the other employees. It is quite easy for managers, once they pick up the scent of a problem employee, to accumulate some information to support the general impression that he or she is worse than everyone else.

A side effect to this kind of problem occurs when a manager is chewing out an employee because of lateness and the employee responds with, "Why are you are picking on me? Everybody is late." The employee knows that everybody else is late occasionally, therefore, the employee thinks the boss's position is unreasonable.

Let's look at it another way. Let's say you call in the employee because of excessive tardiness, and you tell her she must clean up the tardiness problem. Let's say you have spoken to her several times about it and it has not improved; you warn her that if she is late again you are going to have to fire her. That certainly sounds reasonable doesn't it? But do you mean that if she is late again ever in the next 20 years (if she stays in the company that long) that you will fire her? Of course, you don't mean that. Well, do you mean that if she is late once in the next two years you will fire her? Well, it is doubtful you mean that. Well then, what do you mean? If you don't really mean that, then why would you say, "If you are late again, I'm going to fire you?" If there is some level of lateness that is acceptable by policy or practice, that is what must be stated as the proverbial *thin line* that people must not step over. If you will accept lateness of no more than 30 minutes and in no greater frequency than one day per month, that is what you must say. "If you are late more than 30 minutes any more frequently than one day per month, I am going to have to fire you."

Another common situation is when the boss observes an employee spending what appears to be too much personal time on the phone. The manager tells the employee, "Stop spending so much personal time on the phone." Unfortunately, the manager never identifies to the employee what *so much* is. Does the manager really mean no personal phone calls can be made during business hours, or does the manager mean if you keep it down to one call in the morning and one call in the afternoon, it's okay?

Many of the performance outcomes that are unsatisfactory in business are usually caused by the same kind of behaviors that everybody else is involved in, except this employee is doing it more than anyone else. You must identify the frequency of that undesirable behavior before you can know it is a problem and before you can start to deal with it. The best way to do that is to use a technique called *work sampling*. In brief, this means you actually make a record of your observations of what the worker or workers are doing at specific intervals. For example, let's assume you have concluded the reason somebody's productivity rate is down is because of excessive time away from his workstation. Your impression is *Every time I walk through there Charlie doesn't seem to be around*. The next step is to conduct a work sampling. On an 8½ by 11 sheet of paper draw vertical lines to make a column for each employee. Horizontally draw lines across the page to create boxes. In the left hand column list the times you want to observe the problem employees; once every hour would be good.

Once each hour throughout the day, walk through the work area and observe, not only Charlie, but other workers doing similar work. Then go back to your office and make a record of what you observed for each employee. In this instance it might simply be "A" for away or "T" for there. If you do this once each hour, by the end of the day you would be able to analyze the information you have collected to determine whether Charlie is actually absent more frequently than the other employees and specifically what is the difference. Your work sample might look like this.

Worker	WJ	CF	MP	FW	JW	HS	GP
9:30	T	T	T	A	T	A	T
10:30	T	A	T	T	A	T	T
11:30	A	A	T	T	T	T	T
12:30	' LUNCH		–	–	–	–	
1:30	T	A	A	T	T	A	A
2:30	T	T	T	A	T	T	T
3:30	A	A	T	T	T	T	T
4:30	T	T	T	T	T	T	T
	2	4	1	2	1	2	1

If you cannot do it once an hour, you might do it three or four times a day, but be sure to repeat it for several days. The end result will be the same. You will have recorded observations of a group of workers giving you a factual comparison of the problem employee's behavior compared to the other employees. With this factual base, you can say, "Charlie, you are absent from your workstation twice as much as everybody else. Will you please correct that?" A repeated work sample after the discussion will tell you whether performance improved.

The important requirement for your success is this: *If you are going to direct your management effort to coaching the behavior of the people who work for you, it is necessary for you to know what the behavior is now, so that you are able to recognize whether your coaching interventions are helping it to get better or worse.*

This first step is of critical importance because if you do not correctly identify the performance discrepancy, later you and the employee will be talking about the wrong things without eliminating the unsatisfactory performance. As mentioned earlier, your efforts to solve problems with your human resources should be just as practical and specific as your efforts to solve problems with your nonhuman resources. Have you ever taken your car in for repair and the problem was not correctly identified which resulted in replacements, adjustments, and unnecessary servicing until the real problem was discovered and fixed? Well, the same waste of time and money, as well as frustration, occurs when managers don't correctly identify problem behavior.

IS IT WORTH YOUR TIME?

Frequently managers become aggravated over, and get involved in, so-called discipline discussions about isolated incidents that are of little importance to the job or company. Why would a manager discipline an employee who has been late for work once in six months, or who has submitted one sloppy report out of a hundred, or who has made any error for the first time? When I ask managers why they pounce on a single occurrence of unsatisfactory performance their usual response is, "I don't want them to get any bad habits," or "I want them to know that I know they did it," or "If you give them an inch, they will take a mile."

On other occasions managers get involved in so-called disciplinary discussions with employees (actually, these are guidance and counseling) about things that are clearly not related to what the employee is being paid for. When asked why, managers say, "It might lead to bad attitudes, I have to help them maintain the right attitude." This appears to be based on the premise that managers somehow have the responsibility to guide their employees' total lives. I have seen workers threatened with the loss of their jobs if they didn't shave off mustaches or beards, or because their hair was too long. I have seen women whose jobs were threatened because they wore miniskirts and others because they wore slacks on the job. There was a president of a small, Midwest company in the news a few years ago whose action inadvertently shut down his plant. He made a rule that employees could not smoke, even on their rest periods, because it was injurious to health.

One company president wanted me to draft a company dress code to legislate against *bralessness,* which could be used as a basis for terminating employment if violated. According to his logic, women who did not wear bras distracted the male workers and visitors. It took quite an effort to get him to understand that he had no right (much less a method) to control what kind of underwear his employees wore. There are companies where if you don't wear a suit you are laughed at; and in others you are laughed at if you do wear a suit. In some being on time is important, and in others it does not matter. In some body piercing is forbidden but in others it and bare feet are okay. In view of managers' predominant complaint that there is not enough time to do the things they have to do, it is amazing how much time they waste, both theirs and their employees', on unimportant subjects and subjects unrelated to work.

One manager asked me what to do about an employee who used expletives when doing his work. She said his work was good but she wanted him to stop using the expletives. She explained that he doesn't use them on her or other employees he just uttered them to himself while he is working. It took me 20 minutes to convince her to ignore the expletives as long as performance was satisfactory. With tongue in cheek I also suggested she might ask the employees whose work was not as good, to try the expletives; it might work.

The sad fact is that your time is not available in unlimited quantities; it does require your time and the employee's time to discuss, argue, cajole, and negotiate. If the subject is not important, why waste any time on it? If you permit yourself to become aggravated over something unimportant, not only will you be wasting your time, but you may be destroying your relationship with the employee. Also, termination of employment is one of the possible, realistic, and logical alternatives when you are unable to solve a problem of unsatisfactory performance. Why would you want to lose an employee's valued performance over some minute aspect of performance that, in all probability, is not related to, or does not detract from, what you pay him or her to do?

That brings us to the only logical alternative for you to choose when faced with unsatisfactory performance, which is, *if it's not important, don't waste your time on it; forget it.* This means that one of the first things you do after you identify a performance discrepancy is to ask yourself, "Is it worth my time?" This is not a *rhetorical question.* Just because you think it is important *does not make* it important. You must defend your decision to yourself that it is important or ignore it. I knew a sales manager in San Francisco who had a rule that if one of his salespeople did not wear a vested suit the salesperson would be fired. When I asked him if he thought wearing a vest was important, his immediate response was, "Of course it is." But when I required him to describe the relevance of wearing or not wearing a vest to the achievement of the sales goal, he could not do it. He admitted he had a strong preference for the three-piece-suit image, but there was no proof that salespeople in his or any other company selling a similar product experienced unique success or failure related to wearing a vest.

An interesting corollary to this occurred when I was training a group of managers in the coaching process. After describing the preceding situation, I asked the managers what would their actions be in a similar situation if one of their employees stopped wearing a vest. One manager replied that he would fire that employee and he went on to explain that his reason for doing so was that the employee had broken a rule established by the manager. He agreed the rule about vest wearing might be ridiculous, but because he had made the rule his only alternative when a employee broke that rule was to fire him. The rest of the class said the better alternative would be to rescind the rule. We finally convinced him that his management decisions should be functionally related to the management of his employees' performance rather than defending his mogul-emperor position by chopping off the heads of those who defy him. Why would any manager choose to waste two people's time, destroy a relationship, and/or incur turnover costs over something that *is really not important?* That would be self-destructive behavior. If you have a high-technology employee who has so much knowledge that he or she would be almost impossible to replace, you could learn to live with a lot of idiosyncrasies.

So if the answer to the first question, "Is it worth your time?" is "no," the only alternative is *don't waste your time on it.*

DOES EMPLOYEE KNOW PERFORMANCE IS UNSATISFACTORY?

The most logical approach to determine what is influencing unsatisfactory performance should start with the most common and easy to correct reasons for unsatisfactory performance. Since lack of feedback is the most common reason for bad performance, your analysis question should be "Does he or she know performance is unsatisfactory?" If you do what I tell you to do, this is an easy question to answer because your first two coaching interventions are to give neutral feedback. You would have gotten to this coaching analysis only after your feedback failed to correct the problem.

Of course, you may not have a coaching problem and are using this analysis to look for ways of improving performance in general. Therefore, you would be searching for answers. A good approach is to ask employees the following:

"How do you know when you are doing a good or bad job?"

"How do you measure the quality of your performance?"

"How do you know when you do something wrong?"

"Describe what good performance would look like."

"Describe what bad performance would look like."

When searching for feedback problems look for specificity and frequency between the work and the worker. *Generalized* feedback at the end of a day does not influence a person's performance during that day. Specific feedback during the day influences a person's performance for that day.

If the answer to the question of whether the employee knows when performance is unsatisfactory is *no,* the only solution is *let him or her know.*

DOES EMPLOYEE KNOW WHAT IS SUPPOSED TO BE DONE?

As you recall, one of the most prevalent responses managers give to the question, "Why don't employees do what they are supposed to do?" was "They don't know what they are supposed to do." There are four parts to this *not knowing* problem. Employees may not know what specifically they are supposed to do or when to begin it or when to end it or what finished is supposed to look like. It is unlikely that all of this information would be missing at any one time but only one missing part is enough to induce failure. The most common missing information which causes project failure is *they don't know what finished is supposed to look like.* When you tell someone to do a good job, does that mean 5 percent error is okay or 2 percent error or errorless performance is expected? What does "Do your best" mean? Does it mean do what is best humanly possible, or your best according to what we are paying you, or your best according to how you feel today, or your best according to the time available for this project? How hard does "Try harder" mean? And what does a "comprehensive" report look like?

Every business consultant and professor I have ever heard talk about increasing worker productivity has preached, "Tell people what you want them to do; give them good job descriptions." And business has flubbed that advice because most job descriptions don't describe the work; they describe the job responsibilities. Unfortunately you can't do a responsibility. Responsibility describes how it will be decided to give someone a medal or to shoot someone tomorrow. To meet or fulfill a responsibility, a person must *do things*. These things they must do are the behaviors for which you pay the rent money. When people apply for a job in your company, they are knocking on your door saying, "I choose to give up doing what I would rather do and do the things you want done for which you will pay me." But the unspoken response by management is, "Okay, we will hire you but we are not going to take the time to tell you exactly what it is we want you to do." As a result, employees do a lot of guessing.

Has an employee ever done a job for you that turned out to be less than what you expected, and when you described how much more work had to be completed, his or her response was, "Oh, I didn't know that's what you wanted. I'll be glad to do that." If so, the problem was *he or she didn't know what finished was supposed to look like.* Too frequently, especially in creative areas, employees are given jobs to do but the only one who can recognize when it is finished is the boss. The result is that employees keep bringing what they believe to be completed work to the boss and are repeatedly told, "No, that's not what I wanted." I am not talking about those ridiculous but common situations where the boss clearly identifies to the employee what finished should look like, but when the completed project is submitted, the boss *decides* something else should be done rather than what was previously agreed to.

Here is one manager's description of how he discovered unsatisfactory performance was occurring because the employee didn't know what was supposed to be done. His employee was a sales administrator with about one year's experience. His major complaint about her was that when she worked on specific assignments she did not analyze situations in depth to reach solutions or suggest alternative solutions. When she presented an incomplete job to him, his usual response was to accept it and complete it himself without explaining what else he wanted and why. He justified his actions by telling himself he had hired the wrong person for the job, that she was incapable of handling it. Before firing her, he decided to try coaching analysis as an alternative and here is his story.

"Mary, on the recent market price analysis you prepared for me, were you satisfied with the finished product?" Her response was, "Yes, I gave you what you asked for." I then showed Mary the form she had completed and asked her if there was any additional information she could have included that would have helped me reach a decision as to the price we should charge for our product. I had already taken my analysis from the file folder so the additional information I had included, which she should have done, could not be seen.

After some thought she suggested we could add the strength relationship of our product versus the competitive product. I told her that was a good idea, and asked if there was anything else.

"Not really," she said, "all I can think of now is to plug in a price for our product based on the amount of gross profit we think is necessary." I continued with, "Can we sell a product in the market at a higher price than competition?" She agreed that we could not, and said that if we are looking at a product where the strengths of our product and the competition's product are equal, we could only plug in the same price of the competitive product on the form and then compare our cost figure, and list the gross profit in the appropriate place. She was correct.

The analysis was now complete and ready for review and approval by top management. Knowing that pricing is not always that easy, however, I asked Mary how we could arrive at a price if the strengths of the two products were not equal or if other running properties were different. *She did not know.* I then showed her step-by-step how to figure it out, if we knew what the competitor's prices were and what prices we would have to charge to be at parity. I was surprised to see that she even wrote down the step-by-step procedure. I further explained that if our product had superior running properties how much premium we could, in reality, expect to receive, and, on the other hand, if our product was inferior in some way, how we must reduce our prices by a certain factor. I told Mary that when I asked for a market price analysis I expected a complete job just as we had reviewed. She told me she would include the foregoing information in the future. She also said that no one, including me, had ever taken the time to show her how to compare two products with each other.

She further stated that when I had asked her to prepare market price analysis I had not mentioned that its purpose was to be able to establish a price for our product.

Future price analytical work I have asked her to do has been produced as I requested. I discovered that *if she didn't know what I wanted she could not supply what I wanted.*

Another manager, of an electrical engineering testing laboratory, was complaining to me about an employee who always "went too far" in collecting unnecessary data in a testing project. I asked the manager how the technician could know when he had gone far enough in collecting data. The manager's response was, "If he will come to us we will tell him as he progresses with each project." Invariably the employee was advised by his manager that he had not gone far enough or he had gone too far in collecting data. Here was a situation where the only one able to recognize what finished looked like was the manager. This manager eventually agreed (reluctantly) that the best solution was to give sufficient information to the technician so *the technician* could recognize finished when he saw it.

Certainly if you just told an employee what is supposed to be done, you feel safe in assuming he or she now knows what to do. Your confidence in your assumption would be directly related to how specific and complete you were in describing what *was supposed to be done.* (Unfortunately the sounds came out of your mouth not his or hers.) As you and your instructions to employees get separated by distance, and one-way e-mail, as well as by other managers who must pass on your instructions, you should have less confidence in knowing that employees know what is supposed to be done.

For example, if your company is like most companies, you probably use experienced employees to orient new employees to the job. When you do this, do you give a checklist to the experienced employee to follow as a guide in the orientation, to insure that all the critical information relative to the job is covered? Do you ask the experienced employee to annotate the checklist to indicate that all items needed to be covered were covered, and that the new employee understands what must be done? At the completion of the orientation do you quiz (formally or informally) the new employee to find out for sure he or she knows what is supposed to be done? If your company is like most companies, you probably don't do any of that. So why are you surprised six months later, when the new employee does not do something he or she is supposed to do, and when you face the employee with it, the response is, "I didn't know I was supposed to do that"? Of course, you can feel better if you say such things as, "Don't give me that excuse, you had orientation just like everyone else," or "You have been around here long enough, you should know better." But the real problem is *he or she didn't know what was supposed to be done.* In situations like this, managers usually treat the employee's comments as empty excuses rather than feedback to the manager that the management process is failing, and the employees should be informed about what is supposed to be done. If you don't organize the orientation process there will always be some things left out.

One manager told me that her employees get things right only when she yelled at them. She described how she was usually a caring and sensitive person and generally talked to her employees as colleagues rather than as a boss when assigning work. Invariably she said after assigning a project, the employees would return with incomplete and unacceptable work. She said for the first one or two times she would discuss the problem in a quiet, friendly manner. But about the third time she would blow up and yell. Soon after the yelling the employee would return with a complete and acceptable project. She couldn't understand why this was happening and it was driving her up the wall. I explained to her that many managers who view themselves as colleagues rather than managers of their employees communicate about work in such vague terms that the employees don't know exactly what is expected. When the manager blows up and yells the yelling usually includes a description of exactly what is wanted that the employee hadn't heard before. It simply took that long for the employee to get a complete description of what *finished is supposed to look like.*

In one high-tech company, the development engineers described their frustration trying to develop products requested by the marketing department. They would have a meeting at which marketing would describe a customer's need and request a product to answer that need. The engineers would work to develop product for eight or ten months, bring their product to the marketing people, who would say, "That's not what we had in mind." The engineers would go back and work on it for another six months and return to marketing but get the same rejection. The engineers said that this could go on for years. This was a blatant case of no one knowing what finished was supposed to look like. We solved the problem by having the engineers and marketing people meet in a conference room with the lights out, asking the question, "If we could wave a magic wand and create this product instantly in this room what would it look like?"

Some managers mistakenly believe that telling people exactly what you want them to do is de-motivating. (There is no such thing as *de-motivation*.) They believe if you let people work things out for themselves it is motivating. Unfortunately it is just the opposite. When people have to guess what they are supposed to do it makes them nervous and tense. And when they are told that what they did (by guessing) is not what was expected they are punished and frustrated by failure. Let's use a little logic here. How many situations do you face in life outside of business wherein you need others to do things for you such as in a restaurant or with a service organization and you can get exactly what you want by telling people to "guess"?

If you are renting a person's behavior you owe it to them to let them know what behavior you are paying for. The job description should be a behavior rental list describing what you want people to do. Don't worry about how long the list is, if it includes the important behavior needed for the job to be done perfectly. What you pay for is perfect performance with the understanding that perfect performance can include some allowable error rate. Not even professional ball players sink every shot or complete every pass.

The cause of nonperformance described in this section is not a skill deficiency. In these situations employees know how to do something, but they just don't know when it should be started, or when it should be finished, or what finished is supposed to look like (how good it is supposed to be). Therefore, the next logical step in your analysis of performance problems is to look for a most common reason for nonperformance, by answering the question, *does the employee know what is supposed to be done, and when?* If the answer is *no, tell him or her* and the problem will go away.

DOES EMPLOYEE KNOW HOW TO DO IT?

You will recall that the second most prevalent response to the question, "Why don't employees do what they are supposed to do?" was "They don't know how to do it." This is a common reason for nonperformance primarily because of the assumptions we make that learning has taken place.

You may be aware of the practice of social promotion in many public schools. This is the practice of promoting unprepared students to the next grade so they can stay with their age group. In some large cities as many as 40 percent of the elementary school population would not be promoted without social promotions. This means that you will eventually be faced with managing people without basic skills of reading, writing, and arithmetic. But did you know that social promotion is the prevailing procedure in business training? Those responsible for training in business have not universally accepted the binding axiom for all trainers, *If the student hasn't learned, the teacher hasn't taught.* As a result, there are lots of activities going on that are *called* training, but there is very little *learning* taking place. Approximately 80 percent of those people I contact in business responsible for creating or conducting training programs have never been taught how to teach. They are designing and conducting programs that concentrate on teaching rather than learning. They concentrate on what is taking place with the instructor, rather than concentrating on what should be taking place with the student. The most telling clue to identify teachers who don't know how to teach is their comments about the students, such as "Boy, that was a dead group," or "They sure were unresponsive," or "That group was not too sharp."

Another remarkable failing trait all company business training programs share is *the lack of testing* to indicate whether learning has in fact occurred; everyone graduates.

Recently a conversation with the director of training of one large corporation went something like this:

> Me: Do you use testing to determine whether or not your training is achieving learning objectives?
>
> Trainer: Yes, we do.
>
> Me: How do you do it?
>
> Trainer: We don't use paper and pencil tests; actually each trainer makes those observations.
>
> Me: How do they do that?
>
> Trainer: They gauge the responses of the participants throughout the training session and at the end of the session.

> Me: Do the instructors have a checklist, or something specific they can use to help them identify those responses that would indicate whether or not learning has occurred?
>
> Trainer: No. Because of the trainers' long experience in these areas, they have a feel for this.
>
> Me: Well then, do they apply some kind of specific measurement to determine the levels of learning in each individual?
>
> Trainer: No, they just get a general feel for how each individual is doing.
>
> Me: But if you don't have a checklist or a guide to specify the learning that is expected to take place, how does the instructor recognize it when he or she sees it?
>
> Trainer: The things we have to teach are quite complicated and cannot be measured quantitatively. We rely a great deal on the experience and knowledge of the trainers; after all, their experience has to be worth something.

Subsequently I had the opportunity to view one of the trainers in action; he talked and the students listened; they were not required to respond in any way. At the end of a two-hour session only one student had taken notes and only two asked any questions, and the students were not required to demonstrate learning. Not only was there no testing, verbal or otherwise, to determine whether learning had occurred, there was no teaching.

Another cause of nonlearning in business is that common practice of assigning experienced employees to train new employees. The question is, "Who taught the experienced employees how to teach?" The answer is invariably *no one*. Experienced employees are usually selected as the trainers because they do their jobs better than most. Unfortunately, the moment they are asked to show (teach) the new employees how to do it, they are being given a new job as teachers, which they don't know how to do. If there is no teaching happening how can you expect learning to happen? Just because two people spend a certain amount of time sitting or standing close to each other, looking at and talking about the same things, does not mean that teaching or learning is happening. Because the manager has said, "Let there be training," the manager's reaction to a new employee's performance discrepancy in the future will not include the possibility that "that person doesn't know how to do it." It will be assumed that because the new employee was exposed to the training, the learning occurred.

In my five-day seminar "Training for Trainers" there is resistance on the first day because experienced trainers can't understand why they should be there. But on the last day they express their amazement at how much they learned about something they thought they had been doing well for five to fifteen years.

One manufacturing supervisor wanted to know what to do about those employees that obviously "don't give a damn." When I asked him to give me an example he described a situation in which a new employee had been trained by an experienced employee on a custom-designed automatic manufacturing machine. When the training period was over the new worker was assigned to operate his own machine. Almost immediately he did something wrong, which caused $15,000 damage to the machine. The supervisor explained that the expensive damage to the machine was obviously the result of the worker's "I-don't-give-a-damn" attitude. The rest of our conversation went like this:

> Me: This doesn't appear to be a problem of attitude. It appears that you made a bad $15,000 decision.
>
> Supv.: What do you mean by that?
>
> Me: Did you know that a mistake in operating the machine could cause $15,000 worth of damage?
>
> Supv.: Yes.
>
> Me: Then what facts did you have to lead you to believe that the new worker would not damage the machine?
>
> Supv.: He was trained in how to operate it.
>
> Me: You told me that he went through something called training, but how did you know at the end of the training that he knew how to operate the machine?
>
> Supv.: Look, you have to assume some things in the world; if a man is trained in how to do something I have to assume he knows how to do it.
>
> Me: Who was the trainer?
>
> Supv.: Our most-experienced machine operator.
>
> Me: Was he ever taught how to teach?
>
> Supv.: No.
>
> Me: Did he have a written outline to follow in carrying out the training program?

Supv.: No.

Me: At the end of the training did the trainer give you a list of those critical aspects of machine operation that must be covered in training and indicate that they were covered and understood by the worker?

Supv.: No.

Me: Then how do you know the new worker knew how to operate the machine after the so-called training was finished?

Supv.: What do you want me to do, train every new employee myself? I just don't have enough time for that. That production floor is like a mad house.

Me: No, it wouldn't be logical to expect you to carry out the training. But why wouldn't you conduct some kind of test at the end of the training to find out whether learning has actually occurred?

Supv.: Look, I'm not a college professor. I'm a production supervisor trying to produce the product as economically as possible. I just don't have time for all that stuff.

Me: Let's look at this another way. How much justification does your company require if you want to spend $15,000?

Supv.: Well, they would want quite a bit of justification. If it's a purchase they would want at least three estimates, and they usually want to know why it can't be done without the expenditure in the first place.

Me: That sounds typical, and rightly so. But it appears that you didn't go through any justification to spend the $15,000 on the machine that your employee damaged.

Supv.: Wait a minute. I didn't damage the machine. It was the worker who made the decision to screw it up, not me.

Me: It appears that way, but these are the facts: (1) you knew that the machine could be damaged to the tune of $15,000 if it were operated improperly; (2) you assigned the worker to the machine without having any facts to indicate that the worker *would not damage the machine.*

Supv.: Wait a minute. I didn't assume the worker would damage the machine.

Me: Right. But you did assume that the worker would not damage the machine. When you assigned that worker to that machine, you were actually stating, "I, the supervisor, sound of mind and body, am making the decision to assign the new worker to operate this expensive machine, which could be damaged to the tune of $15,000. I have justified this decision by gathering enough facts to lead me to believe that the worker will not do those inappropriate things to damage the machine." You, in fact, made that $15,000 decision without any justification whatsoever. You merely assumed the worker knew how to operate the machine because he was exposed to something called training.

Supv.: I understand what you are saying. When I assign somebody to do something, that decision is worth the value of the highest cost to the company if that worker screws up. But I am not capable, nor do I have the time, to sit down and design training programs and high-class tests.

Me: You are certainly right, and it wouldn't be reasonable to expect you to design a training program. Nevertheless, if you are aware of the combination of those critical conditions and worker actions that lead to destructive results, then it would be fairly simple at the end of training for you to ask a list of questions that would face the workers with those critical conditions to determine whether or not they select the appropriate alternative action (and, therefore, prevent the destruction from occurring).

The problem is that because you see training taking place, you assume that learning is taking place; because you assume learning has taken place, you have to find another reason for the screwup when it occurs, such as, "They don't give a damn."

Let's consider another question. If a student attending a five-day training program in your organization does not attend for one of the five days, is the student scheduled for a sixth day to make up for the day missed, or does the instructor spend twenty minutes with the student on the following day to make up for the lost time? If your company is like most companies, the instructor will spend the twenty minutes with the student to make up for the lost time. You might ask yourself, "Then why isn't the training program four days and twenty minutes instead of five days?" How can a student make up for a day's training in twenty minutes? Because the worker's record indicates he or she attended the training program, the manager assumes learning has occurred.

Another aspect of the learning problem relates to that big difference between knowing what should be done and having the opportunity to do it. For example, reading how to fly an airplane is quite different from flying a real airplane. Reading how to bowl is quite different from doing it. Reading how a skill should be carried out is entirely different from the actual practice of using that skill. A significant amount of training in business is not successful because it exposes employees to knowledge about how a skill should be performed, but does not provide them with the opportunity to apply that skill until the real job must be done. They don't get a chance to practice. You may be faced with a performance discrepancy of an employee who possesses all the innate qualities necessary to perform, who may have a high desire to perform, and there are no obstacles beyond the worker's control to prevent him or her from performing, but nonperformance is occurring because *he or she doesn't know how to do it.* It could be the employee did it so long ago he or she has forgotten how to do it, or it could be the worker learned what he or she *should do,* but was never provided the opportunity of *doing it.*

It serves no practical purpose for you as a manager to make such observations as, "I can't believe that anyone who has been around here as long as you have does not know how to do that," or "If you have been to the training like everybody else you should be able to do it," or "You should have learned that by now." When training is supposed to take place, test to determine whether learning has occurred, and you will not make wrong assumptions. In your quest to answer the question, "What is influencing unsatisfactory performance?" one key question you should answer is, *do they know how to do it?* If your nonperformance problem is occurring because "The employee doesn't know how to do it," the solution is *provide training or practice.*

DOES EMPLOYEE KNOW WHY IT SHOULD BE DONE?

Does the employee know the importance of what he or she is supposed to be doing? Does he or she understand how this task or project relates and impacts on his or her own total job, fellow workers, internal and external customers, the organization's mission? Does he or she know the value of the desired performance relative to profit and loss, safety, and legal considerations. This is a common problem when employees are new in a job or when people are faced with changing the way they do things.

When employees ask, "Why do we have to do this dumb thing?" do you consider it an attitude problem and tell them, "Just do what you get paid for and stop complaining"? If you do, you missed answering a real good question. If you understand that your employees are not robots or automatons, ask yourself why would they do things well, if at all, if they don't know why they should do them. If you are too busy when assigning projects to explain the importance of each project, you will have these problems. It continues to amaze me when executives complain about their workforce not supporting their organization's increased need for profit, market share, or customer satisfaction yet they have not communicated these needs to employees beyond a single one-page message. It is not enough to tell people to "ask closing questions" or "slow the machine down when you do this" or "don't change the system unless you first tell me" unless you can explain why they should. If you can't explain to people why they should do things, either you don't know why or what you want is not important. In one high-tech company all the employees at each location assemble in the company cafeteria each day to hear executives report on current status of sales, product problems, customer gains and losses, new product developments, marketplace changes, internal changes, and anything else management thinks everybody should know. You can bet everybody in that company knows why they should be doing what they do.

Without considering any motivational theories common sense would lead you to conclude that knowing why something should be done is an important element influencing people's performance. If you are not sure of the answer to the question, *"does the employee know why it should be done,"* ask employees if they know. If the answer is *no* explain it to them and performance will improve.

ARE THERE OBSTACLES BEYOND EMPLOYEE'S CONTROL?

Hardly anyone is able to do his or her job without some type of support services from other employees, departments, or vendors. When things go the way they should this support is like breathing; it is just there. But all too frequently these support services are late, deficient in quality or quantity, or don't arrive at all, becoming obstacles to performance. Too frequently the employee needing this support knows it is not there but the manager does not know.

The next logical step in your coaching analysis is to determine whether there are obstacles beyond the employee's control blocking performance. It is important that you pursue this question early to avoid blaming an employee for a problem when it is not his or her fault. If the employee's performance is being adversely affected by obstacles beyond his or her control, it is really your problem, not the employee's problem. As the boss, you may have to use your knowledge, experience, and influence to modify or remove those obstacles to solve the problem.

Occasionally you may observe obstacles hindering performance merely by observing the work process. But most of the time you will only learn of obstacles when you ask why a project is late. Most managers don't follow up frequently enough during a project to check progress so they only discover there are obstacles when the project fails. It is then too late to prevent failure.

Examples of obstacles beyond the employee's control could be such things as nondelivery of raw materials, unfinished prework, late or incorrect reports or data, inaccessible data, equipment or program failure, or conflicting instructions. Picture an employee scheduled to come in on Saturday to run a special program on the computer only to find the building's electrical system not working because the elevator system is being repaired. The result is nonperformance. There are other obstacles, such as 36 inches of snow, floods, hurricanes, accidents, illness, and death (of others). You may not be able to eliminate some of these obstacles, but you may be able to help lessen their effect on performance.

Besides observation, the most direct source of collecting information to determine whether there are obstacles beyond an employee's control is to talk to the employee. People are not reticent to point out the many obstacles that interfere with their performance if you are available to talk to. Unfortunately, managers make up their minds in advance that the reason for nonperformance is caused by poor attitude, lack of self-motivation (whatever that is), or stupidity; therefore, any comments about obstacles are written off as excuses. This *magic* that managers perform, is to judge whether an employee's comments are valid reasons or excuses without investigating to collect the facts.

I know it is embarrassing to be in high gear chewing out an employee only to be presented with factual information about obstacles to performance of which you were unaware. When it happens to you, you feel like an idiot. You can become a bigger idiot by waving it away as unimportant, or you can swallow your pride, apologize, and go away to investigate.

Many years ago I was teaching a seminar in a hotel in Kansas City when I became annoyed by one of the participants who was sitting on my left about the third seat in on a U-shaped table setup. About every three or four minutes he would emit a whistle and everyone would laugh. I suspected this to be some kind of prank these Westerners were dumping on me, the big city slicker from New York city. So I said to him, "Your whistling may be funny to you and the rest of the group but it is interfering with my conducting this seminar, would you please stop it?" He turned to me and pointed to a hearing aid in his left ear which I had not seen and said, "The whistling coming from my hearing aid is caused by the hotel paging system. Every time they page someone it causes my hearing aid to whistle although you can't hear the page in this room. If I turn it down so it doesn't whistle, I can't hear you talking." Wow! Although it was only 9:45 A.M. I was ready to get out of town. How dumb can you get? Of course a better response to the whistling would have been, "Excuse me, sir, I wonder why we are hearing whistling every few minutes." You can bet that was the last time I implied motive to a situation before collecting some information.

The best alternative, of course, is not to get into a chewing session until you find out who is to blame for what. If there really are obstacles beyond the employee's control, then your concern is not about the employee's behavior, but about the obstacles.

Some obstacles cannot be eliminated such as citywide power failure when you have no backup generators. But some obstacles are only obstacles to that employee because he or she does not know how to circumvent them. If you teach them how to circumvent an obstacle you have in effect removed that obstacle as an impediment to performance. If you really want to be a "can do" manager, forecast obstacles your people could face working on a project and discuss in advance how to handle them and encourage your employees to come to you quickly for assistance when unforeseen obstacles arise.

When trying to answer the question, *"Are there obstacles beyond the employee's control?"* it is your responsibility to collect enough information to determine whether the obstacles the employee talks about are real or imagined. If the obstacles are real, it is also your responsibility to do what is necessary to remove them or circumvent their influence. In your quest to answer the question, "What is influencing unsatisfactory performance?" you should answer the question *are there obstacles beyond their control?* If the answer is *yes, remove them* or explain how to get around them and performance will become satisfactory.

DOES EMPLOYEE THINK YOUR WAY WILL NOT WORK?

When employees have been doing their jobs a certain way for a long time and you ask them to change and do it your way, a common response is "I don't think it will work." You usually don't hear it because they say it to each other. This reason for nonperformance pops up at the most critical time—when you are trying to make changes you believe are needed. This reason for nonperformance may also occur with new people who don't fully understand all aspects of the job but have doubts about the effectiveness of what you are telling them to do.

But it is not enough for you to be right; they have to believe you are right or your way will not be implemented. Some will even try to prove your way will not work by sabotaging it. If your relationship with your employees encourages open discussion about work you will hear, "I don't think that will work"; and you can answer that as a question. If that question does not come from them you should ask it yourself. "Can anyone think of any situation we might face when this new way will not work?" But, "Yes, it will" or "Trust me, it will work" is not enough of an answer. You have to do some *selling* not just telling. If your way has been done successfully in the world before, present detailed explanation of how it worked and where it worked. If after your explanation you still hear "it will not work" and they can't explain why they think that, or if your way has never been done before, just ask them to try it your way and you will take responsibility for the consequences.

So if nonperformance is occurring because *employees think your way will not work,* convince them and performance will improve.

DOES EMPLOYEE THINK HIS OR HER WAY IS BETTER?

Employees having better ways of doing things than your way is a very pleasant condition and something we strive for in business as long as changes are coordinated to prevent disruption in the general work process. But this cause of performance problems is when an employee thinks he or she has a better way but it isn't better. This commonly occurs when an employee quantifies his or her new idea without relevance to other workers, departments, customers, legal considerations, or long-term consequences. Frequently the employee's idea is good for that individual but not for anybody else. This problem usually arrives when there is little or no discussion before the work begins and you have people doing things wrong because they think their way is better. If you hear "my way is better" when assigning work or making a change in how the work is done, discuss the proposed new way in detail to discover if it is in fact a better way. If it is not a better way you must be convincing in exposing it. You will not get this opportunity if you don't have time for discussions. When introducing your way it is a good idea to ask, "Does anyone think they have a better way?" If the answer is *no,* you are homefree on this one, but if the answer is *yes,* you must deal with it, not dismiss it. If you conclude the employee *thinks his or her way is better,* explain convincingly why it is not.

DOES EMPLOYEE THINK SOMETHING ELSE IS MORE IMPORTANT?

Under this question we are talking about priorities. The employee is working but he or she is not working on the right things; the employee thinks something else is more important. The employee could be working on your work but it is not the highest-priority work, or the employee could be working on things helping others or even a personal project all of which are a lower priority than what you need done now. Many jobs present a myriad of things that an employee may choose to work on at any moment in time, and it is easy to be working on the wrong thing from the manager's viewpoint. In these situations managers don't have a problem deciding what is the highest priority because they have an unwritten formula in their head which guides them. The solution is for the manager to teach the employees how to use the formula. If your work process involves frequent changes in work priorities you have to spend a lot of time keeping people informed of the current priorities to avoid this reason for nonperformance. If the employee *thinks something else is more important,* explain the work priorities and performance will improve.

ARE THERE POSITIVE CONSEQUENCES TO EMPLOYEE FOR PERFORMING APPROPRIATELY?

This question takes us back to the discussion of the scientific evidence that behavior followed by a positive consequence to the performer will increase in its frequency. Also true is any behavior followed by no consequence will decrease in its frequency. So with this question you are looking for what rewards if any come to the employee from the employee's point of view for doing the job the way it is supposed to be done. If the job is not intrinsically rewarding during the day and rewards are not forthcoming from fellow workers, you the manager are the only source of rewards for the employee. If you deliver none, then it is safe to assume the employee isn't getting any. This is especially true with routine jobs which seem to have no beginnings or endings and project work which takes months and even years to complete. You can put the opportunity for winning in routine jobs by setting performance goals by the hour and provide feedback to the employee about performance toward the goal. Project work should be broken down into smaller steps to provide more beginnings and endings with target dates. For example, if our goal is to drive from New York City to Los Angeles in 10 days, where are we supposed to be tonight at six o'clock? If we don't know, it is just another day of driving; if we do know, we either win or lose at six o'clock.

Of course, your verbal reinforcements of the employee's gains or achievements in performance are the most effective and least expensive. In many companies where positive reinforcement is understood as a powerful influence on performance, tangible reward are used to drive all kinds of performance. There are rewards for attendance, safety, quality and quantity of productivity, customer service, customer satisfaction, sales, product delivery, creativity, and profit. Contests running continuously are good as long as you follow the scientific rules. Don't reward the one who does the most of anything; you don't influence enough peoples' performance. Set a goal and everyone achieving or exceeding the goal is eligible. Put their names in a hat and draw one name as the winner. But don't have groups larger than 15 people. Also all contests should be short range: the next hour, the next day, week, or month. Long contests reveal potential winners long before the end of the contest and 85 percent of the group seeing no chance of winning drops out. Keep your rewards small but desirable and have lots of them. I know one vice president who gives out silver dollars to members of his staff when some one accomplishes a targeted activity. Some companies print up fake money ($100,000 bills) with no monetary value and give one to employees achieving something beyond the normal. It may sound dumb to you but you would change your mind if you saw the $100,000 bills prominently displayed on desks. Some companies give $100 cash to each manager each month to give to employees in $1 to $5 amounts to reinforce performance. If you give prizes keep them under $50 and choose things of which people would be happy owning more than one. For example, if you give someone a hat or a jacket, why would a second one be a reward to them?

Nonmonetary rewards work well, such as giving easy or more desirable projects to someone who just finished a difficult, unenjoyable project; extra rest breaks or coffee breaks with you; e-mail praising performance; introduction and praising comments about employee to higher-level managers; special business business trips; special parking place for a week, and so on. If you work on it, you will come up with many more ideas relevant to your work situation. But the verbal reinforcements are easy to do and very effective. If you conclude that there are no *positive consequences to the employee for performing appropriately, give positive reinforcement.*

DOES NEGATIVE CONSEQUENCE FOLLOW PERFORMANCE?

You will recall that the science of behavior management is based on the premise, *all behavior is a function of its consequences.* The scientific practice of behavior modification has demonstrated that behavior followed by a positive consequence will increase in frequency; behavior followed by a negative consequence will decrease in frequency. Your understanding of this contingent relationship between behavior and consequences provides you with new alternatives in answering the question, "What is influencing poor performance?" For example, it would be perfectly logical for you to explore the possibility that desired performance is not occurring because a negative consequence or a painful event is experienced by the performer following the desired performance. As mentioned earlier, it frequently happens in business that workers who do the nasty tasks well, get to do all the nasty tasks.

One of my early work experiences while in high school was for a large furniture store as a part-time lamp assembler, paid by the hour.

One of the consequences of getting my work done quickly was to go home early. Now going home early from work could be construed as a positive consequence under certain conditions, but not if you needed the money and I did. As you might guess, my speed on the job was quickly replaced by thoroughness; a thoroughness, I might add, that was far in excess of what was expected. The consequence was that I rarely went home early.

About two months after I started the job, the manager told me they occasionally needed someone to help with furniture deliveries and, if I wanted to, I could go out on the delivery truck after my lamp assemblies for that day were finished. Now it might appear miraculous to some, but it so happened that my accumulation of two months lamp-assembling experience had the sudden effect of improving my speed, so that all the assigned lamp-assembling work was completed in about half the previous time. The consequence was that I was available to help on truck deliveries every day they needed me. Incidentally, the work on the truck turned out to be just as great as I thought it would be.

Recently a manager who supervises five secretaries, who work for eight executives, described a situation where performance was being followed by negative consequences to the performer. He said the rule was that when any secretary finished her work she was supposed to contact the secretary with the most work and take on part of that work herself. But in practice it was not occurring. Each secretary was apparently stretching her own work to avoid finishing. This is a frequent occurrence where the only consequence to those workers who work fastest is to get more of somebody else's work.

In an ice cream company one job the workers considered most undesirable was on the popsicle machine. The operator had to bag the popsicles being made and place them in a carton. The job was undesirable because of the speed at which the machine produced popsicles, and because the worker had to stand and work alone. Because the popsicle machine was considered such a "bad job," the workers were rotated through that job one day at a time. The manager complained that most of the workers did not do this job very well; the popsicles would pile up and fall on the floor and frequently the machine would have to be stopped so the worker could catch up. To his surprise, even the workers who did well on that job at first couldn't seem to do well later on. Although the workers were rotated, those who did this job best tended to be rotated through that job more frequently than the rest of the workers. There was an obvious negative consequence to good performance.

As another example, a manager was having difficulty getting members of his staff to recommend programs that would contribute to the organization's overall effectiveness. He complained about their lack of creativity, initiative, and interest in contributing to the organization. But in his staff meetings where these suggestions came forth, his response to an idea was to imply that it was impractical or unbusinesslike. If an idea was accepted, his usual response was, "That's a good idea; because it's your idea why don't you follow through on it." The consequence of coming up with ideas was to be embarrassed or to end up with more work.

In labor-intensive production situations, supervisors frequently talk about new workers who *start off with a bang,* showing potential as future high producers, but who seem to *fizzle out* and their production gets just like the rest. In some work situations one of the consequences of producing more than your fellow workers is to drink your coffee alone lose your teeth in the parking lot or have a lot of flat tires. Rate busters are not very popular people.

One common complaint of executives in smaller organizations is, *people in this organization don't think for themselves or do anything on their own; they look for the bosses' okay on everything before they do it.* You might wonder whether anyone ever does anything on his or her own in those organizations. The answer is yes, once in a while. But when someone does do something individually and if it works, the best thing that can happen is for the boss to tell him 11 other ways it could have been done better. If the independent action didn't work out, the consequence varies from being ridiculed by the boss in front of peers to being ostracized by the boss for several days or being permanently damaged by the label of *screwup.*

Incidentally managers are unaware that, in their dealings with employees, they fall victim to *thought transmission* and thereby unknowingly dispense negative consequences intended as gems of wisdom. One thing that happens when an employee presents an idea to the manager is that he or she frequently thinks of another idea. Because the mind is a reactive instrument, the presentation of the employee's idea created a thought reaction in the manager's head, which caused that other idea to appear.

Quite naturally because the manager's idea was triggered by the employee's idea the manager's idea will probably be a better one. If you combine this with another occupational disease of management which is *the boss thinks the boss's ideas are always the best* (even if they are not) you create a situation where there is only negative consequences to an employee who presents ideas to the manager. The manager always comes up with another idea, and it has to be done the boss's way. As a manager you can't stop thought transmission from occurring when your employee presents ideas to you, but you can prevent it from being a negative consequence by using thought transmission to make your new idea come out of the employee's mouth.

There are situations in the work world where the obvious negative consequence to performance is failure on the part of the performer. These failures frequently occur because the performer does not know how to perform correctly. When workers are required to do things they don't know how to do or are incapable of doing, they usually fail; this is a negative consequence to them. Frequently salespeople do not try to sell one or more of their company's products because (1) they know the product does not perform the way it should; (2) the product will invariably not be delivered on time; or (3) the salesperson is not technically conversant with that product and, therefore, will not be able to answer a real customer's questions. The result of the first two is the customer will be aggravated and will vent that aggravation all over the salesperson. The third reason results in an embarrassment and most frequently a lost sale. Who wants to lose sales?

A salesman with a company that introduces five to fifteen new products a year was recently explaining that he was in danger of losing his job. He was in trouble because he rarely sold any of the new products until 10 to 12 months after they were introduced. This is the reason he gave:

> When this company introduces new products, the situation is always screwed up. One time they come out with the literature, but there is no product available; the next time they come out with the product, but there is no literature available. Another time they will release a new product, but then someone in Engineering decides to modify the tool used to apply it, which results in the new product being available but the tools needed to apply it are on back order.
>
> I used to sell these new products, but I felt like an idiot in front of the customer when I couldn't explain why the new products I just sold couldn't be delivered.

There are certain jobs such as in customer phone centers with exposure to customers or the public, wherein the worker is subjected to above-average verbal abuse, which may include four-letter expletives. Under these conditions the consequences of talking to customers is to suffer. Occasionally new workers entering these positions perform poorly, by overreacting argumentively, just as though the complaints were directed at them personally, rather than at the company or the product. Perhaps they shed tears, absent themselves from the workstation, arrive late for work, or don't come to work at all. It is easy for us to accuse them of making mountains out of mole hills and label them as emotionally unstable for that job. Nevertheless, a vital part of the training of workers in high-volume, customer service jobs is to teach them how not to react personally to the customer's comments. By teaching a worker how to behave appropriately, you are eliminating a skill deficiency, which has the effect of eliminating the negative consequences to performance.

On rare occasions you will be faced with situations when nonperformance will occur because a worker will persistently overreact to what is customarily accepted by the rest of us as normal pain in that job. If you cannot remove the pain (negative consequence) or lessen it through training, remove the worker from the job.

As an example, a young woman employed with a retail company for about five years was suddenly on the verge of losing her job because of high absenteeism. Her manager thought her absences were due either to "female problems" or personal problems, neither of which she chose to discuss. He was resigned to losing the employee because he had to take a hard stand on absenteeism.

When I interviewed the employee it was revealed that her absenteeism began only after she was transferred from the merchandise labeling department to the garment labeling department. Both jobs paid the same. The only difference was that in the merchandise labeling department the labels were put on merchandise with an adhesive, whereas in the garment labeling department the labels were put on the garments by using a pinning machine. The pinning machine was like a handheld gun that actually shot straight pins through the label and the material. It was quite common for new workers to occasionally shoot a pin into their fingers, along with the label and the garment. The injury was painful when it occurred, but never serious, and it rarely happened to experienced pinning machine operators.

The worker in question had never had a pinning accident, but she expressed a strong fear of having one. She related that when a job opened up in the merchandise labeling department she had asked the supervisor to transfer her back again, but he had refused. When I asked the supervisor why he would not transfer her back to the other department, he said, "Of course she told me she didn't like the pinning machine, but she was blowing it out of proportion; I showed her the right way to do it; she's just going to have to grow up and learn how to do this job. I told her I would transfer her to the merchandise department when she learned how to do the pinning job and stopped being so childish about it." (Sounds like the dark ages, doesn't it?)

The action taken was to transfer the woman immediately to the merchandise labeling department. The miraculous result was that the absenteeism problem disappeared. The moral of the story is that the manager could have solved his own problem (the worker absenteeism) had he accepted the employee's view of the negative consequences of performance.

These are all examples of negative consequences happening to workers when they perform the desired task. Managers usually search for a lack of a reward (positive consequence) as a reason for nonperformance, but rarely does it occur to them that unsatisfactory performance is occurring because the worker is punished when the job is done right. If logic would lead managers to believe that *workers do not do things they are not rewarded for doing,* why wouldn't the same logic lead managers to believe that *workers do not do things they are punished for doing?*

The obvious solution to this kind of problem is to remove the negative consequences. But you may say, "Every job has negative consequences; after all work is not play; and suppose you can't remove the negative consequences." Of course, you are right. But you will have to admit that *all play requires work and includes some negative consequences.*

The most popular participative sports today require physical exertion, cause blisters and minor injuries, as well as social embarrassment for failure far greater than what might be experienced on the average job. So why are these sports so popular? Is it because we love punishment? The reason is that these sports also provide positive consequences that compensate for, or outweigh, the negative consequences. It is logical to remove negative consequences that are causing nonperformance, but if the negative consequences cannot be removed, the solution is to provide positive consequences where there are none, to counterbalance the negative consequences.

If you recognize the scientific fact that *behavior is a function of its consequences,* you will expand your analysis of reasons for unsatisfactory performance and will be able to solve more performance problems. In your search to discover what is influencing poor performance, answer the more specific question: "Does a negative consequence follow performance?" If the answer is *yes,* the solution is *change the consequence or transfer the individual,* as follows:

1. Change the consequences by eliminating the negative consequence.
2. Change the consequences by providing an immediate positive consequence for the same performance to outweigh the negative consequence. (Verbal reinforcement works well: "I see you are responding in a friendly manner in spite of the customers' yelling; keep up that professional approach.")

DOES EMPLOYEE ANTICIPATE FUTURE NEGATIVE CONSEQUENCES?

Fear is merely people's anticipation of future negative consequences if they take an action. When people say, "I'm afraid to do that," you have to get them to describe what they are afraid of. The more specific the better because it will help you reduce a general fear to a specific fear you can most likely deal with. If the fear is imagined and will not even happen, it is nevertheless real to the employee. You have to be very convincing that it will not happen. If it is real and the negative consequence could happen and it is something the other employees live with, you have to show that the reward for doing it is of more value than the negative consequence for doing it. Determine whether they anticipate a future negative consequence for performing appropriately or for failing to perform appropriately. The former will probably not happen and since the latter will only happen for failure you can offer your support to guarantee success. There are a lot of things in life people are afraid to do but they do them anyhow. Fear does not incapacitate everyone. If their fear is incapacitating (mental illness), there is nothing you can do about it. If the employee *anticipates a future negative consequence,* correct his or her understanding.

DOES POSITIVE CONSEQUENCE FOLLOW NONPERFORMANCE?

Because the scientific study of behavior modification has demonstrated *behavior that is followed by a positive consequence will tend to repeat itself,* we should try to discover if our nonperformance problems are occurring because nonperformance is being rewarded.

It is clearly evident that one of the reasons workers don't do what they are supposed to do is because they receive more reward for not doing it. Amazing as it may seem, frequently it is the manager who rewards the worker for not doing it the way the manager wants it done. This occurs because most managers interpret what is happening to employees in view of how they, the managers, view the world, not how the employees view the world.

For example, let's take a look at a worker with an absentee problem. From the boss's point of view the worker appears to be capable of doing the job; he may even have done it well at one time. Because of the high absentee rate, however, the boss is now unable to assign important jobs to the worker. The boss spends a lot of time talking to the worker trying to get to know him better, to understand his motivation. The boss discusses loyalty, teamwork, personal growth toward building a future with the company, and has even asked the worker which jobs he would rather have. In the boss's eyes the worker is unreliable. Because of this unreliability there is certainly no future in the company for this worker. This unreliability gives the worker a low value in the manager's eyes, and if the problem is not cleared up, it will eventually lead to the worker being fired. The boss cannot understand how anybody can go through the world doing such a thing. If he were to be absent for obviously unimportant reasons, he wouldn't be able to face himself in the mirror.

Now let's look at it from the worker's point of view.

1. When I take days off I get paid for not working (company sick pay policy).
2. I can sleep later on days I don't work, and do lots of other interesting things rather than work.
3. I get a lot of attention from the boss.
4. They put me on the easy jobs (which are not hampered by absenteeism).

5. They keep talking to me, but they don't fire me (it usually takes a year around here).

You can see how the consequences visualized by the worker are personally relevant, immediate, and positive, whereas the consequences to the worker as visualized by the boss are either irrelevant, long range, or actually positive to the worker. You may feel I am pushing you back into the mind-reading business, but I am not. The problem is not difficult if you restrict your understanding of consequences to the work environment. You really know more about that than you think you do.

For example, if you have worked in business for any amount of time you must be aware of the unwritten rule, *if you have important things to do, go to the people you can count on.* This is frequently demonstrated when a manager needs something important done. The more critical the task, the more likely the manager will seek the most capable people to do it. The manager is certainly being logical in using the source where good services will be rendered and avoiding the source where experience has shown that good services will not be rendered. It's the essence of survival.

Unfortunately, the manager is assisting in the metamorphosis of individual workers, permitting them to do little, with the positive consequence that they will be asked to do less in the future. They are learning *the less you do, the less you are asked to do.* This occurs at all levels in the organization. When it occurs at the higher levels it appears almost obscene that someone should be paid $80,000 a year to do relatively nothing.

Efforts are not being made to solve the problem; it is just being avoided. The avoidance is nonetheless resulting in positive consequences to the worker for nonperformance. In some companies the positive consequence of nonperformance is to be sent off to a seminar. I don't mean seminars designed specifically to teach a skill to correct a performance problem caused by a skill deficiency. I mean seminars that are non-skill-oriented and fall under the general heading of *development.*

In discussing performance-appraisal design with the Canadian division of a worldwide company, the director of human resource development was lamenting the scarcity of transfers of high-potential managers between divisions, although these transfers meant promotions for the individuals.

He said, "Each division is willing to give us candidates to fill these promotion positions, but they do not give us their best people. When we ask for their best managers, as indicated by previous performance records, the division heads always come up with reasons why they can't let the individuals go. As a result," he said, "I know we are not getting the best people for these promotions. We are only getting those people they feel they can spare, and in some instances people they are happy to get rid of. The real high-potential managers are being locked into their divisions and the acceleration of their personal long-range development is being slowed."

This is not an isolated incident. It happens to a greater or lesser degree in all organizations, whether it be business, governmental, or academic institutions. The individual managers making these decisions are following the logic of their survival rules. They are keeping what they believe to be the high-level talent in their own lifeboat to insure their own survival and willingly shifting the so-called dead wood to anyone else who will take it. These decisions are perfectly logical to the managers making them. The consequence is that nonperformance is being rewarded by promotion, and performance is being punished by no advancement.

Another example of nonperformance being rewarded occurs under the mistaken heading of something called teamwork. In one college library one of the tasks that every member of the staff had to perform was called *reading the shelves*. The library was divided into sections, and each staff member was assigned a section. *Reading the shelves* required the staff member to read the numbers on every book on the shelves in his or her section to insure the books were in their proper numerical sequence. It took approximately four hours to complete a section and the head librarian required it done weekly. The staff members considered it a boring, detestable job.

By noon each Friday the head librarian checked a chart on which staff members were supposed to indicate whether they had done their assigned shelf reading. Frequently he discovered that various staff members, with the excuse of having too much work to do, would not have completed, or even begun, their shelf-reading assignment. The head librarian would respond by asking other staff members, who had completed their sections, to do the *shelf reading* for the members who didn't do theirs. There were staff members who accomplished their shelf reading every week, and there were staff members who did shelf reading only two out of every three weeks. No one was ever fired or reprimanded for failing to do his or her shelf reading. The consequence of not doing your assigned shelf reading was to have someone else do it for you.

In one of my seminars a manager asked, "How do you handle a secretary who complains about the work she has to do, although the workload is not heavy and she has plenty of time to do it?" He explained that, although the secretary was hired to work for two sales managers, only one was on the staff when she was hired. During the eight weeks it took to hire the second sales manager, the secretary's workload was approximately half of what you might consider to be normal. Soon after the second sales manager arrived, however, she complained that the workload was unreasonable. As he described it, first she complained to either or both of the sales managers and then began to complain to the people near her work area. Now, he said, the problem is worse; she spends a lot of time away from her workstation complaining to other people in the office about her heavy workload. He assured me there were no conflicts in priorities, and the work she had to do was not unreasonable because both sales managers traveled quite a bit.

When I asked him what the sales managers did when the secretary first complained he replied, "Well, the first few times they listened to her complaints and then gave her flowers. But that had no effect, the complaints were increasing rather than decreasing." I asked him to analyze this problem in view of the behavior management concept *all behavior is a function of its consequences.* He quickly recognized that the receiving of flowers by the secretary was obviously a positive consequence to her and was reinforcing her *complaining behavior,* because it was increasing. I told him if they kept giving her flowers every time she complained, they would most likely have her out on the street stopping traffic, complaining to strangers about the unreasonable workload. The managers were doing what they thought was nice, but they were actually rewarding nonperformance. They should have brought her flowers on those occasions when she did not complain about the workload.

This is an amusing example of managers effectively using positive reinforcement to increase the frequency of a behavior they didn't want. The fact is that positive reinforcement increases the probability of a behavior repeating itself independently of the intent of those who dispense the reinforcement and those who receive the reinforcement. For example, have you ever had discussions with employees about their nonperformance in which you discussed their poor attitude and stressed the need for them to change, but they didn't change. In fact you found yourself holding more discussions about attitude. This happens when you play amateur psychologist because your attention is very likely a positive consequence to the employees. In effect your attention may be reinforcing *excuses and promises to change,* leaving the troublesome behavior unchanged. Your behavior may increase the likelihood that the employee will offer excuses and promises to change when the nonperformance again occurs.

One sales manager described a problem salesman who was invariably late with certain required periodic reports. The manager's tactic to correct this problem was to ask the problem salesman to stand up in the monthly group sales meeting and explain why his reports were late. This would usually be accompanied by joking and laughter from other salesman. The problem salesman would be on his feet five to ten minutes talking about himself, his territory, his work, and why the reports were late. The manager's logic was that embarrassing the salesman in front of the other salespeople would eventually result in getting the reports in on time.

The manager did this for almost a year with no change in the lateness of the reports. He said, "It was hard to believe but the problem salesman always had some plausible sounding excuse for his late reports." Then, for some reason, the manager did not get around to using that tactic at three consecutive monthly meetings. At the end of the fourth month, all the required reports were submitted on time. The manager said he had complimented the salesman in private on one occasion about the on-time reports and never had trouble with late reports again. He couldn't understand why.

As frequently happens, managers' actions they construe as negative consequences may actually be positive consequences to employees. Standing up in front of a group and being the center of attention amidst friendly banter is a positive consequence to a lot of people, not a threat.

If your analysis of "What is influencing poor performance?" leads you to the conclusion that *positive consequences are following nonperformance,* the solution is to *change the consequences.* Remove the positive consequence for nonperformance, and arrange for positive consequences to follow appropriate performance.

IS EMPLOYEE PERFORMING INAPPROPRIATELY WITHOUT RECEIVING NEGATIVE CONSEQUENCE?

Do you work for one of those companies that never fires anybody? Is it your strategy with bad performers to transfer them to another department? Do you avoid giving problem people letters of reprimand or warning because you don't want to make them feel bad? Or do you fill their file with warnings and reprimands but never take any other disciplinary action? Do you have some employees who have been performing inappropriately it seems like forever and they are still on your payroll? If you answer *yes* to any of these questions, there are no negative consequences to these people for performing badly and it is your fault. Some employees learn quickly that they don't have to do what you pay for, they only have to do enough so the pay doesn't stop. You owe it to the people who do the job right to take corrective action with the people who don't.

One negative consequence is to appear in their work environment more frequently and ask specific questions such as, "what are you doing?" "when will you start?" "when do you expect to finish?" "why are you doing that?" When you see your people standing around spending too much time socializing, walk over there and listen to the conversation. They will go back to work. If not, ask, "Is this a work-related conversation?" When they say "no" ask them to go back to work. When they do, thank them. One manager told me he had two employees who left their work area early everyday and stood by the exit ready to leave at quitting time. He did what I told him, he stood by the exit a minute before the employees usually arrived. Because he was there they did not leave their workstation, so he thanked them for remaining at their workstations until quitting time. After two days they didn't leave early anymore. His presence at the exit was one-half an intervention to get them to perform appropriately. His reinforcement when they did perform appropriately was the second half of the intervention.

A manufacturing manager complained that he had a group of union press operators who left their press early each day to be first in the wash room. Whenever he talked to them about it, the next day they would claim the press was making funny noises and was unsafe and the press would be shut down for half a day for inspection. We talked a long time about consequences he controlled and it finally came out that these press operators were on the company softball team and left work early one day each week for team practice. At my urging he told the press operators that if they didn't stay at their press until quitting time they would not be permitted to leave early for softball practice. The problem went away.

One manager related a unique use of negative consequences to turn around the performance of Jack, one of her eight salespeople. Jack, who covered the downstate area selling athletic clothing to retailers, had the lowest sales in the manager's region. For the last three months every time she met with Jack to discuss how to increase sales he always came up with the same excuses: the economy was bad, unemployment in his area was up, his stores' customers were mostly blue-collar people living on tight budgets who weren't spending their money on athletic clothing. The manager had other salespeople selling in similar demographics and their sales were good so she knew it had to be Jack's fault. She scheduled another meeting with Jack and went into a speech about what an important service Jack had performed for the company in his detailed analysis of the sales potential in his territory. She told Jack that he had convinced the company that there really was not much sales potential in his territory and it didn't warrant a full-time salesperson. Therefore, the company would combine Jack's territory with Franny's upstate territory. "Of course," she said, "that means that you don't have a job anymore but we really appreciate your fine analysis." She said Jack looked as though he was going to have a heart attack. But after a moment he said, "Wait a minute. Maybe there are some things we can do to get more sales in my territory," and went on for the next two hours outlining plans to increase sales. She said that within 30 days he exceeded his monthly sales targets.

Negative consequences may be written reprimands and warnings, assignment to less-satisfying work, loss of privileges at the manager's discretion, low appraisal ratings, denial of transfer requests, time off without pay, and so on. In most companies with union contracts managers don't realize the freedom they have under the contract. Because they are intimidated by it they tend to avoid taking actions that could help productivity.

If the employee is *performing inappropriately without receiving negative consequences, deliver negative consequences.*

ARE PERSONAL PROBLEMS INTERFERING WITH PERFORMANCE?

A personal problem is a situation in an employee's life, not business-related, which conflicts directly with the employee's job performance or which creates an emotional condition which affects job performance. It could be a babysitter quitting or not showing up, car failure, sick relatives, broken romance, doctor or dentist appointments, divorce, a child in trouble with police, house closing, death of a loved one, financial difficulties, auto accident, bicycle seat trauma, bad bowling last night, and on and on. How you deal with a personal problem depends on how much it affects job performance and how solvable it is. Some problems are emergencies such as death of a loved one or an auto accident and the best you can do is accommodate the employee until the emergency passes into history. Some can be planned for, such as house closings or court appearances or picking up a relative at the airport. The ones that give you the most trouble are those which appear to have high emotional content when the employee seems unable to work and absenteeism and lateness continue for many weeks. If somebody is going through a divorce, you can give them a few days off and permit them to arrive late or leave early to see lawyers. But you can't let them come to work and not do their job for six months or stay home and get paid for six months. The question is how do you handle it. The answer is to explain to the employee that there are two problems, the personal problem and the work problem. You can tell people you understand that they feel bad and it is okay to feel bad but not okay to work bad.

The president of a small company told me that one of her employees just started a marriage breakup and was crying a lot and spending a lot of time on the phone with relatives and lawyers but not doing her work. The president said she felt sorry for the employee but in a small company when one person didn't do the needed work it caused big problems. This had been going on for two weeks and she didn't know what to do about it. I told her what to do and this is her story.

> The president scheduled a meeting with the problem woman and began by saying, "I have observed that you are having some problems, would you like to talk about them?" The employee said yes and spent the next 20 minutes describing the marriage breakup. When she finished, the president asked, "Is there anything I can do to help?" and the employee said, "Thank you, but no I just have to work things out." The president then asked, "How long do you think this problem situation will continue?" The employee said, "This is a very messy situation and I'll be lucky if it is over in a year." The president then said, "I now understand more about your personal problem but we have another problem I need your help with. Your job is to schedule meetings with potential customers, arrange for their travel, and prepare materials for sales presentations so we can enter new mar-

kets with our products. You are the only one who does that job. If you don't do it, it doesn't get done and we fall behind in our marketing program. I can understand how bad you feel about the breakup and I can understand that your problems could last a year. But my business problem can't last that long. Can you help make my business problem go away?" The employee said "yes" and although there were no evident changes to her personal problem the business problem ended. No more crying, the personal phone calls became minimal, and her work went back on schedule.

So, if a *personal problem is interfering with performance,* accommodate the problem or get the employee to solve your problem.

COULD EMPLOYEE DO IT IF HE OR SHE CHOSE TO DO IT?

Usually, this is the first question managers ask when faced with nonperformance. They immediately answer it, "Of course the SOB could do it if he would get off his tail." The manager then proceeds with the Y, S, and T approach to get the employee off his tail. Unfortunately, this question, and its answer, have value to guide your management actions only if they are preceded by the coaching analysis previously outlined. If you don't do the coaching analysis, you will invariably get the wrong answer.

Let's assume that you have done your analysis to determine what is influencing poor performance, and you determined the following:

The employee knows that performance is not satisfactory.

The employee knows what is supposed to be done and when.

The employee knows how to do it.

The employee knows why he or she should do it.

There are no obstacles beyond his or her control.

The employee knows your way will work.

The employee knows his or her way is not better.

The employee knows the priority of the work.

There are positive consequences to employee for appropriate performance.

There are no negative consequences for performing appropriately.

The employee is not afraid to do it.

The employee is not rewarded for bad performance.

The employee does receive negative consequences for poor performance.

There are no personal problems.

Therefore, you are at the point where you must make a judgment about the employee, in response to the question, "Do I believe this employee could do this task if he or she chose to do it?" The implication of this question is that if you stuck a gun in the employee's ear and threatened to pull the trigger if he or she didn't do it, would that person do it? If the answer is *no,* you have narrowed down the reason for unsatisfactory performance to that rare case of failure because of personal limits. This means there is something physically or mentally wrong with this person which prevents him or her from performing appropriately. The employee doesn't have the capacity to do it. We are not talking about ability, which is a function of training. People's capacity is a function of the innate characteristics they were born with and how they may have been damaged along the way. A person may have the capacity to write computer programming code but not have the ability to do so because that person has not been taught how to do it. On the other hand, a person may not ever learn how to write programming code no matter how much training he or she gets because that person does not have the mental capacity to do it.

You can have people with temporary personal limits such as laryngitis or bicycle-seat syndrome or pregnancy but you will know about it before you get this far in your analysis.

If the answer to this question is *no,* the only alternative is to *transfer or terminate the employee* (unless you decide to live with the unsatisfactory performance). If your decision is to live with it, you might wonder why you bothered about it in the first place.

If this decision seems too final to you, all I can say is, "Learn to live with the performance problem because you can't do anything about it." It is certainly possible that you hired someone incapable of doing the job or too mentally ill for you to manage (personal limits). There may also be influential variables in your employees' private lives that are beyond yours and their control to limit or to counterbalance. If you have correctly applied the coaching analysis and arrived at the conclusion *they can't do it,* you have no other alternatives as a manager.

If the answer is *yes, they could do it if they wanted to,* the appropriate alternative for you is to *redirect the employee's behavior through the coaching discussion,* described in the next chapter.

The only reason for performance failure not covered in the coaching analysis is, "no one could do it." This does not refer to such things as power failure which is covered under obstacles to performance; when the obstacle is removed performance resumes. Also, this does not refer to situations wherein no one in the past could do it but your team develops a plan to accomplish what no one else could do. This happens frequently in business. This refers to that dumb strategy of giving people "stretch goals"; asking them to do things that everyone knows cannot be done but the expectation is that they will at least try harder. Also, there are lots of other limits to performance such as computer processing speed, production equipment capacities, and the time in a day. Whatever it may be, you can avoid asking people to do what no one could do, if before the work begins you take the time to answer the question, "How are we going to do it?"

10

Coaching: The Face-to-Face Discussion

The purpose of the face-to-face process, called the coaching discussion, is to redirect an employee's behavior to solve a performance problem: to get the employee to stop doing what he or she shouldn't be doing or to start doing what he or she should be doing. (See Fig. 10.1.) The assumption is that you have completed your coaching analysis, which has left you with the conclusion that the employee *could do it if he or she chose to it.*

If you have not completed the coaching analysis, you should not be holding this coaching discussion. You could be giving the employee feedback about performance or you could be trying to gain a more complete understanding of the problem but you should not be having a coaching discussion. The coaching discussion will not be effective if nonperformance is occurring because of one or more of the reasons given in the coaching analysis. The coaching discussion is effective in redirecting behavior only when other reasons have been removed. For example, if someone does not know how to do something (skill deficiency), you will not be able to get her to do it (redirect her behavior) unless she learns how to do it. Sometimes during your coaching discussion you may discover something you overlooked in your coaching analysis. For example, you may learn there is an obstacle you didn't know about, which is preventing performance. Stop the coaching discussion at that point and proceed as you would in the analysis, that is, remove the obstacle.

The coaching discussion is a five-step process which guides you in the face-to-face discussion with problem employees to get them to correct their performance problems.

Figure 10.1 Steps of the coaching technique.

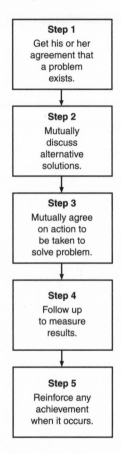

```
┌─────────────────┐
│     Step 1      │
│  Get his or her │
│  agreement that │
│   a problem     │
│    exists.      │
└─────────────────┘
         │
         ▼
┌─────────────────┐
│     Step 2      │
│    Mutually     │
│    discuss      │
│   alternative   │
│   solutions.    │
└─────────────────┘
         │
         ▼
┌─────────────────┐
│     Step 3      │
│  Mutually agree │
│   on action to  │
│   be taken to   │
│  solve problem. │
└─────────────────┘
         │
         ▼
┌─────────────────┐
│     Step 4      │
│   Follow up     │
│  to measure     │
│    results.     │
└─────────────────┘
         │
         ▼
┌─────────────────┐
│     Step 5      │
│  Reinforce any  │
│   achievement   │
│  when it occurs.│
└─────────────────┘
```

Preparation for the coaching meeting should be similar to preparations you have undoubtedly made in the past for appraisal discussions:

1. Hold it in some private place so the conversation cannot be overheard.
2. Do not have a third party present if at all possible. If a third party must be present, talk only to the employee.
3. Take steps ahead of time to insure there are no interruptions, phone calls, and so on.

4. Do not hold it in a restaurant. No matter how good it feels, there are too many distractions to be successful. For the same reason, don't hold it in a car while one of you is driving.
5. Allow as much time as it will take so you don't have to end the discussion before you have completed it.
6. Do not start the coaching meeting until you are able to control your emotions.
7. Have a specific description of the behavior discrepancy that is going to be discussed. If you are going to talk about tardiness, you should have accurate information, such as the specific incidences of lateness and the amount of time late, as related to scheduled work days as well as to the norm or average for other employees.
8. Be prepared to substantiate logically the importance of the desirable performance, as well as the consequences of nonperformance. You are pursuing the coaching process, obviously, because you believe the nonperformance is important.
9. Determine in advance that it is the employee's behavior that will affect the desired change in performance. Obviously, if the employee's performance doesn't affect the change, why would you talk to the employee about that problem?
10. Decide ahead of time what minimum action you will accept as a result of this meeting, what the possible alternative solutions are, and when you expect performance to improve.

STEP 1—GETTING AGREEMENT A PROBLEM EXISTS

The first step in the coaching process is to *get agreement a problem exists*. This is the most critical step in the coaching process and usually will involve half of the total time spent in a coaching discussion. This first step is where most managers fail in their efforts to eliminate performance problems. They fail here because they bypass it. It is a natural tendency for managers to assume the employee knows a problem exists. "After all," they explain, "it is the employee who is doing the thing wrong; therefore, that person must know what he or she is doing." It sounds logical, but it doesn't work that way. However difficult to believe, many problem employees know they are doing something wrong, *but they don't know it's a problem.*

Most managers believe that two people cannot collaborate in solving a business problem unless they agree a problem exists in the first place.

The only reason this logical and most important first step is bypassed with employee problems is because managers assume the employee knows the problem exists.

A good example of this was described by an executive of a small chemical company who told me he was going to fire one of his staff, a Ph.D. chemist. The chemist's performance was satisfactory, except he rarely submitted weekly progress reports to the executive although the executive repeatedly requested them. According to the executive, "I have been trying to get him to submit these reports for over a year now with no success. If he can't do something as simple as that, it's not worth the aggravation to me to keep him; there are enough Ph.D. chemists on the market."

I taught him the coaching process and suggested he try that before he incurred the expense of replacing his chemist. A month later he told me he used the coaching process and was amazed to discover why the chemist was not submitting the reports.

According to the executive, during the first step of the coaching discussion, *getting agreement the problem exists,* the chemist related that because he and the executive met informally each day to discuss progress, the chemist assumed the written reports were merely a clerical detail and not necessary. The chemist said, "I thought you knew everything that was in the reports anyhow so there seemed no necessity to give you a written one." The executive informed the chemist that he did not know enough in spite of the verbal briefings. "Although the verbal reports were informative," the executive said, "I need the complete information between covers so I can study it, remember it, and refer to it as necessary."

The chemist apologized for assuming the verbal briefings were a substitute for written reports, and agreed to submit them thereafter. The executive told me that in the three weeks following the coaching discussion, he had received three weekly reports without any further discussion. He was confident he would continue to receive them.

This is a common occurrence and a good example of the importance of the first step in the coaching process. The chemist knew he was not doing something, *but he didn't know it was a problem.* The important part of this first step is not telling people there is a problem or doing something called *letting them know there is a problem,* it is actually *getting their agreement a problem exists.* The only way to know you have achieved this is when the sounds coming out of the employee's mouth sound something like this, "Yes, I agree that is a problem."

You will use up approximately 50 percent of all of the coaching time in this first step. In fact, you may believe you have spent too much time on this first step, and proceed to step 2, even though you did not get agreement. *Don't do it, because you will not succeed in solving the problem if the employee does not agree it is a problem.* If the performance discrepancy you are working on is really not important, you will not be able to get the employee to agree it is. This points out an additional reason for a realistic answer to that important question at the beginning of the coaching analysis, "Is it worth your time and effort?"

There are only two categories of reasons that will convince a problem performer that there is a problem:

1. If the employee understands the results to your organization of what he or she is doing wrong or failing to do right
2. If the employee understands the consequences to him- or herself if there is no change in performance

The results referred to in number 1 are those things that happen in the world to the people around them because of their nonperformance. For example, an employee's nonperformance might interrupt service to someone who needs it; others might not be able to do their jobs because of late or incomplete data or prework; extra work might be required; additional costs might be incurred; damage or injury might occur; customers might complain; and your boss might yell at you.

The consequences in number 2 refer to those things that will happen to the employee if he or she doesn't eliminate the nonperformance. For example, certain prestigious work normally assigned to the employee may be given to someone else; the employee may be transferred to a less desirable job, fired, or demoted; may not receive a raise, may be denied preferable assignments, may be removed from membership on a prestigious committee, or may be denied attendance at certain enjoyable things such as conventions or remotely related business travel and non-skill seminars. Obviously these consequences will vary widely depending upon the employee's job.

The consequences under number 1 clearly relate to what is happening to everybody else because of the employee's nonperformance, while the consequences in number 2 are clearly what could happen to the employee if he or she doesn't stop it.

You may conclude that the consequences under number 2 sound quite punitive. You are right, although punishment is not our intent. If you relate this to our earlier discussion of George Kelly's ideas, you will recall our conclusion was *people do not go through the world doing self-destructive things on purpose.* If they select what they believe to be the best alternative from those *they see* available to them at that particular time, then what they are doing must seem like a good idea to them, even though we may know it is self-destructive. If you believe that people do not do self-destructive things on purpose, it is quite appropriate for you to assume if you can get people to recognize the consequences of things they are doing wrong, they will agree it is a problem.

The practical result of using this coaching process in business is that 95 percent of the nonperformers will agree there is a problem once they recognize the results of the thing they are doing wrong. Ninety-five percent of that remaining 5 percent will agree there is a problem once they recognize the consequence, or what is going to happen to them if they don't stop it. People do not do self-destructive things on purpose. If they do them, they either don't know the consequences will be self-destructive to them, or they don't believe those consequences will happen to them.

You will note that the preceding percentages do not lead you to believe there is going to be a 100 percent success with this process. The simple fact is that you cannot control all the consequences influencing your employees. On occasion elements of nonperformance will be supported by positive consequences beyond your control. You will not be able to save everybody. You will fire some employees. Some employees will realize, because of your more specific efforts in managing their behavior, that they no longer can dazzle you with fast footwork, and they will resign. One manager told me that in the middle of one coaching discussion the employee said, "Look, I don't want to work as hard as you require in this job so let's save some time and I will resign." The manager was sorry to lose the employee but he was happy that the coaching process accomplished something that with another approach would have dragged on for another six months.

Let's consider what the consequences for bad performance may be for an employee named Herman, who is frequently late for work. You have defined *frequently late* in this instance as three late arrivals of 20 minutes or more every five days, compared to an average lateness of one per month for everyone else. The results of nonperformance as they might occur under category 1 are as follows:

1. His phone rings and is not answered, so callers are not serviced.
2. Callers who don't get an answer call someone else (possibly higher level) and complain.
3. At times other workers interrupt their work to answer Herman's unattended phone.
4. The work of others is delayed because Herman's work does not begin on time.
5. Other workers complain about alleged preferential treatment. (Why isn't everybody required to come to work on time?)
6. Your boss questions your ability to get your employees to come to work on time.

Depending upon Herman's specific job, your list may not include all of these, and may include some that are not listed. What is important is that the results you define are real rather than imagined.

Now let's consider consequences that might occur under category 2 if there is no change. In this particular instance they might be as follows:

1. Failure to follow the rule to come to work on time may bar him from a salary increase.
2. As continued lateness reflects unreliability, Herman may be barred from a promotional opportunity.
3. He may have to be transferred to a lower-level or less-responsible job.
4. You may have to terminate him and replace him with someone who will come to work on time.

You can see that some of these consequences may be beyond your control, but these are things that will happen to Herman you will initiate. You do not have a choice whether you permit Herman to come to work late. It is a company rule that you didn't make; you just have to administer it. Ignoring it is not an alternative. Now if you tell Herman that he must come to work on time and he refuses to come to work on time, he is restricting the alternatives available to you. He is backing you into a corner.

As discussed earlier, neither you nor your employees have unlimited alternatives of behavior available on the job. Both your behaviors are restricted; each of your jobs have specific behaviors that are appropriate to that job. When an employee does not do what he or she is supposed to do, your behavior as a manager is even more restricted. It is the employee's behavior that dictates your behavior. For example, you may know with certainty that if Herman's lateness continued and you recommended him for a promotion or a raise, your manager would not only refuse to approve your recommendation but would question why you would do that for someone who refuses to come to work on time.

In some instances there may be only one consequence under category number 2, such as, "If he doesn't stop it you are going to have to replace him with somebody who will come to work on time." If you do not have a choice to permit him to continue to be late for work, your alternatives are limited.

Your objective in listing these results and consequences of the nonperformance is not to dream up horror stories to scare the people who work for you. You don't want to scare them, you just want to help them. You want to help them stop their self-destructive behavior by letting them know the consequences of that behavior. Remember, we believe that people will always select what they believe to be the best alternative from those alternatives they see available to them. The reasons people do what appear to be illogical things at work, things that turn out to be self-destructive behavior is because (1) they do not truly know what the consequences are, (2) they overestimate their ability to escape the consequences, or (3) they don't know what else to do.

Let's go back to our example of Charlie stabbing his brother-in-law. If, when Charlie was about to plunge the bread knife into his brother-in-law's throat, we had grabbed his wrist and said, "Charlie, do you realize you could end up in jail for the rest of your life if you do this?"

Charlie: But he's driving me crazy and I have to shut him up.
    We: Is there any other way you can shut him up besides stabbing him?
Charlie: He would probably shut up if I punched him in the mouth.
    We: Would you go to jail for life if you did that?

    Charlie: No, they would probably just get me on assault and battery, and I might get 30 days.

        We: Which sounds like the better alternative?

Charlie's most likely response is that he will drop the knife and punch his brother-in-law in the mouth.

In our lateness example, the fact is that Herman is involved in self-destructive behavior. It is destructive both to the organization and to Herman. Because you are trying to eliminate self-destructive behavior, you must identify the consequences of this destructive behavior and the consequences if it doesn't change. You must know what they are before you begin your coaching discussion.

Whatever the consequences may be, it is not enough that they exist, it is necessary they be perceived by the employee as the result of inappropriate behavior. The quickest and most effective method to get the employee to understand these consequences, and for you to know this perception has occurred, is for the employee to *tell you* what these consequences are. You accomplish this through thought transmission using the questioning techniques to make sounds come out of his or her mouth.

To demonstrate the coaching discussion, let's choose the common problem of work being completed late. You have an employee who is assigned projects with expected completion times varying from one to two weeks. Having concluded that her work is late 50 percent of the time you had a feedback discussion with her that went like this.

    You: I don't know if you are aware of it, but about 50 percent of your projects are finished late.

    Her: I know that some of them are late but with all the work I have to do and all the deadlines it's difficult to get everything done on time but I will try to do better.

    You: Thank you.

The next two one-week reports were on time but the following two reports were late so you decide to have a second feedback discussion.

    You: Four weeks ago when we talked about late reports you said you would do better. The next two reports were on time but the next two were late. (You might ask yourself here, "Why didn't I talk

to her when the first two reports were on time to reinforce that
performance?")

Her: I told you the last time that with all the work I have to do I can't
always get your work out on time.

You: (You are surprised at the "all the work" comment. Your view of
her job is that the projects you assign are her primary function.)
Are you saying that you have so much other work to do that you
can't get the projects I assign you completed on time?

Her: That is what I have been telling you. People come to me and ask
me for help and I have projects of my own I have to spend time
on. There just isn't enough time to do it all.

You: (You just learned that the late projects are not the behavior discrepancy; they are the result of her working on lower-priority
work when higher-priority work is assigned.) Look, I think we
have a misunderstanding. I realize that you have a variety of
work to choose from at any one time and these different things
you can choose to do have different priorities. Is it your understanding that some of the things you do have a higher priority
than the projects I assign to you?

Her: Well, yes.

You: I think it will help you if I tell you that the projects I assign to
you should be treated as top priority; they should be worked on
instead of other things you could choose to do.

Her: You are telling me that as a professional I can't use discretion in
doing my job to choose what I think is important? Is this some
kind of dictatorship? Am I supposed to be some kind of robot
without a choice?

You: (This feedback conversation is going no where so cut it off. A
coaching discussion is needed.) Thank you for your time, I will
get back to you about this problem.

You return to your office and use the coaching analysis to better
understand this problem. You conclude that the only reason she is working on lower-priority work when high-priority work is assigned is because
she is choosing to do so. You believe that she doesn't realize how her late
projects affect the rest of the organization or what the consequences to
her could be if she doesn't change her behavior.

Being fully prepared for the coaching discussion is critically important to your success. The most difficult part of the coaching discussion is the first step, getting the employee to agree that there is a problem. To help you succeed using thought transmission, use the following Coaching Discussion Plan (Fig. 10.2). The Coaching Discussion Plan has been designed to guide you in identifying and organizing the specific information you will need to get you through the first coaching discussion step. Please feel free to copy the form for your own personal use.

Figure 10.2   The Coaching Discussion Plan.

1. BEHAVIOR DISCREPANCY (what is employee doing wrong or not doing right)
2. RESULTS OF THIS DISCREPANCY (who is hurt or inconvenienced, what is added cost, etc.)
3. CONSEQUENCES TO THE EMPLOYEE IF IT DOES NOT STOP (list all)
4. WHAT IS THE DESIRED BEHAVIOR (possible alternatives)

In box number 1 of the Coaching Discussion Plan you describe the specific behavior discrepancy including frequency. Keep it simple such as not using sales aids, interrupting people, not following standard procedure, late for meetings, collecting too much data (or too little), and not returning phone calls. In our example, it would be "working on lower-priority work when higher-priority work is assigned."

In box number 2 write the results of the thing done wrong; what happens and who gets hurt when the employee does what you wrote in the first box. In the example, you might list the following:

1. She is not working on assigned work.
2. Assigned work schedule is not being followed.
3. Projects are not completed on time.
4. Late projects delay the work of others.
5. Delaying work of others is giving poor service.
6. Service to customers is delayed.
7. Customers buy the product from competitors.
8. Revenue is lost.

It is not enough that these results of bad performance exist. It is necessary they be perceived by the employee as a result of her own behavior. Using thought transmission will help you do that.

As mentioned earlier, most employees will agree there is a problem when they understand the results of what they are doing wrong. When they do, you don't have to go further in discussing consequences. But to be prepared for the real tough cases you need to fill in the information in the third box which are the consequences to the employee if he or she doesn't change the specified behavior. Some managers have a problem with this because they want to avoid getting too severe with the consequences. But consider, if the employee says, "I will correct the problem" and never does or says, "I don't care what you say, I am going to do what I darn well please." The end result is the same—unacceptable performance. How long are you willing to live with unacceptable performance? What would you do if the employee never improves? Write in box number 3 your alternatives in ascending order of severity. Your list might look like the following:

1. Less interesting work assignments
2. Low performance appraisal rating

3. No (or delayed) raise
4. Loss of perks (specify)
5. No opportunity for promotion
6. Demotion
7. Termination

Some managers don't want to list *termination* as an alternative. That's okay, but it means that when, after all your coaching efforts, the employee either by action or by saying so tells you to get lost, you will have to live with the problem. Fortunately if you use thought transmission correctly with the items in the second box, 95 percent of employees will agree there is a problem. Sometimes in the high-tech business world you will have a techie you can't live without but who breaks all your rules. It is up to you to answer that first question, "Is it worth my time and effort?"

Ninety-five percent of those who did not agree there is a problem after discussing the results of the thing done wrong will agree there is a problem when they understand the consequences to them if they don't change their behavior.

In the last box of the Coaching Discussion Plan write what you want performance to look like when it is done correctly. Obviously it should be related to what you wrote in the first box. In our example you might write, "She will work on work according to the assigned priority and finish projects on time."

Your next step is to have a coaching discussion. Following is an example of how the coaching discussion will proceed. It is important to remember that this is a discussion: two people are participating in a conversation. You are not lecturing someone. It is also important that you don't answer your own questions. Frequently employees have learned that if the boss asks them a question and they don't answer it, the boss answers his or her own question. Don't do that. When you ask a question wait for the answer. If after 15 minutes the employee does not answer, say, "Do you want me to repeat the question?"

Your coaching discussion would proceed something like this:

You: Do you know why I called you in? (Always start with this question to get their attention.)
Her: No.

You: We have a problem.

Her: What problem?

You: It has to do with your working on low-priority work when high-priority work is assigned. We talked about it twice in the last month.

Her: Oh, that again. I told you the last time we talked that I have a lot of things to do and feel as a professional I should be able to choose what work I do in what order. After all I am not a child. But I will take care of it.

You: (Ignore the empty promise "I will take care of it." You have heard that before.) Do you know what happens when you work on low-priority work when high-priority work is assigned?

Her: Yes, I get a lot of things done that I think should be done.

You: Look, all of the work assigned to you are the projects I give you which are high priority. If you are working on low-priority work when high-priority work is assigned, are you working on assigned work or not working on your assigned work? (You are using thought transmission. The sounds you want to come out of her mouth are "I'm not working on assigned work." To accomplish that, ask her a question which ends with two alternatives: the one you want and its opposite. She has to pick one.)

Her: Well, I'm not working on assigned work. But I'm working on a lot of other things I think are important.

You: (You got the answer you wanted; don't pay attention to the rest.) Right. If you don't work on assigned work when you should, are you following the assigned work schedule or are you not following the assigned work schedule? (Notice how the opposite alternative is said completely. If you said "work on schedule or not," the answer you would get is "not." You don't want that.)

Her: Obviously, the assigned work schedule is not being followed.

You: Right. When you don't follow your assigned work schedule, are your projects most likely finished on time or most likely finished late? (You use the words "most likely" because some of them are finished on time.)

Her: I don't care.

You: (She just answered a question which you did not ask. Treat it that way.) I didn't ask you that question. The question I asked was when you don't follow your assigned work schedule, are your projects most likely finished on time or most likely finished late?

Her: Some of them are finished late.

You: That's right. (Notice that you are reinforcing correct answers.) When you finish your projects late, are other people who need your work able to do their work or is the work of others delayed?

Her: (silence)

You: Do you want me to repeat the question?

Her: Delayed.

You: Correct. When you delay the work of others is that good service or is that bad service?

Her: I suppose they think it is poor service.

You: Right. As you know, the work we do eventually becomes products for our customers. If we delay the work of others which delays delivery of product, is that good service to customers or bad service?

Her: Bad service.

You: Right. When our customers get bad service or late deliveries do they ignore that or do they buy the product from our competition?

Her: I don't know.

You: Guess.

Her: They probably buy from our competition.

You: Right. When we lose customers to competition, is our revenue retained or is revenue lost?

Her: Revenue is lost.

You: Right. (You just finished communicating *the results of the thing done wrong,* so ask the big question.) Now do you agree there is a problem?

Her: Yes.

Hooray! you just got through the first step, *getting agreement that a problem exists.* You don't need to use the information in box number 3, *consequences if it does not stop.* Now you are ready for the second step of the coaching discussion (Fig. 10.1, page 157) which is mutually discussing alternative solutions. You begin that step by asking, "How are we going to correct this problem?"

But what if this employee hadn't agreed there was a problem and responded like this:

> Her: Well, I understand those things happening but I think I am a good worker with a broad picture of what is going on around here and I think of myself as professional who should have some freedom of choice in how I schedule my work.

You didn't get agreement, so move on to the consequences to her if she does not correct the problem.

> You: Do you know what is going to happen to you if you continue to work on low-priority work when high-priority work is assigned?

When you ask this question sometimes the employee will say, "You can fire me." If you would not do that, say, "No, I wouldn't; what else?" If you have listed termination as a consequence, say, "You're right. I need someone in this job who will do what needs to be done and I wish it were you; what else?" If the employee says, "If you fire me, there is nothing else," you may reply, "Before we fire you what might happen to you?"

> Her: You will probably keep hassling me.

Your first reaction to this response probably is to defend yourself. Don't bother. Only pay attention to responses which will advance the coaching discussion.

> You: Last year you said you like the projects I give you because they are creative and interesting. If you continue to work on low-priority work when high-priority work is assigned, will you continue to get the interesting projects or will I give them to someone else?
>
> Her: You mean you will not give me any more creative project work?
>
> You: Right. Also what do you think will happen to your appraisal ratings?
>
> Her: You will probably give me a low rating.

You: Right. If you get a low appraisal rating, what will happen to your next raise?

Her: You mean you will not give me a raise because of this?

You: Right. One of your perks is going to the regional customer meetings. Do you think you will continue to attend those meetings or will I send someone else?

Her: You will probably send someone else.

You: Right. If you don't work according to the assigned priorities, will you be recommended for promotion or not recommended for promotion?

Her: You will probably not recommend me for promotion.

You: Right. We have people in lower-level jobs who would like to have your job. Do you think you will keep your job or will you be demoted?

Her: Would you demote me over this?

You: Right. Neither you nor I have a contract which says we will have a job here forever. If you don't follow the priorities in your work will you be here as long as you want or will you be terminated?

Her: You mean you would fire me over this?

Every time the consequence of firing comes up always repeat the statement, "I need someone in that job who will do what has to be done and I wish it were you."

By now you might have concluded that she feels threatened by this conversation. Well, you are right. Nevertheless, there is a clear difference between you actually threatening to take her job away from her and her recognizing the consequences of *her own behavior.* Threats, per se, usually do not work. Sometimes the threatened worker responds with a resignation on the spot. If termination of employment is a realistic consequence of the employee's unsatisfactory behavior (self-destructive behavior), then it is important (and only fair) that he or she be made aware of that consequence. People are free to act as they choose as long as they are aware of the consequences of that action. It is only reasonable that your workers accept responsibility for their own behavior.

You: Right. I need someone in that job who will do what needs to be done and I wish it were you. Now do you agree we have a problem?

Her: Yes. I agree.

Hooray! You just completed the first step of the coaching discussion.

An interesting point you might raise here is why we pursued this so far, when, in the beginning of this discussion, the employee indicated her willingness to correct it. I can explain by asking you: "If someone is doing something inappropriate now, and she does not think it is a problem or important, what makes you think she will begin to do it appropriately? Also, she probably told you several times before this discussion that she would correct the problem.

A common manager's complaint is that employees frequently promise to eliminate a nonperformance problem, but they don't. The only short cut to step number 1 getting agreement, is if you called somebody in and the discussion went something like this.

> You: Do you know why I called you in here?
>
> Employee: Yes, I believe you called me in because I have been late with my projects. I know it creates a problem to the people I service. I am going to correct it.
>
> You: Do you agree that it's a problem?
>
> Employee: Yes, I agree that it's a problem, and I am going to work according to the assigned priorities.

Hooray! You just finished step 1, *getting agreement that a problem exists,* and you are ready for step 2.

One good question that may occur to you is: "What do you do if you can't get an employee to agree that a problem exists?" This will rarely occur if you have done your homework before beginning the coaching discussion. If it does occur, however, it is likely that it will have happened for these reasons:

1. You are not dealing with a behavior.
2. What you are dealing with isn't really important.
3. It is important, but you have not identified all of the results and consequences under categories 1 and 2.
4. You are trying to get the employee to recognize unrealistic consequences or hypothetical consequences, which are not likely to occur.
5. You are not using *thought transmission;* instead of the consequences being verbalized by the employee, you are verbalizing them, and the employee is nodding his or her head or merely saying *yes* or *no.*

6. Your past relationships with your employee have proven to him or her that you threaten a lot but never do anything about it.
7. There is a positive consequence for the employee if he or she is fired.
8. The employee is too mentally ill for you to manage.

STEP 2—MUTUALLY DISCUSS ALTERNATIVE SOLUTIONS

The next step in the coaching discussion is to mutually discuss alternative solutions. In this step you and the employee together will identify as many alternative solutions as may be necessary to solve the problem. Because experience is merely increasing the number of alternatives an individual has to select from when faced with a requirement to act, this step actually compresses experience for the employee; it increases his or her alternatives quickly. Because you are dealing with behavior, it is necessary to specify those changes in behavior that are needed to influence the outcome or result. The employee may not know what to do to solve the performance problem.

For example, if the nonperformance problem you are working on is *increased typing errors,* you will get nowhere if the solution is to *decrease typing errors.* Effective alternative solutions might be as follows:

1. Type slower
2. Don't leave typing for the last thing to be done each day
3. Stop typing if people stop by to gossip
4. Wear your glasses in the office
5. Proofread each page before going to the next one rather than proofreading as you type
6. Identify the errors you make most often and slow down when you get near one

I don't suggest that all of these alternatives are necessary to decrease somebody's typing errors, but one or more might be. For example, possible alternative solutions to an employee lateness problem might be as follows:

1. Set the alarm clock early enough
2. Buy an alarm clock that works
3. Get an alarm clock with a louder alarm

4. Put the alarm clock far enough away from the bed so he must get out of bed to shut it off
5. Catch an earlier bus or train
6. Drop out of the carpool that usually arrives late
7. Get to bed earlier during the work week
8. Change babysitters to one who shows up on time
9. Get the car fixed so it will start in the morning

Again all of these solutions will rarely be needed to solve a late arrival problem, but I hope you are surprised there can be that many possible alternatives. It is important to recognize that whatever the employee is *doing now* results in unacceptable work; what he or she is doing is not working. Therefore, the purpose of the second step is to identify *what the employee could do differently so that he or she will produce acceptable work.*

Many discussions about performance problems end when the employee says, "Okay, boss, I'll try harder." And the manager responds with something like, "I am glad to hear that," believing the problem is solved. It is certainly nice that the employee will try harder, but the question is: *what will employee do differently so that when we see it we will know he or she is trying harder?*

Unfortunately, we have many workers who try harder, but are still doing the wrong thing. That is, they are doing *more of* something, but what they are doing will not result in solving the problem. Unless you specify what *trying harder* is, the only result you may achieve is people walking around perspiring with clenched fists, tight buttocks, and grinding teeth. It will certainly give them a feeling of trying harder, but they will not be doing anything to change the outcome.

It is important to recognize that step 2 is not a *selection of alternatives,* but just the listing of what the possible alternatives might be. The selection of specific alternatives from those available will be accomplished in step 3. In step 2 you may list nine possible alternatives to solving the problem, but in step 3 you may select only two of them.

The *mutual* aspect of this step relates to the expectation that both of you will contribute to the solutions. You should assume that the employee will be able to come up with some solutions to solve the problem. But if he or she is unable to do so, it is up to you to furnish the necessary solutions. You can best accomplish this step using thought transmission, making the sounds come out of his or her mouth.

You cannot begin step 2 until step 1 has been completed. You will know that step 1 has been completed when the employee says something like, "Yes, I agree that's the problem." You then begin step 2 as follows:

You: I am glad you agree; now how are we going to solve it? (This is a good time to smile and recognize progress.)

Her: I'll take care of it.

You: That's good but what will you do differently?

Her: I will work according to the assigned priorities.

You: That's good. Can I ask you why you don't do that now?

Her: Well, people come to me and ask me to help them with stuff they are working on, so I get sidetracked.

You: What could you do about that?

Her: I could just tell them that they will have to wait until I finish the high-priority work.

You: Fine. Is there anything else that causes you not to work on the priority work?

Her: Well, we are allowed to work on our own ideas when we have free time and I guess I get involved in my own ideas and I let the other stuff slide.

You: Good observation. What could you do about that?

Her: I could just face the fact that there is a schedule and I will have to delay my own stuff until the high-priority work is completed.

You: Sounds good. Any other reasons why you can't work on the high-priority work when you are supposed to?

Her: No.

If in your judgment you have mutually discussed sufficient alternative solutions to solve the problem, you have completed step 2. You are ready to go on to step 3.

STEP 3—MUTUALLY AGREE ON ACTION TO BE TAKEN TO SOLVE THE PROBLEM

The next step in the coaching discussion is to gain mutual agreement on which alternatives previously discussed will be acted upon to solve the problem. As mentioned earlier, the mutual discussion of possible alternatives is entirely separate from the selection of alternatives that will be acted upon.

A common failure managers experience in their problem-solving efforts is to combine the selection of alternatives with the listing or discovery of alternatives. Unfortunately, these are two clearly separate functions; combining them inhibits the optimum achievement of either. If you argue the merits of ideas as they are given, you are wasting *idea-giving time*. If you reject ideas as they are given, you could be punishing *idea-giving behavior,* thereby decreasing the behavior of idea giving. Of course, you could reinforce idea-giving behavior by recognizing good ideas when they come up, but the common trap is to stop searching for ideas when a good idea comes up and before all the ideas come out. The process of generating ideas depends on the interaction of ideas. The best ideas are rebounds from bad or trivial ones. Finally, when you select ideas as they are given, you inhibit *idea giving* because a worker may not want to act on certain ideas. So the employee rejects the idea, not because it is a bad idea, but because he or she doesn't want to do it. When this occurs it would be appropriate for you to state that your intent at this point (step 2) is not to state actions that will be taken later, but only to list possible alternatives.

In step 3 you will not only mutually agree on which alternatives will be acted upon, but will also specify when the action will take place. You want to identify *what* will be done and *when*. Again, the best technique for accomplishing step 3 is thought transmission.

When you complete step 2 (in your judgment all solutions necessary have been discussed), you begin step 3 as follows:

You: What are you going to do to solve the problem? (Followed by silence.)

Her: What we said.

You: What's that?

Her: When people ask me for help I will put them off until the assigned high-priority stuff is finished and I will work on my own projects only when the high-priority work is done.

You: Sounds like it will work. When will you start doing that?

Her: When do I have to start?

You: When are you going back to work?

Her: Right after we finish this conversation.

You just got verbal commitment as to *what* will be done and *when* as solutions to solve the problem. An appropriate closing response would be to thank the employee for agreeing to solve the problem and to specify a time when you will meet again:

> You: That's great. I am glad we are able to work out a solution to the problem. I am looking forward to on-time projects. Thank you for your cooperation.

STEP 4—FOLLOW UP TO INSURE THAT AGREED-UPON ACTION HAS BEEN TAKEN

The second most common reason for manager failure in all functions at all levels is lack of follow-up. It is also one of the most common reasons managers fail in their efforts to correct employees' unsatisfactory performance. It never ceases to amaze me that managers will take the time to discuss a problem, but will not take the time to check to see if the agreed-upon action has been taken. What usually happens is that the manager is overwhelmed by the employee's *promises to change*. The employee has confessed to the error, has expressed the right amount of humility and thoughtful concern, and has reaffirmed loyalty to the crown; therefore, the manager assumes the change will take place.

This sounds reasonable because we are not dealing with children; we have two mature (sometimes educated) and experienced people dealing on a face-to-face basis. We have to assume there is still some honor and integrity left in the world, so we take the employee at face value and assume that what is expected to happen (or promised) will occur. Too often we discover, three months later, things are just as bad as they were in spite of the employee promises. It really does happen that, although employees promise to make changes, they really don't change, and it takes the boss three months to find out.

But what happens frequently is the employee *does* change initially and, because the manager does not follow up, there is no recognition of this change and, therefore, no reinforcement to support the change. So, the employee returns to the inappropriate behavior. The manager taking a look at the scene three months later just assumes no change has ever occurred. Logic would have to tell you that what the employee is doing unsatisfactorily must feel good to the employee. If the employee changes and does it the way you want it done, you have to be there to make it feel good or that person will go back to the old way.

There are also occasions when the manager adroitly follows up immediately following the employee's promise to change, but will not follow up thereafter. Following up only once is better than nothing, but it will usually have the same result as no follow-up: a return of the unsatisfactory performance.

There are those managers who do not believe that follow-up is a part of the management process for a myriad of reasons. There are also many managers who tried to follow up at one time, but stopped doing it because they could not defend to their employees what they were doing. When initial efforts to follow up with employees result in a confrontation, the manager usually decides to avoid it in the future. Some typical responses from employees when a manager follows up are as follows:

"What's the matter, don't you trust me?"

"Look, if you think I'm not able to do this job, why don't you take it away from me; otherwise, just let me do it."

"Look, if you don't have confidence that I can do this job, why did you give it to me in the first place?"

"If you don't like it when it's finished, tell me then, but let me work on it in peace."

"I wish you would treat me like the professional I am rather than checking up on me all the time."

Managers do not know how to respond to these comments. Although most management-training programs tell managers *they must follow up,* the subject is never covered in sufficient detail to explain the *why* and the *how,* or even *what it is.* So, let's see if we can clear up some of the confusion here.

The first important point is to know what follow-up is. *Follow-up is the process of finding out whether an employee is doing what he or she is supposed to be doing.* The important prerequisite is that you and the employee both know what it is that is supposed to be done, which includes how much of it will be done when, and what it is supposed to look like if the right amount is done at the right time. To convince you this is not double talk, let's relate it to a performance problem. For example, let's assume the performance discrepancy you are trying to solve with coaching is an excessive absence from the workstation, and you have gotten the employee to agree that he will decrease his absence from the workstation. The next step, of course, is for you to follow up tomorrow to find out whether he has done that. You will observe him tomorrow to determine whether he is at his workstation. But suppose I ask you:

Me: How will you know if the problem is corrected?

You: He will not be absent from his workstation.

Me: You mean he will never be absent from his workstation?

You: Well, he has to be absent sometimes to take a coffee break or go to the restroom. After all, there are times when it's okay to be absent from his workstation.

Me: That makes sense. Well, how many times is it permissible for him to be away from his workstation before you will say the problem is improved?

You: I haven't thought of a specific number, but just so it's better than what it was.

Me: That sounds logical. What was the average number of times he was away from his workstation each day?

You: Well, I don't have an exact number, but it would be more than anyone else.

Me: Well, how many times is normal for everybody else?

You: I think about three or four times each day.

Me: Is that an exact number based on your observations, or is that what you think it ought to be?

You: Well, I can't stand around and observe people all day long. I just think that's probably what it ought to be, with a coffee break in the morning and a coffee break in the afternoon and maybe one or two unscheduled visits to the restroom.

Me: Okay, how many more times a day than three or four was the problem employee away from his workstation?

You: I don't know exactly, but it seemed like he was gone every time I passed his workstation.

Me: Do you have a record of how many times you passed his workstation and how many of those times he was not there?

You: Of course not. I have more important things to do than sit around keeping records on that sort of thing.

Me: But if you don't know how often he was away from his workstation, how will you know if it gets better?

You: Well, he will just be there whenever I pass his workstation.

Me: But you just said that under normal conditions he could be away
from his workstation three or four times a day.

You: Well, I mean if he's away from his workstation other than those
three or four normal times.

Me: That sounds reasonable. Does the employee know how many
times it is okay to be away from his workstation?

You: Well, we didn't talk about that specifically.

Me: That brings us back to the basic question. If neither you nor the
employee knows specifically what is the allowable number of
times and when it is allowable to be absent from the workstation, how will either of you know when the employee is doing
what is expected?

You: You mean I have to be *that* specific?

Me: No, you just have to be specific. If you don't know the appropriate numbers of absences or the appropriate times when allowable absences from the workstation could occur, how will you
be able to determine whether the employee is doing what is supposed to be done?

You: You mean I should specify that allowable absences from the
workstation are no more than two times in the morning and two
times in the afternoon, and two of those times may be coffee
breaks not to exceed 15 minutes and two of those times can be
unscheduled breaks not to exceed 10 minutes?

Me: That sounds great. Now both you and the employee know what
acceptable performance will look like when you see it.

As strange as this conversation may seem to you, it occurs numerous
times when I discuss performance problems with managers. It is easy for
managers to tell employees to *shape up, get with it,* or *start earning your
pay,* but without defining specifically what it is supposed to look like, neither the manager nor the employees will be able to recognize improved
performance when it occurs.

If you had really progressed to step 4 in the coaching process, you
would have had more facts than you appeared to have in the preceding
conversation. For example, in order to identify the performance discrep-

ancy of excessive absence from the workstation you would have had to use a work sampling as described in Chap. 9. You would have a record of the number of times you had observed the employee away from his workstation compared to the other employees. You would have known that the other workers averaged two absences per day, while the problem employee averaged four absences. Without that information you couldn't have gotten the employee to agree there was a problem.

Many managers who know what follow-up is, don't know the reasons for it. In other words, they confuse the reason for follow-up as being synonymous with the definition of follow-up, that is, the reason I want to know whether people are doing what they are supposed to be doing is because I want to know whether people are doing what they are supposed to be doing. That is good stuff to know only if you do something about it. The two reasons for follow-up are

1. If people are doing what they are supposed to be doing, the purpose of follow-up is to *maintain performance* by
   a. Giving feedback
   b. Reinforcing good performance (verbal is best)
2. If people are not doing what they are supposed to be doing, the purpose of follow-up is to improve performance by asking, "How can I help?"
   a. Giving feedback
   b. Find out why it is happening
   c. Removing obstacles
   d. Letting them know priorities
   e. Removing negative consequences for good performance
   f. Removing positive consequences for poor performance
   g. Working around personal problems
   h. Teaching them what you thought they knew but don't
   i. Delivering negative consequences for poor performance

As you can see, the purpose of follow-up is not score keeping but to change the score. Follow-up is your management delivery system after the work has begun. It is what you do during the race to get all of your people to tie for first place. If you don't follow up, you are left with laughing or crying about results.

In this step in coaching when you follow up and observe that a problem worker has partially improved, you must reinforce that partial improvement by saying something like, "I see you have made the effort to correct that problem. I appreciate that. If you keep that up, pretty soon you will be achieving our target. Thank you very much." The sounds coming out of your mouth recognizing his or her achievement reinforce the increase in that specific activity. This is quite different from saying to yourself, "Well, I see the SOB did it right at least once."

The second reason for follow-up invariably escapes most managers. If they have a discussion with an employee to correct a problem, and their follow-up reveals no improvement, their typical reaction is, "That SOB is still screwing up."

Remember the earlier, obvious conclusion we drew was *the only reason you are there as a manager is to do everything within your power to help your employees be as successful as you need them to be.* Therefore, if your employee is continuing to fail, your additional help is needed. That help may be in the form of providing additional alternatives because the ones selected didn't work, or it may be using your organizational influence to clear away obstacles, or it may be merely to clarify further *what is expected to be done when and what finished is supposed to look like.*

Therefore, when employees accuse you of treating them like children because you follow up, just explain to them what follow-up is, and tell them you have no choice; it is part of your job. If you didn't follow up, you would be involved in self-destructive behavior as a manager.

One critical aspect of the follow-up process is timeliness. If you are playing amateur psychologist and dealing with changes in attitude, it is necessary to observe many behaviors over a long period of time to establish a basis for your guesses about the attitude. Likewise, if you are dealing with sales results and cost figures, you will most likely be unable to follow up until the appropriate computer run comes out at the end of the month or quarter. Both of these lead to ineffective follow-up because they are not soon enough and don't deal with specific behavior.

Because the coaching process directs your corrective efforts to specific behavior, you don't have to wait too long for the opportunity to observe that behavior in the normal work environment. For example, in our problem with wrong priorities, you don't want to wait to see if projects are completed on time. You want to follow up daily to find out if she is doing what she said she would do to correct performance. The more specifically you define the behavior that must change, the easier it is for you to determine whether the change has taken place.

Continuing our example, your follow-up the next day may go something like this:

> You: Hi. I was wondering how things are going after our discussion yesterday.
>
> Her: Everything is fine. I felt the urge to work on one of my hot ideas but I just told myself the quicker I finish the high-priority stuff, the quicker I will get to work on my own stuff.
>
> You: Sounds good. How about requests for help from other people?
>
> Her: Haven't had any yet today but I am prepared to deal with them as we discussed.
>
> You: Sounds as though you have things under control. I am looking forward to on-time projects. Thanks for your cooperation.

This is not the end of it; your follow-up must be scheduled to examine behavior weekly or monthly until you conclude that this behavior is a part of the employee's customary behavior.

When I teach managers how to use thought transmission in coaching discussions, they express concern that they will not be able to memorize the intricacies of asking each question correctly and might screw it up. I tell them that it is customary to write down all their thought transmission questions like a script, practice reading it to a friend, and then read it to the problem employee (but wait for the employee's answers). But "that sounds too formal," they say or "I would feel funny doing that," or "won't the employee think it is weird?" But when they have to do it in the real world, they write it and read it and later tell me that it worked fine; the discussion worked and the employee didn't comment on the reading. If you do it and the employee asks you why you are reading, you can say, "Because this is an important discussion for the both of us and I don't want to leave anything out."

STEP 5—REINFORCE ANY ACHIEVEMENT

The last step in the coaching process has the greatest potential to sustain improvements in performance; that step is *reinforce any achievement* when it occurs. The complimentary sounds that come out of your mouth concerning his or her behavior are a reinforcement of his or her achievement, which is a vital part of your efforts to correct performance problems and maintain improvements. The influence of your reinforcement of improvements is of such major importance in the coaching process it is treated as a separate step.

The timeliness of your recognition is of critical importance to its influence on sustaining improvement. The sooner reinforcement occurs after the actual performance achievement, the greater is its influence. The longer the period of time between the actual performance and the occurrence of the reinforcement, the less influence it has. For example, if your intended follow-up on this priority problem was to check her activities daily, but not to reinforce any improvements verbally unless her reports were on time, at the end of the week, it is not likely you will get a sustained change. You will not be doing anything to support daily actions.

If someone corrects something today, it is better to thank that person face to face today than to send him or her an e-mail a week from now expressing your appreciation. If someone working for you at another location corrects performance by sending in a report on time, it would be more effective to call that person when you receive the report than to thank the sender the next time you meet face to face weeks later. If someone corrects a performance problem today it is more effective for you to tell him about it this week, than to give him a raise eight months from now and tell him at that time how much you appreciated his performance. If someone must improve her performance today, which will result in a change on the computer printout next month, it is more effective to call her today to find out whether she did it or not today, and if she did it, to recognize her achievement during that phone call. If someone is supposed to behave differently at 10 o'clock today, and he does it, it is more effective if you reinforce that change at 10:15 rather than at 5:00 tonight or tomorrow. The guide you should follow in reinforcing any achievement is *when in doubt, do it now.*

Unfortunately most managers working to correct performance usually expect it to go from failure to perfection in one jump. An employee failing by 15 percent who shows only a 5 percent improvement is still considered by the manager to be failing by 10 percent. Obviously there is nothing to reinforce because failure is still occurring. But reinforcement theory tells us that reinforcing people's little bits of achievements will get you more bits of achievements. What this means to us in business is that if someone failing by 15 percent manages to improve performance by 5 percent, and you reinforce that 5 percent improvement, you have a greater chance of getting the other 10 percent improvement. If this is so, why would any manager choose to ignore the 5 percent improvement? That would be self-destructive behavior.

If you have an employee who arrives late for work three out of five days per week and after feedback or coaching the employee is late only one day per week, that would be a 60 percent improvement. It does not mean the entire problem is solved, but it does mean you should reinforce the improvement. By doing so you are using the most appropriate means of achieving total improvement.

An appropriate reinforcing statement you could make at the end of the week where only one lateness had occurred (rather than three) might be as follows: "You have improved your performance. You came to work on time almost every day this week, four out of the five days; that is a 60 percent improvement. If you keep this up, pretty soon you will be meeting our attendance standard as we planned. Thank you." Your complimentary remarks will function to increase the frequency of *on-time behavior.*

Behavior management research has demonstrated that positive reinforcement is more effective if it is not continuous; that is, if it does not occur each time performance occurs. As a matter of fact, studies have shown that when reinforcement is continuous the behavior being reinforced will cease to occur once the reinforcement is removed. Once somebody has changed *late arrival* behavior to *on-time arrival,* your recognition would cease to have the effect of reinforcement. If you frequently thank someone who normally comes to work on time for coming to work on time, the likely response would be, "Why are you doing that? I come to work on time all the time." When the desired behavior change becomes a part of the individual's repertoire, and occurs with normally expected frequency, your reinforcement should decrease.

The most effective schedule of reinforcement would be intermittent scheduling. For example, with the priority problem situation you might reinforce daily behavior three days a week for a couple of weeks then once each week for three weeks, then switch to reinforcing on-time reports. For other situations such as on-time arrival for work your follow-up and reinforcement might be daily for two weeks, once a week for four weeks, and once a month for two months, then twice a year.

CONTINGENCY RECOGNITION

Another form of recognition is a positive consequence within your sphere of influence you prearrange to happen to the employee when the behavior improvement occurs. For example, in step 3 of the coaching discussion, when you are getting agreement on what actions will take place to solve the problem, you may tell the employee if he or she can do a certain thing for the next 60 days, you will assign certain important projects to him or her. This would establish a contingency relationship between a specific reinforcement that the employee will receive and his or her behavior, when it changes appropriately. It is important this positive consequence you promise actually is a positive consequence to the employee. What you construe to be positive work may be just *more work* to him or her. Second, if a contingency is promised, you had better deliver when the time comes.

Contingency recognition is not a new concept to managers. Unfortunately, they use it as a con job. For example, managers hand out sticky jobs to employees and mention should the employees do this sticky job well, the boss will remember the employee come raise time 12 months from now. There is nothing wrong with that until two months later when the boss hands out another sticky job to the same employee and again promises if it is done well the reward will come at raise time. Is the boss increasing the anticipated raise increment each time a sticky project is handed out, or is the boss really promising the same raise several times?

Managers would be a lot more successful if they recognized they are insulting the intelligence of their employees by promising the same reward for several jobs. Even more important, there are other things in a manager's sphere of influence that have nothing to do with spending money, but are more effective as reinforcers because they can be administered immediately. Here are some contingency recognitions of achievement that cost a lot less than salary increases.

"If you complete this difficult report on time, I will give you the next easy job that comes into the department."

"On any day you produce zero errors, you can go home a half hour early."

"If you can keep your cost within budget for six months, I will take you to the convention."

"If you meet all your schedules, I will give you the next new executive chair we receive."

"If you will stop arguing with that department, I will give you a cubical with a window."

These are just some examples to trigger your thinking. You could very quickly make up a list twice as long.

If you know that a consequence within your sphere of influence is a positive consequence to your employees, consider it in step 3 as a possible reinforcer to the employee, contingent upon his or her changing behavior. But make certain you and the employee agree on how and when performance improvement will be recognized. Otherwise, your contingency agreement will lead to arguments and conflict rather than a reinforcement of a desired behavior.

Although reinforcement of achievement is part of the follow-up process it has been treated as a separate step in the coaching process because of its vital importance. If you do not reinforce the change from unsatisfactory to satisfactory performance, you will not sustain the change; you will have wasted your time. Getting a person to change is only one-half of your performance improvement intervention; maintaining that change is the second half. Only when you have achieved a sustained change, have you completed the coaching process.

11

But What If It Doesn't Work?

One logical question you might ask at this point is "What if after you coach someone about priorities and they agree to change, the next day there is no change?"

You should undertake a new coaching discussion, except the problem this time is not priorities, it is *not doing what the employee said he or she was going to do.* The conversation may go something like this:

> You: Do you know why I called you in?
>
> Her: Yes, I was not working on the priority work. I will not do it again.
>
> You: That's not why I called you in.
>
> Her: Then why did you call me in?
>
> You: We have a problem.
>
> Her: What's the problem?
>
> You: Let me ask you a question. Did we have a meeting yesterday?
>
> Her: Yes.
>
> You: What was it about?
>
> Her: About my not working according to your priorities.
>
> You: Did you agree that it was a problem?
>
> Her: Yes, and I said I was going to change it.
>
> You: What did you say you were going to do?
>
> Her: I said I was going to work according to the priorities.
>
> You: Did you?
>
> Her: No.
>
> You: That's the problem. You didn't do what you said you were going to do.

Her: I know. I'll begin tomorrow.

You: Let me ask you a question. If you don't do what you say you are going to do, what basis do we have for an employment relationship?

Her: I know I promised, but I got side-tracked. I'll get right on it tomorrow.

You: Please answer the question. If you don't do what you say you are going to do, what basis do we have for an employment relationship?

Her: You mean if I don't tell you the truth how can we work together?

You: That's right.

Her: Well, I guess there is no basis for the relationship.

You: You are exactly right. If there is no basis for a relationship, what happens to you?

Her: Well, I guess I get fired.

You: That's right! That certainly could happen. Now don't you agree that's a problem?

Her: Yes, I agree that's a problem, and I told you I am going to get right on it tomorrow.

You: Well, I'm glad you agree it's a problem. How are we going to solve it?

Her: I am going to do what I said I was going to do.

You: What's that?

Her: I'm going to work according to the priorities.

You: When?

Her: Tomorrow.

You: I'm glad you have agreed to solve this problem. I'll see you tomorrow. Thank you very much. (End of conversation.)

Now you ask: "But what if she doesn't do it tomorrow?" You should conduct the same coaching discussion again, but when she promises she will work on priorities the following day, you ask one additional question, as follows:

You: Let me ask you a question. What will happen if you don't do what you said you were going to do tomorrow?

Her: Then I guess you and I will be talking again.

You: No, we won't. What else could happen?

Her: I don't know.

You: Guess.

Her: Do you mean I'll get fired?

You: You have agreed that if you don't do what you say you are going to do we have no basis for a work relationship. So if tomorrow, for the third time, you don't do what you said you were going to do, how can that relationship continue?

Her: You mean if I don't work according to priorities tomorrow I am fired?

You: That's right; I will process the paperwork to terminate your employment.

Her: You mean I am going to lose my job in spite of what I do for you only because I am not following your priorities?

You: No, you are going to lose your job because three times in a row you said you were going to solve a problem and three times in a row you did not do what you said you were going to do. I assume that since you know there is no basis for our relationship, that it doesn't matter to you if the relationship is terminated. I don't have a choice.

Her: Well, I guess you are right. You don't have anything else you can do.

You: You are exactly right. Now what are you going to do about it?

Her: Well, I'm going to work according to your priorities.

You: I'm glad you agree to solve the problem.

If in actual practice someone promised three times he would behave in a certain way and three times in a row he did not, it would be my guess that on the fourth try he will also not do it. Therefore, you will be terminating that employee. You may conclude that since the purpose of the coaching process is to improve unsatisfactory performance rather than fire employees, the coaching process has failed. I would certainly agree with you on that. You should not assume that if you use coaching you will never have to fire anyone. But you could assume that with the proper use of the coaching technique you will be firing fewer people, not because you will learn to live with nonperformance but because you will correct nonperformance problems quickly.

In the preceding situation, an employee may be fired after four daily failures to correct performance. This is in contrast to what I currently see happening in business, where the same employee might fail for eight months and then be fired. The time would be longer, but there would be a lot less functional effort to solve the problem than has occurred in the four days of coaching. In both instances, the employee was fired, but in one instance it took eight months to discover the situation was not correctable.

As mentioned earlier in the book, when you hire someone you do not buy that employee's body or mind, you only rent the person's behavior. When someone whose behavior you are renting chooses not to deliver what you have rented, there is no basis for a work relationship. Because you are dealing with behavior rather than internalized attitudes and motives, neither you nor the employee can evade your corrective efforts. Because you are dealing with behavior, it is most likely that behavior must occur in the next work day. If it does not occur, it is clear the employee did not do what he or she said he or she would do. If your union contract precludes terminating employment without written warnings, you would have given three warnings in three days. You will end up firing some employees and some of them will quit, but you will have a lot more confidence you did everything possible to correct the problem. There will be times when you will not get a change in behavior because *you failed* in the coaching process.

Let's suppose you had a coaching discussion with an employee, Herman, who had been coming to work late for a couple of days each week. He agreed there was a problem and agreed to "come to work on time" but the next day he is late again. When he finally arrives he says, "Gee, boss, I wanted to be on time, but my alarm clock didn't work."

Surprise! The reason you didn't get improvement is because in step 2 of the coaching process you didn't actually identify what the employee *had to do different* to arrive at work on time. You didn't discover the other influences preventing punctuality, the malfunctioning clock. At the end of step 1, when he agreed there was a problem, the discussion should have sounded like this:

> You: I am glad you agree that a problem exists. But what are we going to do about it? (step 2 beginning)
>
> Herman: Well, I'll just try harder to come to work on time.
>
> You: That's great that you are going to try harder, but tell me what are you going to do differently so that will be the result?

Herman: Well, gee, I do everything I possibly can now.

You: Why are you late for work?

Herman: Well, sometimes my alarm clock doesn't go off.

You: I see. How could we solve that? (Of course, you know how but you have to make the sounds come out of his mouth.)

Herman: Well, I guess I could buy a new alarm clock.

You: That's a good idea. What else goes wrong?

Herman: Well, lots of times the person I ride with doesn't show up.

You: What could you do about that?

Herman: Well, I guess I could find somebody else to ride with.

You: That's a good idea. Is there any other reason you don't come to work on time?

Herman: Well, I guess a lot of times I go to parties during the week and stay out too late because I am having such a good time. Then I hate to get out of bed in the morning.

You: What can you do about that?

Herman: Well, I guess I could go to fewer parties or come home a little earlier during the week.

You: That's a good idea. Is there anything else you can think of?

Herman: I can't think of anything else.

If you can't think of any other alternative solutions, you have just finished step 2, and you should begin step 3.

You: They sound like good solutions. Now which of those are you going to do?

Herman: Well, I am going to buy a new alarm clock.

You: Good idea. When?

Herman: Right away.

You: When is that?

Herman: On my lunch hour.

You: That's a good idea. What else are you going to do?

Herman: Well, like I said, I'm not going to go to as many parties and I'm going to get home earlier.

You: That sounds effective. How much earlier do you think you need to get home?

Herman: Well, I haven't thought about it.

You: Okay, I'll wait while you think.

Herman:	Well, I guess I ought to be home before 1 A.M. If I get home any later than that, I usually don't want to get up in the morning.
You:	Getting home by 1 A.M. sounds like a good idea. What else are you going to do?
Herman:	Well, I'm going to change the person I ride with.
You:	When will you do that?
Herman:	Well, that may take me a little time. I will have to ask around, and I don't know exactly how to go about it.
You:	Do you think the personnel department might know who lives in your area?
Herman:	Yes, it might be a good idea to call them.
You:	Yes, I think that will work. Do people looking for rides sometimes advertise?
Herman:	Yes, they put a little blip in the company newsletter. I could probably do that.
You:	That sounds like a good idea. Is there anything else you could do?
Herman:	Well, I see notices on the bulletin board sometimes with people asking for rides. I guess I could do that.
You:	That's a good idea.

Your alternative solutions should counteract the reasons for nonperformance if possible.

When your initial follow-up reveals a cause for nonperformance that could be counteracted by an alternative solution, resume your coaching discussion at step 2. But during that same coaching process you should also try to uncover any further influences preventing punctual behavior. You should discover then, and not two days later, that additional reasons for occasional late arrival may be the carpool or partying.

When you have identified *who* was going to do *what, when,* to solve this problem, you are ready to go on to step 4, which is *follow-up.* If the employee said he was going to buy a new alarm clock at lunch time, your follow-up step should be to see him after lunch to find out whether he did in fact buy a clock. If he did, you can recognize his action. You should follow-up similarly on his actions to call the personnel department, to place an ad in the newsletter, and to put a notice on the bulletin board. The remainder of your follow-up efforts relate to his arrival for work.

We could go on and play the game *but what if* forever and still not cover all the possibilities you might be faced with. The important point is that this coaching system permits you to adapt your approach to the specifics of each situation. It is not necessary for you to solve every influential nuance in an individual's life to achieve a simple behavior change such as arriving at work on time. If you get the employee to agree that a problem exists and you reinforce any punctual arrival for work, the result very likely will be that he will buy the clock, eliminate the carpool problem, and come home from parties earlier without you discussing it. The only reason we went into that much detail is to provide you with some alternatives to the *but what if* problems.

Tardiness appears to be one of the most frequent problems managers have difficulty solving. With flex hours it becomes even more difficult for managers to know whether there is a lateness problem. Excessive absenteeism is also a common problem. If you substitute the absence problem for the tardiness problem with Herman, the approach would be quite similar, although there are other influences that may interfere. For example, one company has a policy of providing workers with 12 paid sick days per year. Their policy does not permit workers to accumulate sick days. If the 12 days are not used by the end of the year, the worker loses them. If you analyzed this problem with coaching analysis it would be clearly evident that one of the positive consequences of being absent one day per month is to have a day off and be paid for it. (Nonperformance is rewarding.) Also, the negative consequence of coming to work every day is to lose 12 day's pay that you are entitled to. (Performance is punishing.) The result is that the majority of the employees in this company are absent from work 10 to 12 days per year. It is common knowledge that people use the sick days to do many things besides being sick. In some departments it is common for people to call in and say, "I am taking one of my sick days." Recent surveys report that the average number of sick days employees are taking without being sick are increasing. Employees say that they are working so hard they feel they need a day off now and then.

The managers try to keep absenteeism below 12 days per year, but when they pressure employees who have missed 7 or 8 days before the end of the year, the employees claim the managers are in conflict with company policy and have no right to set up a different policy in each department. The managers tell me their hands are tied. The employees are only taking advantage of a company policy; it would be highly ridiculous for them not to.

Certainly you could undertake the coaching process to get agreement that a problem exists, but you do not have the alternative of the ultimate consequence of termination until the employee exceeds the 12 sick days that are allowed.

One manager in that company asked me what was the most serious consequence she could use in her coaching discussion with someone who was missing 9 or 10 days a year. The manager wanted to correct the problem because she thought the employee would be in line for promotion sometime in the future. I asked her what the average absenteeism was for the supervisors and managers in her organization. Her reply was 3 to 5 days per year. My suggestion was that her discussion of the consequences with that subordinate go something like this:

Manager: Do you know what the average absenteeism is for the workers?

Employee: Probably 12 days a year.

Manager: You are right. Do you know what the average absenteeism is for supervisors and managers?

Employee: I don't know.

Manager: What would you guess?

Employee: A lot less?

Manager: You are right. It's no more than 5 days per year. Now are you interested in being a candidate for future promotion?

Employee: Of course.

Manager: What do you think are some of the things upper management looks at when deciding to promote someone?

Employee: Work performance.

Manager: Yes, what else?

Employee: Reliability.

Manager: You are right. Do you know how we measure reliability?

Employee: No, but because you brought it up, I guess absenteeism has something to do with that.

Manager: Right. It has a lot to do with it. Let me ask you a question. Suppose I have one promotional position available and I am considering two employees for that promotion. With all else being equal, one of them has an absenteeism of 12

days per year, and the other has an absenteeism of, let's
say, 5 days per year. Which one do you think I'll choose?

Employee: You would probably choose the one with 5 days per year.

Manager: You are exactly right. Now don't you agree 9 to 10 days
absence is a problem?

Employee: Yes.

The most practical way to solve this company's absentee problem
would be to change the consequences by changing the policy. For example, if the policy were changed to permit people to accumulate sick days
forever, rather than to lose them each year, the consequences to the individual worker would change. The consequence of coming to work every
day would be a positive consequence of adding to the individual's bank
account of sick days that would be available in the future should a major
illness occur. The consequence of taking 12 sick days a year when you
really didn't need them would be a negative consequence of wasting paid
days for potential future illness. If the policy were changed, frequent periodic feedback reports should be given to workers showing their current
accumulated bank accounts of sick days. This problem points out the
importance of the coaching analysis to identify important influences that
support nonperformance.

12
Coaching Cases

Let's run through another coaching discussion, this time without all the interruptions. In this case, which happens to be based on a real one, you are a sales manager. Your company has recently introduced a new product that is a substitute for a former product. Although the new product is available for sale you still have considerable inventory of the former product. About a month ago, you called all your salespeople together and asked them to help clean out the inventory of the old product by selling it before they sold the new product. At your request, they all agreed to sell a specific amount within the next 90 days. Thirty days later, the sales figures showed that everybody was selling the older product except Jack, your star salesperson. He had high sales for the month, but all his sales were the new product.

At that time you called him in (first feedback discussion), told him you noticed that he had not been selling the old product, and asked him why. Jack told you he owed it to his customers not to sell them a product that was going to be immediately replaced by a new one. It was up to him to maintain integrity in his relationship with his customers. Since his customers bought a lot of product from him, he thought it would hurt his sales in the long run if he pushed the old product on them and then in 60 or 90 days announced the new product's availability. He said the company ought to bite the bullet and junk all that old product.

You told him that it was company policy to move the old product first and it was his responsibility to move his share of the older product before selling the new product. You explained that if he didn't help to move the old product, the region would be stuck with half a million dollars in old product. You also told him that some customers may be unhappy they bought the old product when they learned there was a new product but every company in your high-tech business faces that problem. He left the meeting saying "I will try to move it if I can, but I just don't want to screw up my customers by selling that older product the company should dump anyhow."

It is now 30 days later, and the sales figures reveal that Jack is still not selling the old product. You have just finished reading this book and you want to use the coaching process to solve your problem. The symptom of the problem is that the older product is not being sold in Jack's territory. This is occurring because Jack is not presenting this product on his sales calls.

Let's first go through the coaching analysis of this performance discrepancy to determine what is influencing unsatisfactory performance.

Question: What is the behavior discrepancy?
  Answer: Jack is not presenting the old product to customers when he makes sales calls.
Question: Is it worth your time and effort?
  Answer: Yes.
Question: Does Jack know his performance is unsatisfactory?
  Answer: Yes, I told him 30 days ago.
Question: Does Jack know what is supposed to be done and when?
  Answer: Yes, I told him 60 days ago in a meeting with all the salespeople and 30 days ago when I talked with him about this problem.
Question: Does Jack know how to do it?
  Answer: Yes, he out sold everybody else in that product until the new product came out.
Question: Does he know why he should do it?
  Answer: Yes, I told him we have to clean out the old product inventory.
Question: Are there obstacles beyond Jack's control?
  Answer: No.
Question: Does he think that my way will not work?
  Answer: No.
Question: Does he think his way will work better?
  Answer: No. If he doesn't sell the old product we will not clean out the inventory.

Question: Does he know the priority of doing it?
  Answer: Yes. He knows the new product delivery date.
Question: Are there positive consequences to him for selling the old product?
  Answer: Yes, he will make commission.
Question: Are there negative consequences to Jack for selling the old product?
  Answer: No.
Question: Does Jack anticipate negative consequences for selling the old product?
  Answer: Yes, but I told him that the consequence he is worried about is faced by every company when they come out with new products.
Question: Is there a positive consequence to Jack for not selling the old product?
  Answer: No.
Question: Is he not receiving a negative consequence when he fails to sell the old product?
  Answer: Not so far.
Question: Are there personal problems influencing Jack's performance?
  Answer: No.
Question: Could Jack sell the old product if he chose to do it?
  Answer: Yes.

It appears that you should redirect Jack's behavior using the coaching discussion. Before you begin the coaching discussion, use the Coaching Discussion Plan to identify the results of what Jack is doing wrong and the consequences if he doesn't stop it, as follows:

What are the results of Jack not selling the old product?

1. The old product inventory is moving slowly, and the region will not meet the deadline for cleaning out the old product.
2. The other salespeople are complaining because they are selling the old product and Jack is not. They also would rather sell the new product; they think it is unfair.
3. Your boss is complaining to you because you are not moving the old product fast enough.

4. If you don't get the old product out within the 90 days, it is going to be almost impossible to sell it because of the national advertising campaign for the new product.

What are the consequences to Jack if he doesn't start selling the old product?

1. Would you fire him?
   Answer: No.
2. Would you demote him?
   Answer: No.
3. Can you transfer him into a less-desirable territory?
   Answer: No.
4. Can you give him a lower raise?
   Answer: No, his high sales dictate his raise.
5. Is he interested in future promotion?
   Answer: Yes, very much so. He wants to be a national sales manager someday.

That's great. One of the consequences of his not selling the product he is supposed to sell is that he is displaying unreliability. Part of a manager's job is doing what has to be done whether he or she likes it or not.

Now we are ready to begin our coaching discussion with Jack. So you set up an appointment to coach Jack and Jack has just arrived. Step 1—
Getting agreement a problem exists:

You: Do you know why I called you in?
Jack: No.
You: We have a problem.
Jack: What's the problem?
You: It has to do with your work performance.
Jack: What's the matter with my work performance? I've been carrying the highest sales dollars in the region, and I'm number three in the country.
You: The problem is you are not doing what you are supposed to do.
Jack: I guess you are talking about selling that old product.
You: Right. That's the problem. (Followed by silence.)
Jack: Yeah, I know you talked to me about that before and I was

going to move it, but after all I just can't see my way clear to push that old product on customers when we have that new product out there and it's so great. It just isn't fair for the company to make us do this to our customers. We are the ones on the firing line trying to make sales happen, and the company just doesn't give a damn. Let those other guys move the old product. I'm concentrating on moving the new product, so the company can move ahead. You certainly can't complain about my sales, can you?

You: Do you know what happens when you don't sell the old product? (Notice you didn't get sidetracked.)

Jack: Yeah, I sell the new product and make just as much money for the company.

You: What else happens when you don't sell the old product?

Jack: Well, I guess you get a little bent out of shape.

You: I mean, what happens in the company when you don't sell that old product?

Jack: The other people sell it.

You: That's right. The other salespeople are selling their share of the old product. Do you think they know that you're not selling it?

Jack: Well, I guess they do. The sales information floats around the branch. Everybody knows what everybody else is doing.

You: You are right. They know that you aren't selling that product. Do you know what they do when you don't sell that product?

Jack: I told you, they sell the product.

You: Yes, they sell it, but what else do they do when they sell it and know that you don't sell it?

Jack: I don't know.

You: What do people do when they have to do something and they see someone else who should, but is not doing it?

The coach in this session is using thought transmission but it is a looser structure than asking a question that ends with two alternatives, one of which you want to communicate. The looser approach takes longer and sometimes fails because you can get sidetracked, but it works.

Jack: I guess they complain.

You: You are exactly right. They do complain. What do you think they complain about?

Jack: Well, I guess they don't think it's fair.

You: You are exactly right. They don't think it's fair that they have to sell the product and you are not selling it. What else happens when you don't sell the old product?

Jack: I don't know.

You: Well, do we have a date by which the inventory of the old product should be cleaned out?

Jack: Yes.

You: If you don't sell your share, what's going to happen regarding the inventory and that date?

Jack: I guess we are just not going to have the inventory cleaned out by that date.

You: You are exactly right. We are not going to meet our regional objective for cleaning out that inventory. What else happens because of that?

Jack: I don't know.

You: Where do you think that deadline came from?

Jack: The regional manager.

You: Right. What do you think he has to say when we don't meet our deadlines?

Jack: Well, I guess he chews you out a little bit.

You: You are exactly right. He wants to know why I can't meet the company objective. Now what else do you think will happen if we don't clean that inventory out within the allotted period?

Jack: I don't know.

You: Well, if the company releases a heavy advertising program on the new product and the customers are getting smarter everyday about the new product, what will happen, let's say four months from now, when we try to sell the old product?

Jack: We won't have a chance in hell of moving the old product because the customers just won't settle for anything less than the new product.

You: You are exactly right. We will be stuck with inventory we can't move. Now don't you agree that's a problem?

Jack: Listen, I agree all those things can be a pain, but after all the objective here is to make sales happen, and I know my customers and I know my territory, and I just don't think it's right that I should destroy our relationship by pushing all that old product on them when I know I've got this great new product that will help them out.

You: (He didn't agree. Now you have to go to the consequences to him if he does not correct the problem.) Jack, did I tell you how much of the old product you had to move?

Jack: Yes.

You: Do you think I have a choice to permit you to choose to sell that product or not?

Jack: Sure you do. I'm the best salesperson you have; let those other people move the old product. Let me make bucks for the company selling the new product.

You: Would you like to know the real answer?

Jack: I suppose you are going to tell me you don't have a choice.

You: You are exactly right. I don't have a choice. I work for the company just as you do, and I take orders from the company just as you are supposed to. Now if I tell you that you have to move that old product and you don't do it, what alternatives are left open to me?

Jack: Don't tell me you are going to fire me over something that small. I'm bringing in more sales than any two other sales reps. You really need me around here.

You: That's right, Jack. I wouldn't fire you, but what other alternatives do I have?

Jack: Well, you can do anything you want. After all you are the boss.

You: No, as a matter of fact I can't do anything I want. Your behavior restricts my behavior. Let me ask you a question. We had a long conversation at the end of last year about your interest in moving up in the organization as a manager; is that still your interest?

Jack: Of course. I want to get to be national sales manager for this company. That's why I work so hard at selling.

You: Well, let me ask you another question. What are the kinds of things upper management looks at when they are trying to decide who should get promoted as a manager?

Jack: Well, I guess they look at someone who can produce, someone who can bring in the sales, someone who is intelligent and aggressive and has those kinds of qualities needed to be a manager.

You: Jack, you are exactly right. Where do you think they get that input?

Jack: Well, I guess they get it from you, from those evaluations you make and any recommendations you make about my promotions.

You: You are exactly right. What are some of the other things you think they consider when making a promotional decision?

Jack: Well, I guess they look at things like dependability, reliability, emotional maturity, and things like that.

You: You are exactly right. They do look at things called reliability and dependability. Now if I'm the one who makes comments and recommendations about your promotion, what are the kinds of things I look at as a basis for making judgments about your reliability and dependability?

Jack: Well, I guess it's whether I do the things I am supposed to do and so on.

You: You are exactly right, whether you do the things you are supposed to do. Now, if you know that you are supposed to be moving that old product and you refuse to do it, what comments do you think I must make in your folder about your reliability and dependability as it concerns promotability?

Jack: You mean you would louse up my future just because I won't move that old product?

You: Jack, you are lousing up your future by not doing what you are supposed to do. Your self-destructive behavior limits my choice of behavior. If you don't do what you are supposed to do, the facts are that you are not dependable or reliable.

Jack: Boy, this is getting to be some kind of chicken outfit when a guy brings in a lot of sales and you give him a hard time just because he isn't selling some product that the company has obsoleted anyhow.

You: Jack, it's not the product we are talking about, it's your refusal to do what you are supposed to do. If you refuse to do what you are supposed to do, I don't know what else to call it except refusing to do what you are supposed to do. Now, if that's going to affect your future promotion, don't you agree that's a problem?

Jack: I think you are being unfair about this, but you are certainly right it's a problem if that's what you are going to do to me.

You: I'm glad you agree that it's a problem. How are we going to solve it? (You just finished step 1 of the coaching discussion and began step 2.)

Jack: Well, I guess I'm going to go out there and sell that product.

You: That's great. What specifically are you going to do?

Jack: Well, I'm going to start presenting that product to the customers instead of the new product.

You: What was our agreement at our meeting two months ago when we decided to push the old product?

Jack: We said we would sell only the old product until we ran out of it.

You: That's right. How will that influence you now?

Jack: Well, I guess I'm going to present only the old product until we run out of it.

You: That's great. But if you have sold some new product in your territory, how are you going to get over that obstacle?

Jack: That's no problem. I've got a lot of customers that I haven't sold any new product to yet, and I will just go in there and load them up with the old product.

You: Well, I am glad to see you have so much confidence in being able to move the product.

Jack: Why shouldn't I have confidence? I'm your number one salesperson.

You: You are certainly right about that, Jack. (You have just finished step 2 and are starting step 3, which is to mutually agree on action to be taken.) Jack, what kind of a time framework do you have now that you are going to be selling that product?

Jack: Well, things look a little tight. Everybody else has been selling that product for 60 days now and we only have 30 days to go before the regional deadline for moving that product.

You: That's right. What are you going to do about that?

Jack: Well, according to my current rate of selling I ought to be able to move all of my inventory 30 days after the deadline.

You: Jack, that's not an alternative. What can you do so we can meet our deadline?

Jack: You mean you expect me to move all that product in 30 days that the other reps have been moving for 60 days?

You: Jack, the regional manager didn't give me a deadline different for you than for anybody else. They didn't tell me to treat Jack different from the rest of my people. Not only that, a minute ago you told me you are a better salesperson than them, so moving that product ought to be a lot easier for you. What specifically are you going to do?

Jack: Well, if you are telling me I have no choice, I guess I have to move all of that product in the next 30 days.

You: That certainly is a positive approach. How are you going to do it?

Jack: Well, I guess I'll just temporarily delay all other sales efforts and put all my emphasis on moving that old product. I will increase my number of sales calls per day, as well as make some deals with some of my biggest customers.

You: That sounds great. How many dollars worth of sales orders will you have to write each day?

Jack: About $5,000 a day.

You: When are you going to start?

Jack: Right away.

You: When is that?

Jack: Tomorrow.

You: You mean by tomorrow night you will have brought in a minimum of $5,000 sales, and each work day hereafter you will bring in a minimum of $5,000 in sales?

Jack: Do I have any choice?

You: Is that what you are going to do?

Jack: Yes, that's what I am going to do.

You: That's great. I believe you are capable of doing that. I am pleased that you have decided to do what must be done. It looks like you are demonstrating that you have those additional qualities necessary to be a successful manager. Tomorrow night after you come back to the office, bring in your sales orders so we can discuss your production. Thank you for your time and help in working out a solution to this problem. (You just finished step 3. All you have to do now is step 4, which is follow-up, and step 5, which is recognizing achievement.)

What you just read was almost a verbatim record of a real coaching effort to solve a real problem. Jack did move all of the old product in slightly less than the 30 days left.

I hope you noted in the preceding dialog that the manager did not react to comments that might be considered disrespectful, smart alecky, or as having hidden meanings. Any effort you devote to these unimportant aspects of the discussion detracts from the main objective of coaching. The purpose of the discussion is not to reaffirm Jack's allegiance to the king, but to change Jack's behavior, to get him to stop his own self-destructive behavior. In your coaching discussion, don't respond to emotional comments. Deal with the words people say, not their intent. (You can't read minds.)

Let's take a look at another performance problem related to personal problems. You are an administrative manager, and one of your employees, Pete, a long-term employee has been stretching his lunch hour to two hours, and appears to be drinking during it. When he comes back from lunch he smells like a brewery and sometimes slurs his words.

When it happened the first time you didn't say anything to Pete because you felt it might be an isolated incident. If it happened only once it wouldn't be worth your time and effort. By the end of the week, however, you realize Pete did it four out of the five days. So, your first step was to have a feedback discussion with Pete to let him know his performance was unsatisfactory. You called him in Friday afternoon and told him you noticed he had been taking two hours for lunch and apparently had been drinking on his lunch hour; you explain this was unsatisfactory, and you asked him to please discontinue it.

Pete's response was to tell you he had a lot of things on his mind. He related he was in the process of getting a divorce because he found his wife playing around; his daughter was coming home from college because she was pregnant; his son had just been arrested for selling pot in school; his bookie was after him because he was behind in his gambling payments; and his car needed a new transmission. Your five-minute feedback discussion turned into an hour-and-a-half crying session. You suggested that he contact a counselor to help him sort things out. You also asked him if he needed some time off, but he said no. You were overwhelmed by his personal problems but you told him that the other employees were talking about him, and you asked him to stop taking long lunch hours and to stop drinking on his lunch hour. He said he would try, but he had a lot on his mind.

At the end of the following week you didn't talk to Pete, but you noticed he had again taken two hours for lunch and had returned intoxicated four out of the five days. You used the coaching analysis to pinpoint the problem.

From the coaching analysis you conclude that in spite of Pete's personal problems his long drinking lunch hours were his behavior choice. He now had two problems: his personal problem and his work problem. If you could let him do the lunch thing forever you would ignore it, but you couldn't do that. You realize that if you and Pete can't eliminate the work problem, firing him will add significantly to his personal problems.

You prepare for the coaching discussion using the Coaching Discussion Plan. The behavior discrepancy is "he is taking long lunch hours (2 hours) and drinking at lunch."

The results of Pete's long, drinking lunches are as follows:

1. His phone is not answered when he's not there.
2. Other workers answer his phone and grumble about it.
3. People don't receive service on time.
4. Other workers know what Pete is doing and are complaining about unfair treatment.
5. Because he slurs in his conversations, the people he deals with know that he drank at lunch.
6. Your boss told you there have been comments from executives in other divisions hinting that he is running a country club in permitting employees to be drunk on the job. He has told you to correct the problem or get rid of Pete.

The consequences to Pete if he doesn't stop are as follows:

1. Pete is also a special member of a management committee. If he doesn't stop, he could be removed from membership on that committee.
2. He will be prevented from attending the monthly professional meetings around the country.

3. You will be forced to fire him.
4. If Pete gets fired, his personal problems will get worse.

The desired behavior is "regular lunch hours and no excessive drinking."

Now you are ready to begin your discussion with Pete. You start with step 1, *getting agreement a problem exists.*

You: Hello, Pete. Have a seat.

Pete: Hi.

You: Do you know why I called you in?

Pete: No, but I can make a pretty good guess.

You: What do you think it is?

Pete: Well, I guess it's about my lunch hours.

You: You are exactly right.

Pete: Well, I know I shouldn't be doing that, but as I told you, I have a lot of things on my mind lately. I have been trying not to do it, but things just get the better of me.

You: Do you know what happens when you take two hours for lunch, and you act as though you had too much to drink when you return? (You can't say he was drinking too much because you weren't there to observe how much he was drinking. You were only able to observe his behavior afterward.)

Pete: Nothing. I do my job.

You: What do you think happens when normal lunch hour is over and you are not here to answer your phone, or to see the people who come to do business with you?

Pete: Well, I guess the phone doesn't get answered, and the people have to come back some other time.

You: You are exactly right. The people who come to be serviced by you are not serviced. What else do you think happens?

Pete: Well, I don't know.

You: What do you think your fellow workers do when your phone is ringing and you are not there to answer it?

Pete: Well, I guess they answer it sometimes.

You: You are exactly right. They interrupt their work to do your work for you. Do you think that bothers them?

Pete: Well, I don't know. I suppose it might.

You: That's right. It does bother them. What do you think they do about it?

Pete: I don't know.

You: Guess.

Pete: Well, I guess they might complain to you about it.

You: Yes, you are right. They do complain to me about it. They want to know why they have only an hour for lunch and you are able to take two hours. What else happens?

Pete: Well, the heck with them. If they had as many problems as I do, they would have a lot more to worry about.

You: What else happens?

Pete: I don't know.

You: When you come back from lunch do you believe you speak normally or do you slur your words like someone who drank too much?

Pete: I can hold my liquor. Besides I don't drink that much.

You: Guess again.

Pete: You mean I come across as a drunk?

You: Right. When people talk to you and you sound drunk, do they ignore that or do they complain about you?

Pete: They can go stuff a chicken.

You: That may well be your feeling but do you think they ignore it or do they complain about you?

Pete: They probably complain but they can still stuff a chicken.

You: Right. They complain. Do you think they complain to each other or to their managers?

Pete: Probably both.

You: Right. When their complaints get back to my manager what happens?

Pete: I guess he gets on your case.

You: You are exactly right. He wants to know if I am running a country club down here. Now don't you agree that's a problem?

Pete: I just never thought the time would come when I would realize that, in spite of the years I put into this company, it doesn't really make a damn bit of difference. I worked my tail off and, now when I have a few personal problems, there is just no sympathy. All that management talk about loyalty and security isn't worth a damn when it comes down to an individual with problems.

You: Don't you agree it's a problem?

Pete: Yeah, I agree it's a problem that the company can't meet me halfway with my problems.

You didn't get agreement on results of the thing done wrong. You now have to review the consequences to him if he does not stop it.

You: Pete, I work for the company just as you do, and I have to follow the rules, and make sure everybody follows the rules. Now let me ask you another question. If you continue to take two hours for lunch and come back from lunch smelling of alcohol and slurring your words, what is going to happen to you?

Pete: How come you are hassling me? Is it because I am old, and you want to get rid of me? I'm a good worker. I've given this company good productivity over the years, and now, when I have some personal problems, you young people just don't help me, you hassle me.

You: I am trying to get you to stop your self-destructive behavior. Because if you don't stop it, you leave me very few alternatives and none of them are in your best interest. Now what is going to happen to you if you don't stop the drinking lunches?

Pete: You can do any damn thing you please.

You: No, I can't. Your behavior limits my behavior. Now if you don't stop it, what is going to happen to you?

Pete: Well, I guess you could fire me.

You: You are right. I need somebody in that job who will do what needs to be done, and I wish it were you. But if we don't fire you what else could happen?

Pete: I don't know.

You: Well, you are our representative to the management committee. If you don't fix the lunch problem will you remain on the management committee or will you be removed from the committee?

Pete: You mean you are going to remove me from that management committee?

You: You are exactly right. You leave me no choice. What else will happen?

Pete: I don't know.

You: Well, you are also our representative at the monthly professional conferences. If you don't fix the lunch problem will you continue to be our representative at the monthly conference or will you be replaced?

Pete: You will probably take me off as conference representative. Boy, it's one heck of a note that when you get a few personal problems around here, people threaten to screw up your job.

You: Right, you will be removed as conference representative. Let me ask you another question. With all the personal problems you have now, will they be better if you lose your job or will your personal problems get worse?

Pete: Well, of course they would be worse if I didn't have a job.

You: Right, do you agree then there is a problem?

Pete: Well, if you are going to put it that way, it certainly is a problem.

You just got agreement there is a problem so move on to step 2, *mutually discussing alternative solutions.*

You: Great. How are we going to solve it?

Pete: Well, I won't do it anymore.

You: You won't do what anymore?

Pete: I won't take two hours for lunch.

You: That's great. What will you do?

Pete: Well, I'll take an hour for lunch.

You: That's fine. What else will you do?

Pete: That's what you wanted, isn't it?

You: Yes, that will be beneficial to both of us. But, what was the other part of the problem we discussed?

Pete: Well, you said that people accused me of being drunk after lunch.

You: That's exactly right. What will you do about that?

Pete: Well, I'll just drink less on my lunch hour.

You: That's great. How much will you drink on your lunch hour?

Pete: Well, that's my private business. After all, you don't pay me for my lunch hour.

You: You are right. We don't pay you for lunch hour, but if what you do on your lunch hour affects your work, then it's important to both of us. Tell me, before these personal problems occurred, did you drink on your lunch hour?

Pete: Of course I did.

You: Approximately how much would you drink?

Pete: Well, I would have one martini for lunch.

You: And did anybody ever accuse you of acting drunk after having one martini?

Pete: No.

You: Then how many drinks do you think it would be safe to have on your lunch hour without people accusing you of being drunk?

Pete: One martini.

You just finished step 2 so you may work on step 3, mutually agreeing on action to be taken to solve the problem.

You: That's great; what are you going to do?

Pete: What we just discussed.

You: What is that?

Pete: I will keep the martinis down to one per lunch and I will not exceed one hour for lunch.

You: That sounds like it will solve our problem. When will you start?

Pete: Well, today is Friday, I'll start next week.

You: That's fine. When next week?

Pete: On Monday.

You: That sounds like it will work. Thank you for your cooperation in working out a plan of action to solve this problem. I'll see you on Monday right after lunch.

You have just finished step 3. Your next two steps are to *follow up* to see if performance did change and *reinforce any improvement.*

You should certainly be there next Monday at the end of Pete's lunch hour to observe that he does take less than two hours and does not appear under the influence. And you should do that each day for the next week. The following three weeks you should check every day to make sure he is doing what he said he was going to do, but it will be necessary to recognize him for it only twice a week.

In dealing with unsatisfactory performance allegedly caused by personal problems, it is important to determine whether you can survive with nonperformance until the personal problems go away. If you can, then don't deal with the problem. Just hold your breath until it goes away. If the performance must be corrected, you and the employee have no alternative but to correct it. Some people will accuse you of being heartless because you will not ignore performance problems allegedly caused by personal problems. But if you don't have the choice of accepting the unsatisfactory performance, it means that unsatisfactory performance is self-destructive behavior. Therefore, if you do whatever is necessary to make an employee stop self-destructive behavior, your efforts are really in his or her interest. If, as a manager, you are unable to get an employee to stop self-destructive behavior, then you are involved in self-destructive behavior.

If you use the coaching process as described, and in the order shown, you will be amazed at the results you will achieve. The coaching process works. But let me caution you that if you change the order of the steps of the coaching process or leave out a step, it will not work. Short cuts will not work, so don't delude yourself into believing you are using the coaching process and expecting to get effective results if you don't follow the steps completely. If you find yourself saying, "I use the coaching process, but on an informal basis," you are not using the coaching process; you are doing something else.

If you want to increase productivity, do the following:

1. Let people know what they are supposed to do. Create accurate job descriptions and when starting projects spend more time talking about the details of expectations; tell them what you want.
2. Use follow-up as your management delivery system after the work begins to maintain appropriate performance or fix inappropriate performance.
3. Whenever possible create feedback systems by the minute or by the hour between the workers and their work. But report achievement levels not failure levels. On long projects establish many beginning and ending points of steps along the way. Feedback puts winning and losing into the workday.
4. Increase the amount of verbal positive reinforcement your employees hear coming out of your mouth. But reinforce specific behaviors and avoid useless generalized comments.

13

The Requirements for You to Be Successful in Eliminating Employees' Unsatisfactory Performance

YOU MUST ACCURATELY IDENTIFY WHAT BEHAVIOR CHANGE YOU NEED

When you manage performance results, it is easy enough to specify desired changes in expected results. There is no problem determining how much more or less of what it is you want within a specific time frame. As we mentioned earlier, though, the manager's job is not to manage results, but to manage those aspects of performance (behavior) that will cause the result. If the results you are obtaining from your employees now are not satisfactory, you have to define what the employees must *do differently* so the desired results will occur.

It is not enough, as a manager, merely to identify what is being done wrong. Although it is helpful to know what is happening, the most important benefit from knowing what is wrong is to use it as a basis to decide what it is the employee must do right. If you have done an effective coaching analysis and used the Coaching Discussion Plan, you will be able to know in advance of your coaching discussion what behavior change you desire. If you can't identify the behavior change you desire, that means any discussions you have with the employee are for the purpose of collecting more information to find out *what is going on.*

THE EMPLOYEE'S BEHAVIOR
MUST AFFECT THE RESULTS

It may seem obvious if obstacles beyond the employee's control are causing nonperformance, a change in the employee's behavior will not affect
the results. What is not so obvious is that many times managers observe
a lack of performance outcome at the same time they observe some
aspect of the employee's behavior that is clearly unacceptable, undesirable, or downright aggravating. Unfortunately, managers do not always
take the time to ascertain whether a change in that particular behavior
will have any effect on the consequences. If a employee's behavior does
not, or will not, affect the consequences, why are you talking to that
employee?

THERE MUST BE MAXIMUM INVOLVEMENT OF THE
EMPLOYEE IN THE FACE-TO-FACE DISCUSSION

I am not suggesting you have actual physical contact with the employee
and win two out of three falls. By maximum involvement, I mean involvement of the employee's head. The only way for you to know whether you
have that involvement of the employee's head is if you can make sounds
come out of the employee's mouth. It is not enough to have a clear *yes* or
no in response to the gems of wisdom you toss out as solutions. You must
use thought transmission to make those wonderful solutions go from
your head to the employee's head. You will know this has occurred when
the sound of that gem of wisdom comes out of the employee's mouth.

THERE MUST BE MAXIMUM COMMUNICATION
AS SPECIFIC FEEDBACK TO EMPLOYEE
ABOUT BEHAVIOR

As mentioned earlier, approximately 50 percent of the nonperformance
problems occurring in business can be related to feedback problems.
That is, the performer is not aware of the results of his or her performance. Maximum feedback does not mean you have to yell loudly when
telling someone he or she is doing something wrong. Having the
employee keep his or her own score is more beneficial than when you
keep score and report it to the employee. The best way to give feedback
about bad performance is neutral feedback; "Do you know you are drip-

ping coffee on your shoe?" "Are you aware that your last three weekly reports have arrived on Wednesday instead of Monday?" "Did you know that when you use a sales aid you hold it so the customer can't see it?"

If somebody says to you, "I didn't realize I was doing that," the person is telling you he or she was lacking feedback relative to the behavior. Remember that the first discussion with a problem employee is to supply feedback, that is, for you to tell the employee what he or she is doing is not acceptable and that you require it to change.

Also, feedback should concentrate on achievement scores rather than failure scores. Don't report people's failure level; report their achievement level. Those people failing by 10 percent are also 90 percent perfect. This feedback is equally important after the employee does agree to change. Employees often promise to do something different to change the outcome, and they truly believe they are doing something different when in actual fact they are not. A high frequency of feedback during the improvement process will support the improvement efforts. Your positive feedback as recognition of previously agreed-upon changes will reinforce the changing behavior.

YOU MUST IDENTIFY FOR YOUR EMPLOYEE THE NEED FOR THE CHANGE

Managers frequently complain about employees who either do not do those obvious things necessary for solving problems or who continue to do the same thing over and over again, although it doesn't work. The things an employee is doing wrong seem so obvious to the manager he or she can't understand why the employee doesn't make the obvious changes. Unfortunately these managers are interpreting their employees' actions in view of the alternatives they see available to the employee rather than the alternatives the employee sees available. Remember what we learned from George Kelly: people do not do illogical things on purpose. They may find out later that something is illogical either because it didn't work or because they discovered a better way to do it.

If the only reason for you to be there as a manager is to help your employees be as successful as you need them to be, you must initiate action to help them improve. Remember that one of the answers to the question, "Why don't employees do what they are supposed to do?" was "they don't know why they should." If employees don't know the reason they should be changing, it is your responsibility to identify that need for change for them. It is not only important you communicate that they must change, it is equally important to communicate the reasons why they must change. In the steps of the face-to-face coaching discussion, step 1, *getting agreement a problem exists,* accomplishes this by communicating to the employee the results of the thing done wrong and the consequences to him or her if it doesn't stop.

If the need for change appears to be blatantly obvious to your employees and they do not change, you should assume, "It may not be as obvious to them as I think."

EMPLOYEES MUST UNDERSTAND THAT THEY ARE RESPONSIBLE FOR THEIR OWN BEHAVIOR

Frequently employees blame others as the reason for their own unsatisfactory behavior. Their assumption is they did what they did because others made them do it.

If you are trying to teach a young child to walk, you will be faced with unsatisfactory performance because the child does not yet have full control over his or her musculature. Therefore the child's attempted body movement will result in the placement of arms and legs in positions that are totally inappropriate and unintended. In the work environment, however, you are dealing with adults, and you are not asking them to perform in ways that are beyond their personal control.

The basic aspect of the employment process is that people are renting their behavior to you. A basic assumption is they are responsible for the behavior they are renting; otherwise, how could they offer it for rent. Although a plea of temporary insanity may be appropriate in a court of law as a defendant's reason for committing a heinous crime, it is not an alternative reason for continued nonperformance on the job.

If the performance problem you face is really occurring because the employee cannot control his or her own actions, the employee is too ill to be managed. He or she certainly can't be responsible for his or her own behavior, and you certainly can't solve the problem. Your only alternative is to get the employee out of there and, perhaps, to encourage medical assistance.

EMPLOYEES MUST PERCEIVE THAT YOUR COACHING IS IN THEIR INTEREST

The only way to know what people perceive is to get them to write about it or verbalize it. The best way to do that is using the thought transmission techniques.

The only purpose of the coaching process is to help you improve employees' performance; to help them stop their self-destructive behavior so you are not forced to administer consequences that are not in their best interest. The coaching process defines solutions to problems, rather than creating a weighty record that will be tied around the employee's neck when you throw him or her overboard. The employee's perception of coaching will be based on your action to solve the problem. If you really believe the only reason for you to be there as a manager is to help them be as successful as you need them to be, you will be *doing* helpful things, rather than just keeping score.

When people accuse you of hassling them or picking on them (if you really aren't), you should explain in detail the things you have learned in the earlier part of this book that relate to self-destructive behavior, management, and what managers get paid for. It is equally important to explain that their behavior dictates your behavior; that the more their behavior deviates from the appropriate behavior of their job, the fewer behavior alternatives you have to choose from. It is not enough for you to know you are trying to help them, and it is not enough for you to say, "I am trying to help you." It is up to you to say and do all those things that will transmit the thought to their minds: "Ah, the boss is trying to help me stop my self-destructive behavior."

YOU MUST BE COMMITTED TO THE SAME THINGS YOU WANT EMPLOYEES TO DO

In a division of one large company, an executive who came to work late, left early, took long lunch hours, cheated on expenses and overdrank his lunches, complained continuously about his employees doing the same things. If you do not come to work on time each day, not only is it difficult for you to know which of your employees come to work on time, but your employees will have difficulty differentiating between what is important and what you say is important. If honesty is a practice you want employees to follow, then honest is what you must be. If you make speeches to your employees about loyalty and commitment to the corporation, but your own behavior demonstrates lack of loyalty and lack of commitment, it will be an inconsistency that prevents you from managing them successfully. You will not be able to get them to follow rules if you do not follow them yourself. For example, if you want them to have minorities on their staff but you have none on your staff, you have a credibility gap. The converse is not true, however; you will not get employees to do what you want them to do merely by doing it yourself. Being a good example helps but alone is not enough for you to change behavior. In addition to being a good example, you must do those other management things discussed in this book.

YOU MUST ACKNOWLEDGE AND PRAISE EMPLOYEE ACHIEVEMENTS

The last step in the face-to-face coaching process is *reinforcing any achievement*. Reinforcement to maintain performance is the first important reason for follow-up. Behavior modification, the scientific approach to managing human behavior, emphasizes the importance of your praise and recognition as a positive consequence to influence your employees' actions. It is not enough for you to observe and record change when it occurs, you must respond to it by saying and doing things to the employee as recognition of their improvements. Remember that achievement is not only winning, it is also losing by less than you ever did before.

WHAT YOU CAN DO TO GUARANTEE FAILURE IN CHANGING YOUR EMPLOYEES' BEHAVIOR

1. Don't get the employee involved, just talk *at* him or her.
2. Don't give specific feedback; talk in generalities.
3. Concentrate on attitude, rather than behavior.
4. Assume the employee understands that a problem exists.
5. Assume the employee knows what has to be done to solve the problem.
6. Don't follow up to insure that the agreed-upon action has been taken by the employee.
7. Don't acknowledge or praise the employee when he or she corrects the problem.

14
Answers for Critical Questions and Problems

Isn't this coaching a little too drastic talking about such things as demotion, no promotion, and termination? You have to put the coaching discussion in prospective. You have an employee whose performance is unacceptable and is causing problems in your operation which must be corrected. You have talked to him or her twice (feedback discussions) and performance has not gotten better. Your coaching analysis tells you that the only reason the employee is performing badly is because he or she chooses to do so. That is when you use the coaching discussion. It is your last ditch effort to save the employee in spite of him- or herself.

Doesn't the coaching discussion create tension and stress for the employee? Yes, but the tension and stress are considerably less than what occurs when you yell or when you tell the employee he or she is fired because of self-destructive behavior.

Isn't all of this manipulation? Sure it is. But so is everything else you do that has the effect of getting other people to do what you want them to do, such as promising raises, terminations, and promotions. Besides, by definition, management is manipulation. In order to manage something you have to be able to manipulate it.

But isn't it less humanistic to deal only with people's behavior? A popular management belief is that it is more humanistic to deal with people's motives and value systems, assuming that if you change them, you will get a change in behavior. This is a shockingly contradictory concept. No employer has the right, or the ability, to mess around with people's motives and value systems. It is, in fact, more humanistic to deal with the behaviors you rent without requiring people to change as people.

Are you telling me that I should talk to people only about their work behavior and have no other discussions with them?   Of course not. This book deals only with those face-to-face discussions relative to increasing productivity and helping employees eliminate their self-destructive behavior. You should maintain your other work relationships. For example, if employees normally seek your advice about personal problems, continue to advise them, as long as your action is not supporting unsatisfactory performance.

How long does it take before you get good at this?   It depends on how closely you follow the steps, and how frequently you do the things in this book. You will get better at it each time you do it. The greater the frequency, the faster you will improve.

Why do you wait to ask for agreement only after you communicate all of the results of the thing done wrong or after all the consequences? Why not ask for agreement sooner if you can get it?   First, I don't know how to tell you how to know when you *could* get agreement. I don't know how to predict which consequence is the one that will move any employee. To some people losing a prestigious perk on the job is more horrible to contemplate then losing the job. In fact, it is quite common for people to resign because of losing some prestigious aspect of their job. Second, getting out all of the results and consequences has a more dramatic effect on convincing an employee with a problem performance that there is a need to change. But remember that you don't discuss consequences if the employee agrees there is a problem after you communicated results of the thing done wrong.

Is there some secret or rule you can give me to help me be as successful as possible using coaching?   There is a rule, though it is no secret. It applies to everything else in life.

1. Prepare: decide ahead of time what has to be done and what you are going to do.
2. Follow a specific plan of action; don't play it by ear.

3. Give yourself feedback; compare your actions and the actual result to what you had planned to accomplish.
4. Decide what you will do differently next time to more closely approximate your plan.

What happens if I do everything you say, but they still don't change? Transfer or terminate them, or learn to live with the problem.

What happens if I use the coaching process, but not so formally?   It generally won't work. If it does, it is an accident.

What happens if my employee cries during the coaching discussion? One manager told me that he had tried three times to coach his secretary about a problem of record keeping but in the middle of each coaching discussion she would burst out crying. He would give her a tissue and console her but the coaching session would end. He felt frustrated because if he could not complete the coaching and correct the problem he would have to replace her and he didn't want to do that. I explained that crying in the face of pressure or pain of confrontations was a learned behavior. In our society little boys get punished for crying, "cry baby," "did you wet your diaper?" "better run home to mommy"; and they are rewarded for not crying, "there's a little he-man," "you're a brave soldier," "that's my brave little man." On the other hand, little girls are not punished for crying and are rewarded for crying with hugs and encouragement, "Go ahead and cry it will make you feel better." Men and women are not aware that they have learned this behavior over many years, they just act accordingly, mostly without thinking about it. It just happens. So, if someone cries in a coaching discussion, it is a learned response to a challenging situation. If the coaching stops when the crying begins, the stopping is reinforcing crying behavior. I told the manager that when his secretary cries in the next coaching session, don't console her and don't give her tissues. Just look at the floor until she stops crying. Then continue the coaching discussion where you stopped when the crying started just as though the crying had not happened. Two weeks later he called me to tell me about his success. He said that he did exactly what I had told him to do when the employee cried and he finally completed the coaching discussion and the performance problem was eliminated. The punch line was that she actually cried three times in the coaching session but he got through it by ignoring the crying.

What happens if my employee also reads this book?   If your employee is a supervisor of others, he or she will probably get better at coaching.

But if my employee knows what I am trying to do, will it work?   Of course it will. Coaching is not trickery. If you interview somebody for a job and that person knows you are interviewing him or her, does that prevent you from doing it? Of course it doesn't. Your questioning techniques (thought transmission) during coaching direct the employee's concentration to giving real answers to real questions.

What do I do when an employee requests that a union representative be present during the coaching discussion?   If the union contract includes this provision, do it. But direct your conversation to the employee, not to the representative. Most union representatives like the coaching process because it deals with specifics.

How is coaching affected by my union contract requirement to give warnings and reprimands?   It is not affected at all. Go ahead and hold your feedback discussions or coaching discussions, and give out the formal paperwork at the end of each.

If I compliment people for failing by less, even though they are still failing, won't they stop trying?   That depends on what you tell them. If someone improves performance from 80 percent effectiveness to 90 percent effectiveness and you tell him he is terrific, he may assume that 90 percent is all that is needed to be effective. Your reinforcing comments must be specific about the improvement, and include a statement about the expected end result. For example, "Your work today is the best I have ever seen it. You have made a big improvement by going from 80 percent to 90 percent. If you keep that up, pretty soon you will be reaching our departmental standard of 98 percent. Keep up the good work."

What happens if I can't get agreement, but I don't want to fire the employee?

1. Look for additional consequences.
2. Reanalyze why you think it's important.
3. If they ever do what you want, stop coaching them, give them pos-

itive reinforcement, for each improvement and see if the frequency increases.
4. Learn to live with it.

Isn't it unreasonable to expect managers to take full responsibility for the success or failure of their employees?   Of course not. A manager gets paid to maximize the organization's return on investment in their resources. Each manager's success is based on the ability to do that. If a manager doesn't accept responsibility for that success or failure, the responsibility passes to the resource itself. For a manager to expect the resource to be responsible for its own success or failure is self-destructive behavior (by the manager).

It seems as though coaching would work for a lot of employees, but I don't think it would be effective with professionals at the Ph.D. level. That's not a question, that's a statement. It is just as erroneous to assume that all Ph.D.s are self-motivated, all M.D.s are competent, all bank officials are honest, and all college professors are logical. Unfortunately, the more education you have, the more money you are paid, the higher the level of position you fill in the organization, the less you will be managed, and, therefore, the less you will be helped by your boss to succeed. For the last 25 years, coaching has been used successfully at all levels, and your organization should use it at all levels as is necessary.

Are you telling me that everybody I hire regardless of level of education, experience, and position in the organization is going to fail?   Of course not. But I am telling you that everybody you hire in the organization regardless of level of education, salary, and position in the organization must be managed to be as successful as you need them to be.

How long will I have to do coaching before it becomes natural for me? If by *natural* you mean, when will you be able to do it without thinking about it, the answer is never. A good rule to remember is this, *Whenever you are doing what you are doing without thinking about it, worry about it, because you are probably not doing it as well as you could.*

Can I use coaching on my boss?   Coaching is effective only on those people who answer directly to you. Some of the techniques, however, such as thought transmission, positive reinforcement, exploration of alternatives, and getting agreement that a problem exists, are useful in dealing with peers and superiors.

Coaching looks as if it will take quite a bit of time; how do I find time to do that as well as everything else?   The fact is that managers using less-effective approaches waste a lot of time repeatedly talking to problem performers without getting performance improvements. Managers frequently say, "I don't have the time to spend trying to get her to do the job right." They only have twice as much time to spend replacing the employee. The initial coaching discussions do not take a lot more time than the Y, S, and T approach. If you use coaching, however, you will solve more problems in the long run, and you will talk about the same problem less frequently. If you are saying you cannot take two hours now to solve a problem, perhaps the problem is unimportant and you should forget it.

Some of those questions and answers in the coaching discussions seem rather childish. Won't the high-level, sophisticated people who answer to me come up with the same observation?   During my twenty-five years of teaching this process, never has a manager or employee reported this happening during coaching. It is unlikely to happen because, in the process of your coaching them, you will be asking for real answers to real questions. Nevertheless, if you feel better using words with more syllables or speaking in Latin, please feel free to do so, as long as you both understand what you both are talking about.

What do I do when I am complimenting someone to reinforce what he or she is doing and that person says accusingly, "Ha! you are giving me positive reinforcement."   You should say, "Yes, you are right. It is easy to do that with you because of this good thing (specify it) you are doing."

I am sometimes faced with some belligerent employees, what should I do when the employee yells?   You hold up your hands in the "time out" position and say, "You don't have to yell, I can hear you." If the employee says, "I want to yell," You can say, "Okay, go ahead, let me know when you are finished." When he or she stops yelling you then say, "What is it you want to tell me?" If the employee says, "I just did," you reply, "I thought the yelling was for you, I wasn't listening". Another approach to curb any yelling is to say, "I can hear you. You don't have to yell. Please don't yell, it upsets me. Can we discuss this as adults?"

What do I do if the employee walks out in the middle of the coaching discussion?   If the employee has previously walked out of your coaching meetings before this meeting say, "In the past you have walked out of our coaching meetings. I want you to know that today's meeting is a scheduled business event. If you refuse to participate and walk out, we will be dealing with a bigger problem called insubordination, which leads to dismissal." If the employee has never walked out on you before but does this time, as he or she is moving, say that this is a scheduled business meeting and if he or she refuses to participate it is called insubordination leading to dismissal.

I don't know if our company culture is ready for this approach in dealing with performance problems.   First, let me tell you that culture is merely what people pay attention to. The culture of your company or country or club is what the people of that group pay attention to, and how they pay attention. By attention I mean the formal and informal rules; the value system; what is accepted or rejected; what is considered humorous and horrific; what is rewarded and punished by the people (social group) and the administration (governing body); and all formal and informal communications (publications, gossip, forms, etc.). If your company culture pays attention to on-time arrival for work and meetings, people will be on time. If your company culture does not pay attention to that, people will generally be late for work and meetings. I know companies in which employees wander in to work late and leave early and no one mentions it (no attention). The same thing happens at meetings with people wandering in and out without any relationship to what is transpiring in the meeting. In those companies there are a lot of meetings trying to accomplish what could have been done in one meeting if everyone arrived on time and left only when the meeting was over. I have had executives in high-tech companies explain to me that they were a different kind of company, laid back, without the (so called) traditional organized controls and where employees have a lot more freedom of action to be innovative and there wasn't any need for typical formalized systems. In their cultures, people didn't pay a lot of attention to following rules, cost of operation or managers helping people to be successful, much less terminating anybody regardless of poor performance (we never fire anybody). This culture of "hanging around together" worked as long as their product was the only one on the market and profit margins were through the ceiling. But when the marketplace changed with other companies producing a competitive product profit margins sank and the company's culture changed. People started to pay attention to things that affected profit and loss, 700 people were fired and rules emerged to better organize the work process. I was visiting one such company when the biggest news on everyone's lips was "we fired someone today." It was the first person the company fired in its eight-year history. To understand your company culture find out what you pay attention to now formally and informally. If you want to change your company culture change what you pay attention to. For example, if your company does not pay attention to managers following up (checking up) on employee performance, you will experience lots of late and incomplete projects; lots of work that must be done twice because it wasn't done right the first time. But if your company pays attention to follow-up (checking up) on people's performance, you will have fewer unpleasant surprises and more usable projects finished on time, the first time.

In business we pay homage to and try to emulate coaching of professional ball teams. Why don't you include that in your coaching techniques? Your job as a manager is much more difficult than that of a professional team coach. Picture what your employees performance would be like if they practiced doing something Monday thru Thursday and then did that thing for real on Friday; got the applause and cheers or boos from 5000 observers when they did something right or wrong; could read about that days performance and see themselves on television when they go home at night and knew they could lose their job every year. But even without all that, if their job had as much winning and losing each day as ball games do, your job would be much easier. But you may be surprised to know that the pro coaches use a lot of reinforcement, do a lot of planning, spend a lot of time on "Who is going to do what, when," and practice, practice, and practice—but that does not make an exciting video or after-dinner speech.

Selected Bibliography

Ader, Robert, et al. *Experimental Foundations of Behavioral Medicine: Conditioning Approaches.* Mahwah, NJ: L. Erlbaum Associates, 1988.

Agras, W. Stewart, ed. *Behavior Modification: Principles & Clinical Applications.* 2nd. ed. New York: Little, Brown & Co., 1978.

Bellack, Alan S., et al. eds. *International Handbook of Behavior Modification and Therapy.* 2nd ed. New York: Plenum Press, 1989.

Bijou, Sidney W. and Emilio Ribes-Inesta. *Behavior Modification: Issues and Extensions.* New York: Academic Press, 1972.

—— and Roberto Ruiz, eds. *Behavior Modification: Contributions to Education.* Mahwah, NJ: L. Erlbaum Associates, 1981.

Blank, Leonard. *Changing Behavior in Individuals, Couples, & Groups: Identifying, Analyzing, and Manipulating the Elements Involved in Change in Order to Promote or Inhibit Alteration of Behavior.* Springfield, IL: C. C. Thomas, 1996.

Breen, Michael J. and Craig R. Feidler, eds. *Behavioral Approach to Assessment of Youth with Emotional Behavioral Disorders: A Handbook for School Based Practitioners.* Belton, TX: PRO-ED, 1996.

Cochran, Larry and Joan Laub. *Becoming an Agent: Patterns and Dynamics for Shaping Your Life.* Albany, NY: State U NY Press, 1993.

Donaldson, Les. *Behavioral Supervision: Practical Ways to Change Unsatisfactory Behavior and Increase Productivity.* Reading, MA: Addison-Wesley, 1980.

Downing, Lester N. *Counseling Theories and Techniques: Summarized and Critiqued.* Chicago: Nelson-Hall, 1975.

Dryden, Windy. *Rational Emotive Behavior Therapy: A Reader.* Thousand Oaks, CA: Sage Pub., 1995.

Epstein, Robert. *Cognition, Creativity, and Behavior: Selected Essays.* Westport, CT: Praeger, 1996.

Evans, Richard I. *Dialogue with B. F. Skinner.* Westport, CT: Praeger, 1981.

Erveldt-Dawson, Karen and Alan E. Kazdin. *How to Maintain Behavior.* 2nd ed. Belton, TX: PRO-ED, 1998.

Fournies, Ferdinand F. *Management Performance Appraisal—A National Study.* Flemington, NJ: Fournies & Associates, 1973.

———. *Salesman Performance Appraisal—A National Study.* Flemington, NJ: Fournies & Associates, 1975.

———. *Why Employees Don't Do What They Are Supposed To Do and What To Do About It.* Rev. & Updated ed. New York: McGraw-Hill, 1999.

Hackney, Harold and Sherilyn Nye. *Counseling Strategies and Objectives.* Englewood Cliffs, NJ: Prentice-Hall, 1973.

Hall, R. Vance and Marilyn L. Hall. *How to Negotiate a Behavioral Contract.* 2nd ed. Belton, TX: PRO-ED, 1998.

———. *How to Select Reinforcers.* 2nd ed. Belton, TX: PRO-ED, 1998.

———. *How to Use Planned Ignoring (Extinction).* 2nd ed. Belton, TX: PRO-ED, 1998.

———. *How to Use Systematic Attention & Approval.* 2nd ed. Belton, TX: PRO-ED, 1998.

Hamerlynch, Leo A., Lee C. Handy, and Eric J. Mash. *Behavior Change—Methodology, Concepts & Practice.* Champaign, IL: Research Press, 1973.

Herzberg, Frederick. *Work and the Nature of Man.* Cleveland: World Publishing, 1966.

Hills, William G., Andre Van Rest, Richard Kearney, and Stephen Smith. *Administration and Management.* Norman, OK: University of Oklahoma Press, 1975.

Kaplan, Joseph S. and Jane Carter. *Behavior Modification in Applied Settings.* 6th ed. Pacific Grove, CA: Brooks-Cole, 1999.

Kazdin, Alan E. *Behavior Modification in Applied Settings.* 6th ed. Pacific Grove, CA: Brooks-Cole, 1999.

Lapin, Maureen and Raymond Houghton. *Learning and Intelligence: Conversations with Skinner and Wheeler.* Portland, OR: International Speciality Books, 1995.

McGregor, Douglas. *The Human Side of Enterprise.* New York: McGraw-Hill, 1960.

Maher, Brendan. *Clinical Psychology & Personality: The Selected Papers of George Kelly.* New York: John Wiley & Sons, 1969.

Martin, Garry and Joseph Pear. *Behavior Modification: What It Is and How To Do It.* 6th ed. Paramus, NJ: Prentice Hall Press, 1998.

Maslow, Abraham H., Robert Frager, and James Fadiman. *Motivation and Personality.* 3rd ed. New York: Harper & Row, 1987.

Megarry, Tim. *Society in Prehistory: The Origins of Human Culture.* New York: NYU Press, 1995.

Miller, L. Keith. *Principles of Everyday Behavior Analysis.* 3rd ed. Pacific Grove, CA: Brooks-Cole, 1996.

Miltonberger, Raymond G. *Behavior Modification: Principles & Procedures.* Pacific Grove, CA: Brooks-Cole, 1996.

Nye, Robert D. *The Legacy of B. F. Skinner: Concepts and Perspectives, Controversies and Misunderstandings.* Pacific Grove, CA: Brooks-Cole, 1991.

———. *Three Psychologists: Perspectives from Freud, Skinner and Rogers.* 5th ed. Pacific Grove, CA: Brooks-Cole, 1995.

Proctor, R. W. and D. J. Weeks. *The Goal of B. F. Skinner and Behavior Analysis.* New York: Springer-Verlag, 1991.

Rosennthal, Robert. *Pygmalion in the Classroom.* New York: Holt, Rinehart & Winston, 1968.

Sarafino, Edward P. *Principles of Behavior Change: Understanding Behavior Modification Techniques.* New York: John Wiley & Sons, 1996.

Schermerhorn, John R., Jr., James G. Hunt, and Richard N. Osborn. *Basic Organizational Behavior.* New York: John Wiley & Sons, 1995.

Sheldon, Brian. *Cognitive Behavioral Therapy.* Rev. ed. Florence, KY: Routledge, 1994.

Sherman, William M. *Behavior Modification.* New York: Harper & Row, 1990.

Skinner, B. F. *About Behaviorism.* New York: Alfred A. Knopf, 1974.

Smith, Alexander M. *Changing People: The Law and Ethics of Behavior Modification.* Brookfield, VT: Ashgate Pub., 1994.

Smith, Laurence D. and William R. Woodward, eds. *B. F. Skinner and Behaviorism in American Culture.* Bethlehem, PA: Lehigh University, 1996.

Sundel, Martin and Sandra Sundel. *Behavior Modification in the Human Services: A Systematic Introduction to Concepts and Applications.* New York: John Wiley & Sons, 1975.

Todd, James T. and Edward K. Morris, eds. *Modern Perspectives on B. F. Skinner and Contemporary Behaviorism.* Westport, CT: Greenwood Press, 1995.

Index

About the Author

Ferdinand F. Fournies is an internationally known consultant, speaker, former guest lecturer at Columbia University's Graduate School of Business, and adjunct faculty for the MBA program at Fairleigh Dickinson University. His many books and videos have been reproduced in several foreign languages. His hobby is wood carving.